Work Time: English Departments and the Circulation of Cultural Value

WORK TIME

English Departments and
the Circulation of Cultural Value

EVAN WATKINS

STANFORD UNIVERSITY PRESS

STANFORD, CALIFORNIA

Stanford University Press
Stanford, California
© 1989 by the Board of Trustees of the
Leland Stanford Junior University

Printed in the United States of America

CIP data appear at the end of the book

FOR DIANE

Acknowledgments

I want especially to thank Helen Tartar, Karen Brown Davison, and Elizabeth Judd for their many suggestions and careful work with the manuscript, and Sherry Laing, who typed much of it. Charles Altieri, William Johnsen, Roger Meiners, Robert Shulman, and Sandra Silberstein helped me a great deal at various stages of different chapters. Carolyn Allen read an early draft of the entire manuscript, and team-teaching a graduate seminar with her made me recognize in innumerable concrete ways the political potential of classroom work. Besides family support and encouragement, Diane and Chris contributed their considerable knowledges of everything from specific work practices in other occupations to rock music. I am grateful to the Fulbright-Hays Commission for the research year I spent in Italy, which shaped the initial idea for the manuscript.

Contents

	Introduction	1
ONE	English Departments as Workplaces	11
TWO	The Possibilities of Political Criticism: Gramsci's Example	45
THREE	Literary Criticism: Work as Evaluation	77
FOUR	Work and Value	142
FIVE	Cultural Work as Political Resistance	248
	Notes	279
	Index	287

Work Time: English Departments and the Circulation of Cultural Value

Introduction

This is a book about English departments, as workplaces employing a labor force engaged in a multiplicity of specific tasks, and to which a much larger and more diverse population of mainly young women and men routinely circulate as part of their educational programs in the university. It is then also a book about literature and literary study, since whatever these terms are taken to mean exactly, they name a pervasive complex of ways in which much of that labor force represents to itself the work carried out in English departments. For nobody becomes an English professor in order to grade papers, write committee meeting minutes and letters of recommendation, or argue with the dean about the need for a Xerox machine in the departmental office. At the same time, however, what constitute persuasive reasons for becoming English professors or taking a course in English should not necessarily be assumed to supply an explanation for the organization of work in English, any more than how X loves reading blueprints would supply an explanation for her or his work as a building contractor. Nobody becomes an English professor to grade papers or write recommendations; nevertheless, these work practices may well explain as much about the organization of work in English as documenting the frontier myths informing *The Great Gatsby*. To be sure, those who work permanently in English are likely more interested in the latter than in the former. There's no immediately obvious reason, however, to think work in English only a reflection of our interests.

I realize a perspective that focuses first on English departments as organized workplaces rather than on English as a discipline of

study, on work time rather than on work practices, on the circulation of a student population rather than on the values and knowledges at stake in the determination of work practices, is likely to
seem very abstract and specialized. And that sense of remoteness
will be reinforced by my choice of resources in the elaboration of
the argument. Even given all the diversity available, it's rarely recent
critical theory I will draw on, but other things altogether. Bowles
and Gintis's discussion of IQ testing in the schools, *Advertising Age*
editorials, Kettering Foundation and other reports, *Labor and Monopoly Capital*, Alexander Inglis's *Principles of Secondary Education*, James Conant's Carnegie-funded studies, the Bangs and Alford
Production Handbook, Labor Department statistics, and so forth
loom large in my argument. Not because I'm interested in reading
them as texts, in some eclectic extension of the notion of cultural
studies, but because in their different ways they can be made to yield
the kind of information useful for understanding the organization of
work in English departments. Time-motion studies of clerical work,
for example, may seem to have little relevance to what you teach in
your upper division American literature class, and to the ideological
implications of those decisions. But if you turned in your book order
for the class to a departmental secretary, those time-motion studies
will have exerted a powerful influence on everything from the allocation of *her* time, to the fact that she's there in the first place—one
member after all of a labor force in English—to turn in your book
list to, and the fact that she's more than likely a she and not a he.

I see nothing particularly abstract about the presence of working
secretaries in English departments. That is, I'm not conjuring some
heretofore unknown territory for your inspection and considered
decision about the contribution this territory might make to "new
directions" in literary study. Theory, to put it crudely, takes secretaries for granted. But for my purposes, the radically new terms
of X's reading of late Victorian poetics are less important than the
systematic allocation, distribution, and use of work time across a remarkably complex ensemble of social positions, including of course
secretarial typing, within which X's essay is produced and circulated. It's not that X's essay is unimportant; the point is that what
effectivity it might have is realized within this complex, not by measuring the degree of conceptual departure from its predecessors.

Like my emphasis on English departments rather than on English as a discipline of study, a focus on work time rather than work practices will also seem a curious specialization. For the very idea of "practices" has a satisfyingly concrete ring to it, if no longer through that classical (and singular) opposition to "theory," as something that (in the plural) installs us immediately in the interstices of effective social power, in its minute details. If you're a student, however, you might be forgiven for supplying in this context a different twist to that familiar passage in *The Communist Manifesto* about how all that's solid melts into thin air. The air thins routinely, about 50 minutes after the beginning of every class. You have a systematically allocated quantum of (purchased) time within which, if not exactly taken for granted, the direction, significance, values, affiliations, and hierarchies of work practices can occupy center stage to the exclusion of other concerns. At the end of class, however, all these things become a problem in another way. For it's no longer just a matter of puzzling how your instructor divined the configuration of "green" imagery in "Sunday Morning," what social implications that configuration has, what skills and knowledges enable you to see them, or even what you're supposed to "get out of" the work or what grade you'll be assigned if you do get it. What now becomes immediately important is that any or all of the above in whatever combinations require possession of an extended quantum of work time, no longer available as part of your 50-minute allotment but which must be secured in some other way.

Nothing more pervasively divides a permanent labor force of faculty in English departments from students and from others in other social positions than the possession of cultural work time. Doubtless there are many reasons why students, and people who work in fast-food restaurants, say, don't often produce intricate analyses of "Sunday Morning" suitable for publication in *PMLA*. But one very powerful reason is that few people in such positions can take for granted the necessary possession of cultural work time. It's nice to think we can "pass on" to our students at least some measure of the skills and knowledges of work practices that might enable them to engage in some such analysis elsewhere, of TV commercials no less than Stevens poems. We shouldn't be all that surprised, however, if the offer is often perceived as empty, since it doesn't also create the conditions where it might be used. That perception doesn't mark "them" as stupid or anti-intellectual or hopelessly duped by hegemonic ideologies or whatever. It just means "they've" figured out the significance of what "we" apparently have some trouble recognizing, that "we" work in a specific location that among other things determines the possibility of a wide range of work practices by controlling the allocation and possession of work time.

I won't, then, have much to say about the rapidly changing work practices valorized by critical theory, except in the context of charting historically what kind of changes the organization of work in the university has permitted. And again, it's not that I find unimportant the difference between a New Critical classroom reading of *Paradise Lost*, for example, and a Marxist reading of Mötley Crüe's video of "Smokin' in the Boys Room." On the contrary, I think that difference important enough to warrant inquiry into the conditions of its effectivity, where and in what way it might make a difference if circulated beyond the English department classroom. To the extent that there remains a kind of nebulous, abstract weight attached to my use of "work time" in the argument that follows, I don't think it's because the concept has little reference to the reality of organized work in English departments. The reason is that perhaps too often I've also used it as a marker to signal my own conviction that it's been altogether too convenient for theory to valorize as most important those changes in work practices that obligingly occur within territories where some direct, individual faculty control can be exercised. Thus while "work time" does have a range of specific reference, I have positioned it against "work practices" as well, as a reminder of the stubborn intractability of many of the most familiar, everyday, routine details of our working lives. It gives polemical focus to what I can't help but see as the comic inflation of self-importance in sitting down to have a really good think about just what we accomplish when we teach a Donald Hall poem in class, and so forth. For though it's true enough that, given the resource of work time available to a position in a university, a great deal of individual control can be exercised over the details of exactly how you read or teach a poem, to assume the effects of the work involved are directly contingent on the characteristics of the work itself ignores what complex of conditions permits you that resource in the first place. Work practices then seem an immediately concrete reality, and reflection on work practices a gravely portentous undertaking.

My use of "labor force," however, yields not a little comedy of its own. English faculty after all don't exactly appear an exploited mass, thousands of miles away, lining up for day wages so that Ford can price its Escort models "competitively." The term, that is, has been available for some time as a way to extort a desirable accumulation of cultural capital from what in another angle of entry names reason for armed struggle. I'm simply gambling that this necessary deflection of perspective is by now familiar enough to negate any shock value to the use of labor force in this context, and allow it instead to emphasize how—all things being relative—a remarkably large number of people are employed in community college, college, and university English departments in the United States doing a lot of different things besides writing essays about literature, a number that of course increases dramatically if you include secondary schools as well. And for reasons I'll argue later, the connections between secondary schools and university faculty are particularly relevant to English departments.

Several recent sociological studies have focused on the function of community colleges as "gatekeepers," a term meant to image the crucial position of the community college in determining the range of economic opportunities available to an increasingly large group of the population. What occurs to me in reading these studies is the appropriateness of the gatekeeper image to the position of English departments, not only in community colleges but throughout the educational system. In 1918, Alexander Inglis was led to remark that English was perhaps the only "universally" required course in secondary schools, and things haven't changed all that much. Now if you think of English as a discipline of study and then of work practices in English, in relation to this pervasive position within an educational system, you're likely to follow that reasoning to the point of seeing English faculty as ideologically integral to the socialization of expectations accomplished generally by education. And in this sense, "labor force" seems a kind of structural abstraction that ignores the potential in specific locations for groups of faculty to disrupt the process of socialization. For though in general a labor force of English faculty, as intellectual functionaries of the State, might be understood to socialize student expectations to conform to the ends of a dominant formation, the specificity of work practices in certain circumstances surely permits successful challenges to that designated function.

But when alternatively you follow the sequence I've suggested from English departments to work time, rather than the socialization of expectations the immediately functional importance of English faculty lies in their position as gatekeepers of economic opportunity. For within the educational system, English in some form continues to be, as in Inglis's time, "universally" required because it has been marked as an avenue of access to the more economically lucrative and socially prestigious professional occupations. Once understood in these terms, it's then not just an avenue of access that's at issue, but a whole series of transformations whereby among other things social constructions like race, gender, and class are rewritten into "neutrally" distributive categories. In this context, it matters less *how* you were taught Romantic poetry say—what socialization or countersocialization of expectations took place—than what grade you got at the end of the process. Thus so far from an abstraction, labor force seems appropriate enough to designate the activities of a large body of people who in the gross number terms of grades generate over and over, like the intellectual "assembly line" to which it's often been compared, the discriminations on which economic opportunity in part depends. Just as secretaries are far more aware of the power vested in work time than faculty, who tend to take it for granted, students are more familiar with the social importance of grading than faculty, for whom it is either an extraneous and bothersome distraction from their "real work," or taken quite seriously as a way of maintaining "standards" in the quality of student work regarding Romantic poetry or whatever. Beyond the classroom, however, as I will argue, few people ever have a clue about a student's expertise in reading Romantic poetry, or even what such expertise would look like. For what is circulated *systematically* is a grade as an index of performance whose value is read off in relation to other grades, not to the specific qualities of work.

In reality, of course, the socialization of expectations and the distribution of economic opportunity cannot be so cleanly separated. Yet taken together, as they must be, they nevertheless yield a distinctively different perspective than any isolated focus on work practices in English. For what they foreground is a twofold process of circulation in which English departments are involved: on the one hand, the continual movement of a student population through English departments, and on the other a continual stream of evaluative reports on those students, systematically going from English departments to other locations. A focus on English as a discipline of study, like a focus on work practices, points you to the conditions of cultural production and reception. But as Marx emphasizes, most obviously in the second volume of *Capital*, production in any sense is intertwined everywhere with a process of circulation, and models of production—no matter how historically relevant, like his own model of capitalist production in volume 1—remain themselves abstractions unless understood in relation to that process of circulation. It's important to think about an English department as a site of cultural production, and as a site where the skills of cultural reception are trained in specific ways. Recent critical theory has inquired into both at length. Yet it is also important to understand who has access to these conditions and resources of production and reception—that is, who is circulated to English departments and how the evaluations of their performances influence their opportunities to circulate elsewhere. English faculty as a labor force are located at a decisive point within the larger patterns of social circulation of people in the United States.

I have said this is a book about literature and literary study, and in part it is, even though it offers no readings of literary texts, no startling reappraisals of just what is "literature" exactly, and little sustained discussion of major theoretical positions as such. It doesn't take as serious history the swell of concern about how centuries of literary study have "degenerated" into merely one university discipline among many, but looks instead at the historical complex of intraeducational pressures that projected a range of problems whose "resolutions" then helped constitute the variable academic structures of English departments. In some part the book is about literature and literary study, but I don't assume that the most immediately important things to be understood about either can be read off from however variable a range of texts that in one way or another are distinguished as literature or the study of literature, no matter how carefully refined the process of such reading. For like people, texts circulate, and the specific cultural process of circulation by means of English departments is not merely an effect of decisions made about the qualities of these texts as opposed to others, or about the terms of reception of particular texts. Whatever texts are valorized for whatever reasons in English are subjected to a particular kind of circulation, where any two texts—*Paradise Lost*, say, and "Smokin' in the Boys Room"—will have much more in common with each other from the perspective of circulation than either will with the Crüe video as circulated by MTV. It's not that circulation thereby preempts any consideration of production and reception; the latter both remain abstractions, however, unless understood as intrinsicated everywhere in the specific process of circulation in English.

My argument perhaps does overemphasize circulation, at the expense of not talking about literature and literary study in the terms made familiar by recent theorizing. That is of course one reason for the emphasis, since as the example of volume 2 of *Capital* makes clear, so often lost as it is between the dramatic claims on either side, the importance of circulation is easy to ignore. I take the more serious reasons, however, as political. That is, it's not only or even primarily for the sake of some comprehensiveness of understanding that I want to emphasize circulation. Rather, as I'll try to explain, I think it's by exploiting the positions of English departments within a complex ensemble of social circulation, in a great many different contexts, that cultural work in English can function most effectively as an agent of political change.

Whether cultural work in English really can be politically effective at all is indeed an open question. However, it's by no means true, as the current cynical cliché suggests, that the prominence of often explicitly politicized theorizing in university departments is an empty exercise, the self-gratifications of endlessly rarefied debates with no real consequences. For among many other things, theory recruits a labor force into English. There was never a time when English as a twentieth-century university discipline in the United States was "untheoretical," because there was never a time when the persuasion of some fraction of a student population to engage in the lengthy, difficult, and always uncertain process of getting a degree and a job in English didn't require theory in some form to carry out. Yet theory must promise in order to recruit. And what the terms of New Criticism promised successive generations of students, in more and more diverse university locations, has been changed significantly by the multiple directions of post–New Critical theory. Anything that so alters the composition and expectations of a labor force in English cannot be dismissed as empty rhetoric with no political consequences.

Women's studies programs, to take a very visible example, not only work to challenge a literary canon, reorder the curricular priorities of course offerings, contest the dominance of patriarchal ideologies. They also recruit women into English, as ethnic studies programs recruit socially designated "minority" populations, as courses in the proletarian literature of the 1930's or readings emphasizing the portrayal of labor movements and the like recruit working class students, as theorizing the politics of ideological conflicts recruits for cultural activism across a number of positions. The theoretical directions of the recruiting process, that is, promise a certain cultural empowerment to be achieved through the process of work in English, and hence accomplish a certain socialization of expectations every bit as surely as Great Books courses or for that matter Tide commercials on TV. In the circumstances of English departments, however, it's less the morality of potentially false advertising or broken promises at issue than how best to take advantage of what opportunities might exist in order to realize politically what the changing composition and expectations of a labor force might make possible. And that requires not only knowing something about what got you into English in the first place, but what it is exactly you've gotten into, which is not quite the same thing. English as a university discipline always foregrounds theory in one way or another, under whatever name, because it is always in the business of recruiting. As a discipline, however, it recruits a labor force for English *departments*, whose social functions and educational importance were not determined on the basis of recruiting promises. Nor can they be changed simply by rethinking the discipline.

ONE

English Departments as Workplaces

Work is a term used a lot in English. It might designate specifically valorized texts, a "work of literature." But it also appears as a notation of time duly logged on a university paycheck, "88.0 hours" or whatever of work. It joins with numerous adjectives to recognize structural divisions of tasks, as in "committee work" or "scholarly work" or "classroom work," and with others to designate divisions of the labor force: "faculty work," "student work," "clerical work," and so forth. It can easily be a source of confusion to outsiders, who might not understand that when someone asks you what you are working on now, s/he usually expects a brief summary of your latest article or book manuscript, not a report on your intro to Am Lit class or a blow-by-blow account of how you typed up the minutes for the last faculty meeting. Indeed, at least for a great many people not employed in university English departments, there is something curious in the conjunction of "English" and "work" at all. They have terms to refer to the activities of people who are employed in English, but "work" is not one of those terms. Thus part of the work of "work" as it were is to persuade others that what goes on in university English departments is "real work."

One way to explain this range of usage, while avoiding the trap of trying to isolate a common denominator, is to say that work has value. For so far from a common denominator, "value" is of course as multiple as "work." That is, the connection doesn't explain how to define work, but how in any given context the designation of work will also express a particular relation of value. Sometimes that relation has the abstract clarity of an equation; X number of hours of labor time can be exchanged for the money value of X number of dollars. But it is just as likely the equation will be complicated by factoring "work" into both quality and effort. Hence the relation of work and value often represents a force of cultural distinction—the possibility of a "work of literature" say, and the impossibility of a "work of Western." And very often there seems a direct correlation between hierarchies of work and hierarchies of value, for "student work" can designate not only the activities of a specific fraction of the labor force in English, but also a negative judgment on *PMLA* submissions. Likewise, asking someone what s/he is working on now doesn't specify "research" rather than "teaching." If you want to know about the latter, you don't ask "what are you working on now?" but "what are you teaching now?" Nevertheless, often sophisticated inversions of hierarchies are possible, as in "play" theories of literature, for example. Work, that is, can just as easily be "play" as "work." For work doesn't always mean the same thing, nor is there any convenient conceptual substratum of definition. But however it's used, work also expresses a particular relation of value.

Another and very different way to explain the range of usage is to say that the possible activities to be designated as work in English are all location governed, are *in* English. That doesn't mean work always occurs at the same place. If you oversee the insertion of pin assemblies in the rear seat belts of Oldsmobile Cieras, should you find yourself fixing your neighbor's seat belts on a Saturday afternoon, you're not "working" in quite the same sense as you are in a GM plant. Your *work* takes place at a specific physical location. However, it's altogether possible to be grading student papers at a downtown coffee bar or reading Coleridge's letters in the British Museum and still be doing work in English. The physical distribution of workplaces is potentially quite diverse; nevertheless, the work is always tied in some way to a location in an English department. English is not a workplace in the same way as a GM plant, but it governs the designation of work just as surely. The potential multiplicity of physical distribution means on the one hand that it is harder to "get away" from work as it were, but it also means that you have more individual control over the *process* of work than in many other jobs.

A number of current theoretical arguments can be understood as addressing how it is that work in English is location governed.

Perhaps the most familiar concept appearing in these arguments is "institutionalization." Like other such concepts, however, institutionalization involves both a relation of value and a story, a history. The relation of value marks a privilege of literary study in English. No one would bother to argue that writing committee minutes or letters of recommendation has been institutionalized. Such activities may in fact take up much of faculty labor time in English, but when you say work has been institutionalized you mean that noting the imagery of color in a Wordsworth sonnet, for example—which in retrospect seems something that could have happened anywhere or anytime it occurred to a literate person to think about what s/he was reading—now takes place for the most part within the organizational structure of an academic field of education. That is, the usually covert expression of value is also a history, a constructed story of how a particular kind of work *has become* location governed.

For reasons I'll take up in detail in Chapters 3 and 4, both the privilege of value and the construction of history implied by the concept of institutionalization leave a great deal unexplained. But for the moment perhaps an analogy can make the point. Marx's analysis of capitalist production in volume 1 of *Capital* focuses largely on the factory as a model of the transformation of labor under capitalism. In early instances of factory work, Marx argued, workers often performed tasks very similar to the craft work in which they might well have been engaged on their own, using similar skills of work with similar instruments or machines. The crucial difference was that they no longer worked for themselves, in their own shops, but for somebody else in a factory; they had become wage laborers. With the development of machine technology, however, and the growing concentration of these means of production in the factory, work itself was redesigned from beginning to end. That is, while it might be said that early factory work "institutionalized" craft skills of work, full-scale capitalist production required such a massive transformation of labor that it would always remain a mystery to analysis that proceeded from a description of craft skills. A factory is not a giant artisan's workshop, and the organization of work in a factory cannot be understood as if it were.

Perhaps it could occur only to an English professor to think of a university English department in relation to a factory; you couldn't put that one over on an Olds assembly line worker. The analogy doesn't yield a point-by-point comparison. Yet there seems to me good reason to suspect that the dominance of a capitalist mode of production has involved structurally comparable transformations of "intellectual" work as well, such that it would be no more possible to imagine a university English department as Samuel Johnson's study writ large than to imagine a factory as a giant artisan's workshop. As a result, institutionalization would be no more adequate to understand work in English than it is to understand work in a factory. Like a factory, an English department is a different kind of formation; it is specific to a phase of the organization of *culture* under capitalism. To say that work in English is location governed thus directs analysis not to a long history of "craft skills" as it were of literary study, now "institutionalized" in English, but rather to the formation of English as a structured workplace.

The designation of work in English expresses multiple relations of value and marks out a range of tasks that are location governed. The usages of "work," that is, occur within these two systems of specification. But they are by no means complementary systems, even though they continually intersect in any given context. For it's not simply that the latter identifies where work takes place and the former a hierarchical structure of tasks at the location. As a pejorative description of *PMLA* submissions, for example, "student work" is both value expressive and transforms location into a metaphorical vehicle of judgment. It tells you that the "work" is buried down too far in the location for what one expects of "*PMLA*-quality" articles. Conversely, the judgment of submissions as "not really professional work" tells you they're not buried deeply enough. As value expressive, the designations of work make of location itself an expressive term of value. Likewise, the marking out of work as taking place in and through a specific location generates a whole range of value relations. The process is most obvious perhaps at disciplinary boundaries—"that's *sociology*, not the study of literature"—but it occurs in other forms as well. The familiar debates about creative writing programs continually emphasize the effects of location on the qualities and values of work, as of course does the concept of institutionalization. So far from being complementary, work as value and work as location governed always intersect as a problem.

What follows is an essay about work in English, that is, about the intersections of value relations and location. I've chosen a lot of examples to suggest the problems in the reciprocity of value and location, but the point is that there had to be multiple examples because "work" in English covers a large territory. In the second part of this chapter, I'll begin as close to home and as casually as I can, with what I hope will be familiar sorts of value terms involved in the work of teaching contemporary poetry, and try to show how quickly those terms unfold into issues of social authority centered in an English department as a location of work. Contemporary poetry affords a convenient beginning because the complex of value assumptions surrounding work in English not only isolates literature and literary study—out of a whole vast range of actual work practices—but also constructs what I would call ideologies of "the new" as a privileged form of value. That is, there's something "new," "contemporary," about *any* highly valued form of literary study in English, not just about recent poetry. You read X's study of Chaucer because it has "something new to add" to our understanding of Chaucer.

In one sense, the pervasiveness of "the new" is no more than an indication of the specificity of formation of English departments as they now exist. For the study of "modernist" literature wasn't just grafted onto an older disciplinary structure, to bring it up to the present. Modernism was from the beginning the center of gravity of literary study in the English department. The organization of the work of literary study *in English* is always and everywhere modernist, whether the subject is Chaucer or Joyce, because as a location and an organization of work, literary study of all kinds in English was always tied in some way to the claims for modernism. A focus on contemporary poetry merely pushes modernism to the edge as it were; when pressed, contemporary poetry must yield not only the awkwardness of "postmodern" and the like, but also those increasingly familiar gestures toward "institutional history." For in order to imagine a "post" modernism, you can't just have another go at some more conceptually satisfactory definition of modernism as a period concept from which to depart. As soon as you attempt such a definition in any detail, you begin to expose the whole ensemble of work practices of literary study in English.

In another sense, however, the complex of values in any *ideology* of the new is also a political analysis of culture in modern, democratic societies. For what it must explain is much more than why "the new" is valuable; it must explain why "literary work" of all things can produce "the new." If you think immediately of mass marketing or molecular biology, it's not exactly obvious. Thus one frequent recourse of an ideology of the new is not an aspect of current society at all, but instead "tradition," which on T. S. Eliot's inspection at least turned out to guarantee "the really new." In my second chapter, I will use Antonio Gramsci's *Quaderni del carcere* not only as the vehicle for a critique of the politics of ideologies of the new, but also as a way to explain the focus of my study on the organization of work in English departments. For Gramsci's conception of political praxis as a "war of position" poses a challenge to the value complex of the new by redirecting attention to the specific social locations where cultural work of all kinds is carried out. That is, my critique of ideologies of the new doesn't target how they "politicize" the relations of work and value, but rather their ineffectual politics. Such ideologies construct a series of value claims that depend on trying to dislocate work, free it from the "institutionalized" structures where it occurs. Following Gramsci, I will argue instead that the possibilities of political criticism begin in learning to exploit the often quite complex range of social relations intricated through locations of work such as English departments. Criticism can have a certain political effectivity, not despite the fact that it takes place at a specific location like English, but because it does.

When faced in *Capital* with explaining the transformation of work into wage labor, Marx developed two different ways of describing the process and organization of work in a factory. "Concrete labor" names the actual effort of work, the physical/intellectual process whereby a particular material is transformed by work into something else. "Abstract labor" in contrast points to the social organization of work, the relations among people at the work location. The effort of making a chair out of wood is a concrete labor task. Who owns the wood in the first place, who owns the tools and machines to alter its shape and texture, who gives orders and who takes orders about how to accomplish these alterations, who gets what money when the chair is sold—these are all questions about abstract labor, about the social organization of work. The terms were immediately useful to describe the emergence of full-scale capitalist production, and in what is now printed as an appendix to volume 1 of *Capital*, Marx explains that in early factory conditions, when the craft skills of work were carried on pretty much as they had been before, the result was a "formal subsumption" of labor to capital: "*Technologically speaking*, the *labour process* goes on as before, with the proviso that it is now *subordinated* to capital."[1] Concrete labor tasks continue basically unchanged, but they occur within a very different organization of social relations. The "real" subordination of labor to capital, "i.e. *capitalist production proper*," Marx adds, begins when concrete labor tasks are completely re- designed to conform to the requirements of abstract labor under capitalism, "when capital sums of a certain magnitude have directly taken over control of production" (*C*, 1027).

An English department, of course, is not a factory. Yet surely there is a sense in which concrete labor and abstract labor might help describe work in English as well. That is, "concrete" in this context has nothing to do with the "materiality" of the material worked on; it's not an excuse to enter the metaphysical lists on behalf of the materiality of signifiers or whatever. It just distinguishes the physical/intellectual process of work on something from the social organization existing among people engaged in that work in one way or another. The relations of work and value in English, however, are typically conceptualized as concrete labor tasks. If you're teaching *Paradise Lost*, those relations might be discussed—often in very complex terms—as involving the "work" of making the poem, as the cultural and social importance of the poem for those who do the "work" of reading it, as the "work" of educating students to be able to read it, and so forth. All of these are in a general way concrete labor.

At the same time, however, the class itself can be understood as a social organization of work, a particular complex of relations among students and the instructor engaged in the study of *Paradise Lost*. Further, these relations are organized in a way that continually "pro- duces value." It's not value in quite the same sense as one might speak of the value of Milton's altering the conventions of English blank verse. But unless you imagine that the whole process of draw- ing up a syllabus, assigning readings and papers, making comments on the results students generate, "translating" those comments into a number grade, and filing a grade report at the end of the term is just a meaningless ritual, then the social relations that exist in the classroom represent an organization of work whose result is "value" in some sense. Indeed, what *circulates from* the classroom most directly and systematically are not at all the value relations specified through concrete labor tasks, but the form of value derived from "abstract labor," from the social organization of the classroom. For you don't report to the registrar that *Paradise Lost* is a revolutionary fusion of contradictory ethical claims, or even that John has a remarkable grasp of English history for a sophomore. You report that 60239 got a 3.8 in Engl 322, which in turn, in a couple of years, is then circulated to the personnel office at Boeing as 60239's prospective employer. There's a chance the workers in the personnel office at Boeing will hear something from 60239 about the fusion of ethical claims in *Paradise Lost*, but not a very good one. They will, however, hear about the 3.8 in Engl 322, which they can read and exchange against any number of similar "value terms." In fact, of course, many of the most familiar details of work in English concern abstract labor; as I will argue in Chapter 3, the allocation of labor time in English is largely a result of the production of value imposed by the social organization of work.

I've suggested already that "institutionalization" is at best an inadequate way to understand work in English as location governed. For very similar reasons, I think "ideology" inadequate to understand the relations of work and value in English. Institutionalization points you to what are in effect craft skills of work, and emphasizes the effects on such craft skills now carried out in a specific institutional location. Likewise, ideology points you to the processes by which values are constructed, and details the social effects of those constructions of value—what they exclude, what they hierarchize, what they disguise, and so forth. That is, in the sense of concrete labor I have adopted from Marx's account, both concepts focus on concrete labor tasks, and then attempt to read off as it were the social organization of work from the functions of concrete labor and the effects it has. The presence of ideologies in English is unquestionably important; in the next chapter I will have a great deal to say about the construction of ideologies of the new and their effects. My hypothesis in Chapter 3, however, will follow Marx's argument in *Capital* that in a capitalist mode of production, concrete labor is subordinate to abstract labor. So far from determining the social organization of work, *whatever* occurs in English as concrete labor—whatever "ideological" constructions of value—reflect what is permitted by English as a location of abstract labor. My example lets me put it overdramatically: the circulation of grades from Engl 322 doesn't enforce the ideological centrality of *Paradise Lost* to dominant sociocultural values; the range of concrete labor tasks marking the study of *Paradise Lost* (and it can be a considerable range) exists at all insofar as it also functions to circulate grades. This way of putting it is of course overdramatic; as I will argue in Chapter 4, the connections are considerably more complex. Nevertheless, the emphasis is worth it as a reminder of the pervasiveness of the social organization of work in English.

My hypothesis does make clear immediately, however, at least some of the limitations of an analogy to Marx's study of the transformation of labor in factory work. Even if concrete labor tasks are subordinated to abstract labor in English, it's not quite what Marx would call a "real" subordination. And part of what I must explain in Chapter 3 is why that is the case. It's more than a "formal" subordination, yet concrete labor tasks have not been designed through and through to the requirements of abstract labor. That is, there seems nothing inherent in the social organization of work in English that would dictate *Paradise Lost* as a typical focus of classroom work. There is perhaps no more easily available demonstration of Gramsci's insistence on the complex and continually shifting relations of *cultural* authority than the recognition of the relative freedom of concrete labor in English as opposed to concrete labor in the organization of factory work. *Paradise Lost* is very often taught to be sure, but the reasons why are not the same as those involved in how the machine that injects cream filling into Twinkies is always manipulated in an identical way every time. And unlike the worker who manipulates the Twinkie machine, you can within certain limits *work differently*; you can teach different texts in very different ways. In this sense, as I will argue in Chapter 4, the ensemble of values that composes ideologies of the new is hardly an illusion. "The new" becomes a sign of the value of work in English because it testifies to this relative freedom of concrete labor. The power to produce "the new" provides continuing evidence that work is at least relatively free.

In factory production as Marx analyzes it in volume 1, the subordination of concrete to abstract labor is a function of the accumulation of capital. Work is organized to maximize surplus labor, which becomes the surplus value realized by the capitalist when what is made in the factory circulates as a commodity to be sold on the market. It's not quite so clear, however, exactly what can be accumulated from the process of how work is socially organized in an English department. The familiar term "human capital" provides a kind of loose, general answer. But it's a long way from this general concept and the analogy it depends on to an answer for the question posed in Chapter 3 of what "form of value" results from abstract labor *in English*.

An English department is of course part of a massive system of education in the United States, and to that extent the answer to the question will involve some understanding of how education itself functions socially. Louis Althusser's well-known argument in "Ideology and Ideological State Apparatuses" offers a particularly attractive answer, because as Althusser understands "ideology," literature with its relentlessly detailed representations of "everyday experience" can loom as a crucial component of education as an ideological state apparatus.[2] One immediate confirmation of this argument then is the fact that English typically is one of the larger departments in both secondary- and university-level educational institutions. And at some point, almost everyone is required to take courses in English. In another sense, however, that size is deceptive. For just as typically, English is not intra-institutionally as powerful as its size would suggest, and English faculty on the university level are not paid on the same scale as faculty in a great many other departments. Further, the size of English is rarely if ever proportionate to the total amount of labor time—student, faculty, clerical, administrative—generated by courses *in literature*. That literature and literary study is highly privileged work for permanent faculty in English seems much more a result of the relative freedom of concrete labor than a result of how the social organization of work reflects the educational functions of the institution to which it belongs.

If under capitalism, as Marx argues, concrete labor in a factory is "really" subordinate to abstract labor, then the relations of work and value can be exhaustively analyzed by explaining the social organization of work in the factory. But in a location of work such as an English department where concrete labor has a relative freedom, where concrete labor tasks are not always and everywhere designed to the requirements of abstract labor, the relations between work and value become more complex. What is circulated *from* English will be determined primarily by the abstract form of value imposed through the social organization of work, which is my subject in Chapter 3. What circulates *in* English, however, will be determined in part at least by constructions of value that may or may not be congruent with the form of abstract value, which may or may not exert pressures on the circulation of abstract value elsewhere, and which—equally important—will have a certain internal history as it were that a discussion of abstract labor can only outline in the most general terms. That is, among other things I hope my argument in Chapter 3 will help explain something about why literary study is possible in English at all, and why literary study becomes privileged work in English. But it can explain little about why literary study has taken the particular forms it has, and why those forms generate continually changing work practices. Thus in Chapter 4 I will return to the complex of work practices sketched out in the second part of this chapter as "ideologies of the new," but understood now as an internal history of concrete labor tasks as it has developed within the social organization of labor that characterizes the formation of English departments.

As I suggested, the visible sign of this shift in emphasis from Chapter 3 to Chapter 4 involves focusing on what circulates *in* English rather than what circulates *from* English. The immediate difficulty, posed by "radical" ideological analysis no less than by "humanistic" rationalizations of the cultural importance of literary study, is a failure to recognize that there is any difference. For to a greater or lesser extent, both assume that in some form or another what circulates in English—perhaps "simplified" or "appropriated" or "defused," but in some form nevertheless—circulates elsewhere also. Thus it seems to me worth the reminder at the beginning of Chapter 4 just how a general circulation of ideas, values, beliefs, attitudes, and so forth is actually accomplished in a late capitalist society such as ours. It isn't really done after all by hiring thousands and thousands of English faculty to take small groups of students through the poems of John Donne or the novels of Ernest Hemingway, as if cultural production had remained unchanged since the eighteenth century, except that more people can read. Those thousands of English faculty, as I will argue in Chapter 3, are hired for a rather different purpose. What circulates generally in the culture is not what circulates in English, but what is produced at sites, unlike English, where the work is organized toward the end of efficient circulation. Thus the appropriate paradigm for understanding cultural circulation generally is hardly an English department; it is, instead, perhaps that most obvious workplace of circulation, an advertising agency.

Now indeed, the formation of English departments and of advertising agencies reveals a remarkably congruent history in the United States in the early twentieth century. More to my purposes in Chapter 4, the design of concrete labor tasks in English reflects a continual, pressing awareness of what advertising and other contemporary sites of cultural production circulate. Nor is it hard to see why. If for whatever reasons—whether the significance of "humanistic" values or the possibilities of "ideological critique," and everything in between—you imagine that work in English is socially indispensable because of the values constructed in and through concrete labor tasks, then the fact that what circulates generally in the culture does not come primarily from concrete labor in English at all, but instead from advertising and the like, is a continual irritant. And if you imagine further that what circulates from English is at least a version of what circulates in English, then you are left with basically two responses to that irritant: (1) people who work permanently in English can know what is really going on (or what ought to be going on) in the society, and have a political responsibility to disseminate that knowledge against the massive apparatus of advertising, and so on, which dupes the rest of the people; or (2) whether people who work in English can really know what is going on or not, whatever they do will be appropriated for use by the massive apparatus of advertising, and so forth, unless we can invent a new and as yet uncolonized territory just beyond the reach of that apparatus. In all their combinations, these options define the political limits of a praxis dictated by the values of ideologies of the new. For in concentrating on English as a site of cultural production of a certain kind, they ignore how English is actually positioned in the systems of cultural circulation.

Concrete labor in what I will argue to be the forms of Gramsci's "war of position" possible in our circumstances of work begins instead in the recognition that what circulates systematically from English is not necessarily what circulates in English, but rather the result of the abstract form of value determined by the social organization of work. Political praxis then involves learning to use the peculiar features of work as a means to disrupt wherever and whenever possible the circulation of abstract value *from* English. That is, it disrupts the formation of "human capital." Thus political praxis cannot only be a matter of "transforming" concrete work practices in English, making them more "concrete" or "material" or "critical" or "self-aware" or whatever. Such changes undoubtedly are necessary, but in and of themselves they guarantee no particular consequences regarding what circulates from English as abstract value. It is necessary instead to learn *to use* work where we are, to disrupt what the social organization of labor is designed to circulate. Indeed, in any number of places such usages are already practiced and have been for some time, almost oblivious it would seem to the highly visible demands of ideologies of the new to invent something else.

In general terms, my argument in Chapter 3 focuses on abstract labor in English as a way to understand what circulates from English, and in Chapter 4 on concrete labor as a way to understand what circulates in English. But there remains still a third sense of circulation that much more directly defines the "territory" as it were, the field of struggle, where a "war of position" must take place. And once again, a concept of total labor time is the most convenient way to isolate this form of circulation for attention. An example can only compound the obvious, but it is perhaps worth it for emphasis.

Let's assume a university English department with 50 faculty (temporary, tenure-track, and tenured), 3 full-time clerical workers, 3 administrators, and 5 work-study students. For simplicity, assume further that faculty, administrators, and clerical workers all work an average 40-hour week in whatever variety of tasks during the 30 weeks of the school year, and the work-study students an average of 12 hours a week. That yields a total of 69,000 hours of labor time during the school year, exclusive of summer. Keeping things here to a minimum, on the average assume each faculty member has 50 students in classes during the course of the entire school year, and that those 50 students each average 4 hours a week, including class time of course, on all their assigned tasks in English. That yields 300,000 hours of total labor time during the school year, more than four times as much as faculty, administrators, work-study students, and clerical personnel combined. By far the greatest percentage of total labor time in English is generated by a work force who is *circulated to* the locations of English.

Now these percentages could be duplicated roughly at least within most disciplines in the university. Throughout education generally, total labor time is most directly predicated on the circulation of people. But what is true of education generally has a special relevance to the disciplines of the "humanities." Indeed, as specific formations, the humanities in the university might be defined conveniently as those disciplines that have *no other* institutional location than within the system of education. This doesn't mean an "English major" or a "history major" will never work anywhere but in an English department or a history department. But when they do, it is because the skills they possess as English majors or history majors are assumed to be transferable *somewhere else*. Unlike a chemistry or journalism or forestry major, for humanities majors there is no institutional formation outside of education that absorbs their skills in the same way. And within the humanities, of course, English is almost always the largest, most powerful, and most pervasive department. Thus while the percentage of total labor time generated by a mobile labor force of students has a certain relevance to education generally, it has a structurally determining force in English. To the extent that work in English is organized toward circulation in any sense, the primary process of circulation involves neither what circulates from English nor what circulates in English, but *who* is circulated *to* English.

As I've suggested, the quick answer to a question of who is circulated to English is just about everybody. At some time or another, just about everybody takes an English course somewhere in the process of education, if not in the university itself, then from a secondary teacher whose own education likely took place in a university. What is circulated in English has multiple sources and follows multiple directions. But what is circulated *from* English as an abstract form of value depends directly on this massive organization of who is circulated to English. The "territory" of political praxis in English, insofar as it attempts to disrupt the circulation of abstract value, is thus the social circulation of people.

The specific divisions of labor between a permanent faculty and a large, heterogeneous, mobile labor force of students circulated to

English mark in comprehensive ways how concrete labor tasks are carried out. This is true even when that concrete labor involves the "same" texts, for example; that is, even when what circulates *in* English are texts that engage the work of both a mobile and a permanent labor force, and specific fractions of both, such as "temporary" faculty. For students cannot encounter *As I Lay Dying* or *Hamlet* in quite the same way as a permanent faculty. Nor indeed can they encounter these texts in the same way they encounter a Wheaties commercial or the latest Spielberg film (unless of course either is "studied" in English). For students, the texts studied in English are first of all occasions for the performance of work to be evaluated by someone else. And in this sense at least, such texts have less in common with a Spielberg film than with a job application at Boeing, a form for a credit card at Sears, a traffic summons, a rental contract on an apartment, and so on. That is, despite the obvious differences, these texts—*Hamlet* no less than the credit card form—are *first* an occasion where you must perform a certain task of intellectual work. If you think the credit card form asks only for "simple information" rather than work, it is likely because you occupy a social position where the possession of "information" skills and knowledges of work—the possession of certain forms of "human capital"—are taken for granted. Otherwise, you know perfectly well that while the credit card application does not ask for the same kind of work as an English class paper on *Hamlet*, it calls for intellectual work nevertheless. Further, the work you do, in either case, will be adjudicated by the intellectual workers who manage the locations where the work takes place, and whose evaluation of your performance will then have an effect in one way or another on the possibility of your being able *to circulate somewhere else.*

English may not be an efficient organization of work to circulate any specific values or doctrines, or even a single, dominant form of discourse. Other sites of cultural production, such as advertising, circulate such things far more widely and far more quickly. English occupies a marginal position in the circulation of "ideologies." However, English has a relatively crucial position in the social circulation of people in the United States. It is a far more pervasive feature of this process than any of the examples I listed above. Not everyone will work for Boeing, shop at Sears, rent apartments, or lose their driver's licenses for traffic violations. But just about everybody takes

English courses at some time or another, often relatively early in their lives, and the abstract form of value circulated from English continually feeds "information" directly or indirectly to countless other locations managed by intellectual workers.[3]

Despite the familiar clichés of social mobility, people can't circulate just anywhere in the United States. Although they are often made to seem invisible, class divisions limit the circulation of any number of people to specific social positions *of all kinds*. (Try getting a Sears credit card if you have no regular means of income.) Constructions of gender quite visibly operate in the determination of who occupies what position and for how long ("Oh, your *husband* works; then we'll need his name on the application"). Constructions of race perhaps most visibly of all affect the circulation of people. Class, gender, and race can all be isolated for attention as factors that distribute the population through a structuring of social positions. But the *mechanisms* of this structuring, the enormous number of points of interchange, the apparatus for the exercise of local powers, the entire network of control features all take place in their detail as part of the process of the social circulation of people.

Insofar as it is a primary and pervasive feature in the circulation of people, English is also a primary distributive force in the details of constructing race and gender, in the formation of class boundaries. That is, as I will argue in my concluding chapter, it is not only because the literary texts taught in English may hide ideological secrets, political agendas of class affiliation or racial bias or gender marks, that English is such a distributive force. For just by virtue of being taught in English, *any* text—"radical" or "conservative" or whatever—is already caught up in the social constructions of class, of race, and of gender. And they are caught up in ways that may or may not at all be congruent with the direction of values "in" the text or "in" the concrete labor of teaching the text or "in" the effort of ideological analysis to expose their secrets. For as part of the *social organization* of work in English, these texts occur in the midst of the social circulation of people.

I have thus backed into an argument very close to the claims derived from Althusser's "Ideology and Ideological State Apparatuses" that I began by questioning. For it is of course in the details of "everyday experience" that the movements of people are structured. My emphasis, however, is a rather different one. It is not because "literature," the privileged texts circulated in English, are an ideologically powerful weapon in themselves, their naturalizing of "everyday experience" crucial to the organization of State authority, that political praxis finds itself once again on these familiar grounds. It is because these texts are taught *in English*, because they are part of a series of organized locations of work to which people are circulated, where the results of work as an abstract form of value are then circulated to and influence power decisions at any number of other boundary locations. Thus just as a political praxis of change is not only a matter of inventing new concrete work practices, it is not a matter either of changing the texts we teach, reforming the "canon." Such reform can of course be made part of a "war of position," but the point is that it must be *made* so against the working organization of English. Nothing follows automatically from teaching Judy Grahn's poetry rather than John Ashbery's, doing a seminar on *film noir* or MTV videos rather than on F. Scott Fitzgerald.

The social authority designated to English faculty, the authority to determine and evaluate tasks of work in English and to pass on the results, does open a great many possibilities of political praxis. But as I will argue in my concluding chapter, it also poses a peculiar trap for anyone committed to a politics of resistance and a "war of position" in English against the social effects of class division, of racial and gender hierarchies. For while it is true that at some time just about everybody takes English courses, the interval is often short and the *working conditions* permitted during that interval are by no means generally available in the society. Thus the forms resistance can take, the directions of a "war of position" in English, cannot be predicated solely on work practices specific to the working conditions of English. For though just about everybody takes English courses at some time, relatively few people go on to work in English. If concrete labor in English is to have consequences beyond the discipline, the "education" in resistance and positional struggles it affords must begin as an education *for us*, in recognizing and encouraging very different practices of resistance as they exist in other conditions of work, in recognizing that "work" itself is an enormously variegated and complex organization of people's lives.

It is in this context I will argue that the value assumptions of ideologies of the new become not only ineffectual but dangerous. For to the extent they deny the specificity of location, the way in which actual practices of resistance depend on specific working conditions, the assumption follows that the practices of "the new" are generally available, that potentially anybody anywhere could do it too. It is then no wonder that from the perspective of "the new," of the "post-modern" or whatever, the world around us seems a bleak landscape of duped and manipulated "subject positions" generated by an all-powerful apparatus of ideological dominance of the State. We'll look a long time to find something somewhere else that looks like "re-sistance" as we know and love it—in "writerly" texts and trenchant analyses of semiotic codes, and so on. And conversely, it should be no surprise that so few people "out there" can imagine us as poten-tial political allies. This is not just because we work in English, at a contact point in the social circulation of people, but because what should be obvious to us as well is already obvious to others, that the work practices we valorize as "resistance" and "terror" depend on working conditions by no means available everywhere. The most dangerous assumption of ideologies of the new is that our political responsibility lies in passing on our work skills and knowledges to others to practice as we do.

English, however, is situated in a perhaps unique position to func-tion as a place of educative *exchanges* of knowledges and strategies, to affirm and encourage a multiplicity of directions, of work re-sistances elsewhere—to educate a support structure, including our-selves, for resistance. For there is perhaps nothing else located to do that job in quite the same way. That is, the very pervasiveness of English departments in the social circulation of people in the United States, if necessary to the distribution of race, class, and gender posi-tions, can also be made a weapon to support multiple practices of resistance. It is, however, impossible to take advantage of that posi-tion so long as we imagine ourselves as a vanguard of change. For even if we could produce "the new," *we're in no position to circu-late its terms generally*. Political praxis in English can only work to support what is politically possible as resistance as it emerges in different forms in whatever different locations throughout the social formation. That is, the political values of our work are contingent on our *location* of work, and that location I think dictates that we func-tion in the education of a support structure. It will mean giving up the dream of transubstantiation, of a cultural avant-garde suddenly and miraculously emerging as also a political vanguard. But for a change it might also mean that the work we do has consequences for revolutionary change.

I

With a group of very sophisticated graduate students for a seminar in contemporary poetry, I wanted to concentrate on the generation of poets who began publishing in the early 1950's in the United States, many of whom—like W. S. Merwin, Adrienne Rich, Galway Kinnell, Robert Creeley, Robert Bly, Sylvia Plath, Allen Ginsberg, James Wright, Denise Levertov, Frank O'Hara, John Ashbery, and others—now have at least some reputation. It quickly became clear to me that I would have to teach these poets, especially their early poems, working against two powerful assumptions. Neither was ever formulated very explicitly in class, even though their pressure on all of us was apparent. One assumption was that in a crowded curriculum, where it was nice enough to be able to devote a whole term to contemporary poetry, it might be better to spend the time instead on the most recent poetry available, on poets arguably at the cutting edge of new poetic material and radical innovations—poets maybe few had even heard of so far, but the course would afford us an opportunity, collectively, to explore their work. None of the poets I had in mind qualified. Rich, certainly, and in very different ways Ashbery, O'Hara, and the others command a current interest. But they are not "the new" in this sense, and there would not be the same feeling of discovery possible with newer poets.

But then what exactly would we be doing with poems written in the 1950's and 1960's? For the second assumption suggests that the business of the course would have to be to identify among the enormous number of these poems the ones that had some lasting value, that transcended their immediate context, that could be seen as no longer simply poems but Poetry. The editors' preface to one of the most influential anthologies of contemporary poetry, *Naked Poetry* (1969), encourages just such a procedure: "We decided to cut across the schools, ignoring all feuds and other ugliness of literary life, and simply pick the best poets writing.... We will put aside all the traditional modesties and say plainly what we think, that much of the best poetry written in America during the last two decades is collected in this book."[4] Like the anthology itself, the class could then engage in this quasi-Arnoldian operation, retrieving from the immediate past what was generally most worthwhile. As I said, neither this nor the preceding assumption was made fully explicit, for none of us wanted to admit there weren't better reasons for reading contemporary poetry. But then there we were, facing a whole lot of poems with a critical context of values where no matter how slyly we crept up behind our words to surprise them into alternative meanings, they remained stubbornly affixed to some version or another of "make it new" or the tradition of "the best that is known and thought."

I've connected the discussion of "the best" poems from the recent past with Matthew Arnold's claims for culture, and Arnold thought a lot about the function of literary intellectuals, how and in what way our work ought to influence the direction of social organization. For my purposes the most important of his speculations involved literature as a means for intellectuals to gain a critical distance from the demands of ideological interests in the present. ("Ideological" was of course not Arnold's term, but we flatter ourselves indeed to think he wouldn't have understood its use in this context.) Among other things, literature provided an access to the past that gave you two correlative insights: it wasn't always this way, and it need not be this way in the future. The immediate alternatives available in the present do not exhaust the potential of human activities to shape a better world. Thus literature and the study of literature not only allow a certain critical distance, but also keep alive an expansive sense of human possibility against the reductions and boundaries imposed by parochial interests. One identifies "the best" poems, those that should take their place in tradition, in part by identifying the difference between poems that contribute to such expansiveness and those that do not, that wear out because the interests they represent have lost their currency. It's easy enough to make fun of Arnold now (as a number of people in a recent critical colloquium at the University of Washington complained, he's "embarrassing" to read), but at least Arnold rarely forgot that literature ought to have social consequences, that "What does it mean?" is after all a smaller question than "What difference does it make?" It's no wonder that when contemporary critics can bear to pry themselves loose from the former question, they often continue to sound like more complicated versions of Arnold.

But not always. For the other assumption, the focus on the "really new," projects a very different set of values. And from this perspective, the complex of Arnoldian claims is at best something left to academics, to consolidators; at worst it's the major threat to the possibilities of the new. When Ezra Pound declared that poetry was the antennae of the race, he was thinking not only of its capacity to anticipate a future, but also of how the range of economic, political, and even scientific activity might in fact just depend on artists out front, on the "information" they can sniff out from the faint traces in the wind. The qualities at issue then involved potential criteria for "the best" less than the capacity to construct new forms, directions, nodes, and energies of movement. Consequences, however, what might actually happen because of literature, became in some ways even more difficult to talk about than for Arnold, for at least a couple of reasons. One seems little more than a kind of indulgent arrogance; those of us in charge of the new can't also be bothered with computing its effects exactly. (In an echo of any number of similar statements by others, Eliot for example dismissed Richard Aldington's worries over the influence of *Ulysses* as "Mr. Aldington's pathetic solicitude for the half-witted.")[5] The second reason exposes the trap in that arrogance: the more one values the newness and daring of the construction itself, the more *any* use of it must appear as a decline, a contamination, even though presumably it was constructed in the first place to effect something. The conditions of value of the new in these peculiarly literary arguments is that the new can't circulate.

The tension between an ensemble of values that privileges linking "the best" poems to a "tradition," and an ensemble that instead focuses on the constructions of "the new," undoubtedly contributed a great deal to the preoccupation in much modernist literature with artists, writers, painters, musicians, and so forth as central figures. Meditating on this phenomenon in the late 1940's, however, well after it had become a familiar feature of literary life, R. P. Blackmur in characteristically casual fashion adduced another set of factors at work in the focus on artists:

Now this happened at the time of the great burst of population, the great expansion of education, and the profound (as it seems, final) division of the field of knowledge. Man, as he became so many, seemed incompatible with his selves, and he entered upon the era of competition for theoretic supremacy among his isolated and opposed selves. Of these selves the most sympathetic to the artist was of course the artistic self; at once the most isolated and the most opposed, and in an excellent position, because of his work, that he was the higher example of and the only escape from the common predicament: as if all the world had become professional and with nobody left to practice on. Hence it is that the problem of the artist became a version of the problem of man and that the proper human heroism was the heroism of the artist.[6]

The immediate subject is modernist literature, but the terms of reference are Blackmur's questions about what was perceived as a "crisis" of intellectuals, the anxiety about social position evidenced in their very different ways by critics like Irving Babbitt, Julien Benda, T. S. Eliot, Randolph Bourne, Christopher Caldwell, and a whole host of others who had preceded Blackmur's meditation. Blackmur's own emphasis is most obvious after the colon: "as if all the world had become professional and with nobody left to practice on." That is, there seemed no large, homogeneous group left whom literary intellectuals could treat as a native population, expressing their deepest, inarticulate needs and desires, and providing the analytic skills of understanding, the political or moral or religious training in human citizenship. Blackmur's use of "he" and "man" may not have been intended to convey anything particularly, but in the context it conveys a great deal more about what he did intend. For the crisis was not exactly a *trahison des clercs* or some version or other of corrupt intellectual consciousness. It was not really a "crisis" except to intellectuals *of a particular kind*, for nobody else appeared very concerned whether they were treasonable, corrupt, alienated, or whatever. These positions were all star turns played out among other professionals interested in other things and caught up in their own part in that masculine competition for "theoretic supremacy"; they were intricate, compound performances for an audience who might have "known enough," made themselves a fit audience to appreciate—modernist literature after all is not *all* that difficult—but simply never took the trouble.

Obviously literature did not disappear in these circumstances. In all its forms—"high," "popular," "experimental"—arguably it flourished as never before. What it provided, however, was not really heroes but quick-change reactions to what Blackmur would undoubtedly call "momentum": "It is the predicament in which we turn to the radio or to the whole of literature each hour on the hour to see what has happened" (AH, 46). Whether in larger terms modernist literature expressed a reactionary elitism or remained the last bastion of negative consciousness in a commodified world, for Blackmur it was at least singularly appropriate "antennae." Not of the "race," but for intellectuals to get the news. Sentimental romances or election results were not likely to anticipate what has happened to "us," but the move from *Portrait* to *Ulysses*—or "The Hollow Men" to "Ash Wednesday" or "Mauberly" to the *Cantos*—just might.

Following Blackmur I have exaggerated, but not without reason. The moral of his minatory fable is that the major categories of value to justify the importance of literature and literary study emerged as ways to represent a special sense of what literature is and how it functions, as if this could be also and for the same reasons "the higher example" of social direction. The result for Blackmur was a "disconsolate chimera" because the specific set of values by which literary intellectuals had had to specialize the work involved instead conflicted everywhere with the values that might enable that work to influence decisively the organization and direction of modern societies. To put it simply, the more the emphasis on modern refinements of skill and consciousness by which artistic activity had *unique* access to a past that antedated the fragmented and commodified world of the present, the more it became impossible to represent that past as a *generally* available resource to educate the values of the present. (What exactly are the "half-witted" supposed to do with the "mythic method" of narrative?) And conversely, the more the special, creative, prophetic powers of poetry to conjure a future beyond the prison house of the present are emphasized, the more poetry comes to seem a competition for novelty among the elect.

Attempts to circumvent these dilemmas meant a remarkable double burden for criticism claiming any serious consequences for literature: to become expert in exegesis, in following the meaning of each complicated artistic trace as potentially a uniquely signifying moment, while at the same time stretching the limits of representation so that instance looms as exemplary, "the higher example of and the only escape from the common predicament." It is little wonder New Criticism in the university always had to match an apparatus of "close reading" with something very different and continually jeopardized by the competition with science, the composite enemy for "theoretic supremacy." For behind the many visible quarrels about "science" and "literature" inherited from the nineteenth century lay a more intransigent confrontation between two models of social authority available to intellectuals, two different kinds of social function where it was by no means clear from the complex of values that informed literature and literary study how either model might be accommodated.

The first is what Gramsci in the *Notebooks* calls "the traditional intellectual." Every class, Gramsci argues, "which emerges into history out of the preceding economic structure, and as an expression of a development of this structure, has found (or at least in all of history up to the present) categories of intellectuals already in existence and which seemed indeed to represent an historical continuity uninterrupted even by the most complicated and radical changes in political and social forms."[7] Ecclesiastics were an obvious example, but as Gramsci points out, such development soon enough led in an aristocratic age to "the formation of the *noblesse de robe*, with its own privileges, a stratum of administrators, etc., scholars and scientists, theorists, non-ecclesiastical philosophers, etc." (*SPN*, 7). These groups experience an internally constituted self-identity by virtue of a sense of "special qualifications" and "uninterrupted historical continuity," and thus they "put themselves forward as autonomous and independent of the dominant social group" (*SPN*, 7). The immensely complicated changes from aristocratic to bourgeois power then found groups already in place who felt their primary allegiance to neither social order, but rather to intellectual values and traditions independent of both.

In the development of a "literary criticism," perhaps the most striking version of the traditional intellectual can be recognized in the "man of letters," someone casually familiar with the Greek and Latin classics, cosmopolitan enough to know several foreign literatures fairly well, but who nevertheless possessed a particularly acute and penetrating insight into his own national literature and its contemporary tendencies. Toward the latter he was often "critical" indeed, because of course he judged not in relation to the parochial issues of the day, but in the long context afforded by his knowledge of tradition, against standards that had stood the test of time. He (obviously "he" is not gender indeterminate here) would feel in some ways closer to Aristotle's *Poetics* than to the latest rage for blank verse or internal rhymes or extravagantly sensual images. Although seemingly without the direct support of any particular class in the present, he could and often did exert real influence over the circulation of social values, in part because he felt himself free to choose what position *deserved* his support. In Italy Benedetto Croce, Gramsci says, thinks of himself as "closely linked to Aristotle and Plato, but he does not conceal on the other hand his links with [liberal] Senators Agnelli and Benni, and it is precisely here that one can discern the most significant character of Croce's philosophy" (*SPN*, 8).

Obviously traditional intellectuals were not really immune to social changes by any means, and in modern democracies one of the most visible changes involved the standards of recruiting members. "Training" rather than birth, "hard work" along with "native sensibility"—although not without struggle—were increasingly important for standing. In part, too, changes were made necessary by the specialization of knowledges required to exercise an "informed" judgment. Even a very competent Latinist, for example, did little service in assessing the potential significance of what linguistic research claimed about the development of languages. Appreciative noises about the grandeur of a particular cadence from the *Commedia* did not carry much weight against the demonstration of historical study that such a cadence was a common feature of Tuscan dialect. From without and within, that is, literary representatives of traditional intellectuals were forced into significantly altered positions by the late nineteenth century. And by the time those poets and critics now categorized as "New Critics" arrived in literary study, a great many of the prerogatives of these intellectual groups were compounded of selective memory even more than imagined experience.

But a potent memory nevertheless. Early New Criticism at least was motivated less by a "formalist" emphasis on reading than by a sense of exclusion from a literary community belonging to others. F. R. Leavis, a shopkeeper's son, seems to have given as good as he got, but what little is actually recorded of the details of his and Q.D.'s academic itineraries at Cambridge is nasty indeed. Blackmur's dubious educational background was something he felt throughout his career as consigning him to second class citizenship in the university. Allen Tate and John Crowe Ransom certainly felt deeply enough an isolation as Southerners. Not long after Eliot threw up his Harvard education and was mixing in the heady atmosphere of mid-war London and Paris, Yvor Winters (still recovering from tuberculosis and a stay in a sanitarium in New Mexico) was earning a living teaching English grammar in a coal-mining camp. Each of these circumstances was conducive to exposing at least something of the disparity between the internally constituted norms of traditional literary intellectuals and the realities of the exclusions practiced.

At the same time, however, as a model of social authority certain aspects of the role of traditional literary intellectuals remained immensely attractive. Relatively early in its history, when *Scrutiny* was carrying on a running feud with Marxist-oriented critics, F. R. Leavis admitted a community of interest "to the extent," he says, "of believing some form of economic communism to be inevitable and desirable, in the sense that it is to this that a power-economy of its very nature points, and only by a deliberate and intelligent working towards it can civilization be saved from disaster."[8] The limiting adjective "economic" before "communism," however, anticipates that something else will follow: "When I add that I believe one cannot reasonably pretend to lay down what are the right immediate steps without consulting specialists, and that one of the functions of *Scrutiny* is to provide criteria, from the realm of general intelligence, for determining what specialists can be trusted, and how far, the Marxist will smile" (*FC*, 185). This "realm of general intelligence," its properly hierarchical relation to the work of specialists, appropriates to *Scrutiny*'s care and redirects one centralizing function of the traditional intellectual. *For Continuity* begins with a chapter entitled "Marxism and Cultural Continuity" that dramatizes a statement of Edmund Wilson's to justify the following conclusion against what Leavis sees as prevailing Marxist doctrine: "There *is*, then, a point of view above classes; there *can* be intellectual, aesthetic and moral activity that is not merely an expression of class origin and circumstance; there *is* a 'human culture' to be aimed at that must be achieved by cultivating a certain autonomy of the human spirit" (*FC*, 9). It is less Edmund Wilson than a version of the traditional intellectuals' claim to autonomy that provides the model for Leavis's "point of view." *Scrutiny*'s struggle in part, as Francis Mulhern has argued in *The Moment of "Scrutiny*," was to make that model live up to its promise, not to abolish it so much as to bring it into existence as a vital and decisive social influence against what Leavis saw as its debased and class-bound privileged form in English society.

The weapons for this struggle, however, perhaps even more obviously in Leavis's American contemporaries, were provided by a very different model: the disciplinary intellectual, precisely the specialist Leavis would "consult," working within an institutional structure and within a rigorously defined "field." For certainly by the early twentieth century, the disciplinary intellectual offered a powerful competing model—already realized elsewhere, in the "hard" sciences and the social sciences, as well as in a whole range of new, professional fields—to the "man of letters" and the "public critic." In *The New Apologists for Poetry*, Murray Krieger had located the deepest issues raised by New Criticism as a resistance to science and its reductions. But his account must be balanced against what any number of others have pointed out, how New Critics often seemed to imitate in their reading practices the very thing attacked. This was less a "theoretical" confusion that could be straightened out conceptually than the result of confrontations between these two models of social authority, the one as polemically associated with "science," the other with "literature," but with the actual direction of literary criticism poised uncertainly between them.

The complex of values in "tradition" and "the new" offered little immediate help in resolving the dilemmas. An emphasis on the "special" nature of literature, whether directed toward the recovery of a past or anticipating a future, moved in the direction of the specialized work of the disciplinary intellectual: exclusive, hierarchical, jealous of territory, and with an increasingly elaborated power of producing internally the details over which it labored. Yet the significance of such specialization could continue to be perceived in terms evocative of the traditional literary intellectual: ahistorical, humanistic, a privilege of some bedrock "experience" as a final court of appeal to test theoretical speculation, and a cultural mission to preserve a "classless" realm of freedom beyond parochial politics. A dominant form of literary criticism emerged in the university at the point where some synthesis was achieved that could naturalize the prerogatives available to a particular disciplinary home field as the appropriate place to maintain at least something of the social identity of the traditional literary intellectual. That is, the outcome of conflicts between competing models of social authority in criticism was an unstable but pervasive synthesis that included modified elements of both models. And it was at that point as well that the quarrels about "science" and "literature" began to seem a relic of Victorian melodrama, F. R. Leavis's violent attack on C. P. Snow an awful display of bad manners.

On the one hand, this synthesis helped disguise the ambivalence of claims about the consequences of literature and literary study. Depending on what aspect exactly was emphasized within the synthesis, it seemed possible to argue that literature had profound consequences indeed, or conversely that properly *literary* works at least existed for their own sake, their essential nature as an object of study independent of what effects they might have. On the other hand, however, as an unstable and complicated synthesis of very different models, it is also what made the issue of consequences so difficult for literary criticism to negotiate at all.

Clearly the authority of traditional intellectuals involved an exercise of power: the selection, authorization, and legitimation of a whole range of sociocultural values as they circulated. Yet as that model of authority was modified as an element in the synthetic position of literary criticism, what tended to disappear—or at least change in important ways—was precisely the apparatus of circulation, in part because that was what had been attacked in the model to begin with by "New Critics." It was perceived as an apparatus dependent on and limited to the privileged class position of a coterie, a literary establishment hostile to the new poetry these critics admired, to the kinds of educational reform they felt necessary, to their own ambitions and the ambitions they encouraged in their students. At the same time, it was difficult to claim for literary criticism as a disciplinary field, for those elements of the model of the disciplinary intellectual incorporated into the synthesis, the kind of dramatic effects that were visibly the result of specialized research in other fields, from physics to medicine to psychology. Yvor Winters could insist that the power of literature "is one of the facts of life, and quite as important a fact as atomic fission," but it took rare eyes indeed to see the effects of studying that "fact" in exactly the same way that one could see the effects of research on atomic fission.[9]

Thus the sense of a natural disciplinary home and a right to exist independently was also a disconcertingly free-floating achievement.

And in their essays in the 1950's, critics like Leavis, Blackmur, Tate, and Winters—all of whom in retrospect could appear established figures in prestigious positions—showed an astonishing depth of bitterness about this "success." Winters is again the most forthright. Thinking of the suicide of Hart Crane in "The Significance of *The Bridge* by Hart Crane, or What Are We to Think of Professor X?," he produced what remains perhaps the most acerbic portrait of "the literary critic" available.[10] For "the literary critic," Professor X, would seem to occupy a position not unlike the 1950's and 1960's poems in my graduate class, a lost interval between tradition and the new. No longer able to claim the cultural authority of the traditional intellectual, and cut off from the power to generate specific social consequences possible to the newer categories of disciplinary intellectuals, Professor X is then left with poetry as an occasion to construct a victorious resolution, to locate once and for all a value-charged field of authority. But poems such as those I was teaching can only function instead as an embarrassment. They give the game away, exposing in the very midst of the resolution the dilemmas it was to have put behind us in the first place.

I I

In a recent review, Mulhern succinctly summarized a widely felt sense of decline in the importance of new literature:

Firstly, and most generally, we are witnessing—and have been for several decades now—a steady decline in the status of literature within the general ensemble of artistic practices; film and increasingly television, now dominate this ensemble and command a correspondingly large proportion of its total energy. Secondly, and in consequence of this, literature has virtually fallen into disuse as a site of avant-garde activity: the major aesthetic issues of today are debated across the terrain of cinema, and those of tomorrow will probably—and should, in all political responsibility—be increasingly concerned with television. Thus, the oppositional literary practices which alone could force new perceptions of the past and stimulate strategic reflections on the ways and means of a concretely revolutionary literature are for all practical purposes—and especially in England—non-existent. In such circumstances, no serious criticism can entirely escape the gravitational field of academicism.[11]

Mulhern's argument seems to signal a decisive break from the system of connections Blackmur had found linking the itineraries of modern literary intellectuals to the fate of new literature. It belongs, that is, within a multiple series of attempts to decompose Professor X's contradiction-crossed territory on behalf of a far more broadly based "cultural criticism." Thus film and television are said to be the appropriate subject for politically responsible work. Otherwise, there is the specter of "academicism." That last clause, however, is an indication that the break isn't quite as decisive as it appears. Because "academicism" in this context functions as a version of "tradition." Likewise, "film and television" of course stand as a version of the assumption that in a contemporary poetry seminar one ought to do "really new" poetry, only pushed to the point where the really new turns out not to be poetry at all. The difference is less a "break" from the value complex of tradition and the new than an appropriation of different material to which the same values can be attached. But film and television are not simply different material, extending the apparatus of cultural production from print to new media. They represent a fundamentally different organization of the work of cultural production and circulation. And as a result, they alter the social configuration of intellectual positions and redefine the functions of intellectual work.

Historically, the production of poetry was always assumed to involve very highly refined cultural skills. Nevertheless, by the late nineteenth and into the twentieth century, the *material means* of writing poetry were increasingly available to more and more people. Almost any literate person could lay hands on the pen and paper necessary to write a poem. What actually circulated *as poetry* then had to be subjected even more rigorously to a double system of controls. On the one hand, there was a complicated selection process centered in the editorial offices of book and journal publication, and the apparatus of reviewing and the like, which continually monitored how and what poems circulated in print. And on the other, there was an increasingly more complicated and structured process of cultural education that differentiated from the whole susurrus of poetic-like-sorts-of-writing what was "genuine poetry," that is, which elaborated in great detail the refinement of *cultural* means of writing poetry.

Now given this historical context, the immediately salient fact about both film and television is less the source of their "energy" or how a lot more people see "Miami Vice" than read "The Waste

Land." It's that in contrast to poetry, relatively few people can own the material means to produce films, and even fewer the material means to produce a "Miami Vice." Indeed, the facts of circulation —the pervasiveness of shows like "Miami Vice" in circulation— are arguably the result of the massive technological redesigning and *concentration* of material means of cultural production toward the end of an always more expansive potential of circulation and an always more rapid turnover time possible to what is circulated. That is, while the circulation of poetry had been made to depend on intellectual positions where the refinement and continual monitoring of cultural skills (of both production and consumption) could take place, the circulation of films and television shows instead depends most immediately on the technological development and concentration of material means designed to circulate what is produced as widely as possible.

Mulhern is then surely right to argue that film and television should concern a "politically responsible" critic. Anything that circulates as widely as "Miami Vice" has social consequences that can't be ignored. Nevertheless, the responsibility is hardly something to be cast in the light of a brave new cultural criticism forging new territories of analysis, held back by an "academic" attention to traditional sorts of things like poems. What English professors can do with film and television *cannot not be "academic."* The reason has nothing to do with traditional values or "energy." It's simply that as itself a site of cultural production, the organization of work and the material means of cultural production available to university English professors are immediately and finally different from film and television as sites of cultural production. We can "study" them to our heart's content, but what we can produce as "study" will be organized and will circulate not like "Miami Vice," but like "literature" in Mulhern's argument. Thus so long as one understands this situation through the complex lenses supplied by tradition and the new, even Mulhern's guarded pessimism will sound wildly utopian.

As I have been suggesting, however, those values are perhaps not quite the appropriate lenses. For if it is true that English is located outside the constellation of sites of cultural production that concentrate complex material means, that is of course even more true for the great mass of the population. The "gravitational field of academicism," understood now as *any* cultural production involving relatively cheap and available material means, embraces most of the population. The specifically *academic* is distinguished within this enormous "gravitational" field by the existence of working conditions that permit a great deal of work time in the elaboration of what is produced, and often a correspondingly greater freedom of direction in the work. That freedom, in turn, can result in a "traditional" focus on "high literature" with the refined cultural skills necessary to produce or to read it. But it can also result in an imperative for the continual elaboration of "the new," which is just as surely distinguished from what is possible to most people most of the time. The specifically academic, that is, refers not to critical practices holding things like film and television in disdain, but to *working conditions* no more available to most people than the material means of film and television production.

My redefinition of the terms of Mulhern's argument involves a shift of attention from the projection of values through tradition and the new, to a focus on the work organization of cultural production. Thus it is necessary, first, to distinguish the availability of material means. That yields a sharp division between, on the one hand, sites of cultural production like film and television, which concentrate a complex and expensive technological apparatus, and on the other a nebulous "gravitational field" that would include everything from somebody singing at a bus stop to a university English department. In contrast to the former, the material means available throughout this gravitational field are relatively cheap and easy to obtain, and there is no particularly clear demarcation—as there is in film and television—between the work of cultural production and ownership of the material means through which work is realized.

Second, it is possible to isolate within this gravitational field the specifically academic as an organization of work designed in part to permit often very elaborate cultural constructions in and through the use of readily available material means. That both the making and the reading of "poetry" are now so often affiliated in one way or another with the university is no mystery; that is where working conditions permit its elaboration and refinement of *cultural* means. Thus the gravitational field as a whole might perhaps be designated appropriately as a "gravitational field of academicism," because it is within the academic that *labor time* is specifically allocated to efforts of cultural production using cheaply available material means. Elsewhere in this gravitational field, work time must be snatched instead from more directly pressing requirements of other forms of work.

My schematic redefinitions can be understood as a refocusing of "political responsibility" in the following way. Rather than studying film and television in an (impossible) attempt to corral the new in its latest avatars of energy, or to demonstrate how a mass of the population "out there" is duped and manipulated into falling for all that stuff as the real thing (unless we educate them otherwise), responsibility would begin by exploring the "gravitational field" in which we are immersed. What do people *do with* film, television, advertising, mass circulation books and magazines, records, videos, and so forth? After all, few of them are in a position to make films, television shows, and so on, themselves. But that doesn't mean they don't do anything. That is, the immediate point of studying film and television would be to learn what circulates as the material people *work on*. To assume that what people do with that material is pretty much what the material commands—that is, that what people do can be inferred from the "structures" of the material—is to take the point of view of production *as determined by centralized sites of cultural production*. It is to assume that what people do with what circulates is "consumption," whether as "freely chosen" or "induced."

Further, it is a point of view that can only be strengthened by forgetting that a specifically academic cultural production depends on anomalous and privileged working conditions and highly elaborated practices of work. For once that is forgotten, if what people "out there" do is neither film or television or advertising, and so on, nor ideological analyses of "Miami Vice" or syllable counts of *Paradise Lost*, and so forth, then *all that's left* as it were is consumption. From this point of view of production, what people actually do is merely a lost interval between two contrasting forms of cultural production schematized in whatever combinations you want of "tradition" and "the new." Gramsci's frequent discussions of "popular culture" in the *Notebooks* are important because they are located in the midst of such a lost interval; because he assumes that what gets dismissed as only consumption, from both sides in effect, is instead a diverse, multiple, scattered, but nevertheless potentially radical politics of local resistances. Rather than shifting attention to what circulates widely, like film and television in our context, "political responsibility" for Gramsci thus begins in taking the point of view of these resistances: "The premise of a new literature cannot be other than socio-political and popular; it must aim at elaborating that which already exists, whether polemically or not doesn't matter; what does matter is that it sink its roots in the humus of popular culture as it is, with its tastes and tendencies, etc., with its moral and intellectual world, even if it may seem backward and conventional" (*QC*, 1822). Thus in thinking about a "new literature" (and a new "cultural criticism" for that matter), Gramsci was relatively unconcerned with whether it really comes first—or second, or eighteenth —in its power of anticipating social change. What counts is that it take the point of view of "popular culture" understood as that lost interval, what people actually do, dispersed among the centralized apparatuses of cultural production.

In the simplest terms, my argument in this book is a process of finding out what that point of view might involve in the specific conditions of work in a university English department. Thus I want to begin with at least some general considerations of Gramsci's arguments in the *Notebooks*, the kind of analysis he engages in that can arrive at political conclusions so very unlike the assumptions of ideologies of the new. Then from Gramsci's arguments, I will turn to the organization of work in English and what its work time might permit as a political contribution to a war of position.

The Possibilities of Political Criticism: Gramsci's Example

Pessimismo dell'intelligenza, ottimismo della volontà

At the beginning of "The Antinomies of Antonio Gramsci," Perry Anderson remarks that "no Marxist thinker after the classical epoch is so universally respected in the West as Antonio Gramsci."[1] For Gramsci's attention to the "relative autonomy" of cultural formations and the complexity of relations between "civil society" and the State, his attack on "economism," his description of the multiple and often contradictory forces at work in any given situation as an "ensemble of relations," his argument that "hegemony" is sustained by both coercion and consent, his theory of intellectuals—these not only seem brilliant anticipations of recent ideological analyses but also available to a great many radical political positions besides the large organizations of Communist parties in Europe. Further, if made less visible for obvious reasons, Gramsci also comes with impeccable credentials, as it were. Like Anderson, I think it worth emphasizing rather than glossing over the latter point as a factor in Gramsci's popularity on the left, but unlike Anderson I see no particular reason to be embarrassed about it. Gramsci's popularity, as Anderson warns, may well be in part a way to disguise quite placid political behavior under the wing of an Authentic Radical Hero. Yet I am more inclined to distrust the Olympian heights of judgment from which such warnings issue. If Gramsci has become a name to conjure with as well as a source of political analysis and strategies, it seems to me a waste of time to lament how these two things are never quite as purely distinct as one might hope. In any case, I should at least make my own position clear. I have used Gramsci in this chapter not only because I think a number of his arguments politically exemplary, but also because I want to take advantage of his current popularity. What follows is then not really a careful hermeneutics of Gramsci's texts. It is a use of Gramsci. If you don't approve that sort of strategy, you're not likely to be convinced by much else that follows either.

A university English department is a location of work that occupies specific positions in a larger social organization. I am interested in exploiting the political possibilities of the work taking place at such a location. Thus what interests me immediately in Gramsci is the complex of arguments that identify a political praxis with a "war of position," and the many and often disparate examples of positionality that crowd the Notebooks. In an intellectual environment powerfully influenced by poststructuralist theorizing and "molecular" politics, this focus will perhaps already seem familiar. Indeed, that Anderson chooses to direct his criticism of Gramsci at the concept of a war of position should be taken as an indication that his likely target is a broad range of current theoretical developments as much as it is Gramsci. Though Anderson is then always careful to preserve from criticism what he calls Gramsci's "subjective political stance as a whole," which is revolutionary and Marxist, he finds at the same time that the "objective logic" (AAG, 49) of Gramsci's concepts tends in a rather different direction. As a result, Gramsci's prestige as the Marxist "theoretician of culture" cannot altogether be written off as a domestication by later and "reformist" interpreters.

I assume in the course of this book it will become obvious that I share at least some of Anderson's reservations about "cultural politics." Which is why I think it worth beginning my discussion of Gramsci with Anderson's critique. Nevertheless, working as I do in a university, in a country where no broad-based Communist party has ever been able to establish itself as a decisive political influence, it is hard to imagine a quicker dead end than Anderson's realignment of Gramsci's war of position: "In this schema, Gramsci's war of position would correspond to the phase in which a revolutionary party seeks to win the masses ideologically (consensually) to the cause of socialism, prior to the phase in which it will lead them politically into a final (coercive) revolt against the bourgeois State" (AAG, 69–70). That is, crudely, Anderson seems to object to the substitution of a multiple, diffuse theoretical avant-garde for a van-

guard Party in the "cultural" uses of Gramsci. The objection has
some validity, of course; everybody gets tired of innumerable MLA
sessions promising "revolutionary" results from new readings of X
writers. Such things, however, are what university critics work at
and in the midst of, and in those circumstances exhortations to go
thou and commit socialism instead become just one more session.
That doesn't mean the whole show should be dismissed, but that it
ought to be taken more seriously, in less apocalyptic terms. Politics
in English involves a war of position because English departments
occupy specific positions in a larger ensemble of forces. As I understand Gramsci, his arguments offer ways of learning how and why to
exploit those positions without leaping to the exaggeration of either
avant- or van-gard.

I

As Anderson's title suggests, his reading of the *Notebooks* proceeds by what should be familiar from other contexts as a way
of locating Gramsci's arguments in the coordinates of primary, opposed terms. For Anderson, those terms are "East" and "West,"
where the problem inherited for Western Marxism was to secure on
the terrain of Western democracies the success of the revolution in
Russia. Gramsci's discussions of hegemony, the relations between
civil society and the State, and the problems of political praxis may
then be linked with this primary opposition in the following way. In
the West, ruling class power is maintained for the most part through
civil society rather than the State, and it is exercised less by direct
coercion than by the complex means of hegemony available through
gaining the consent of the masses to a specific "direction." Corresponding to this analysis of the nature of power in the West is
Anderson's argument that Gramsci's conception of political praxis
shifts from what is called in the *Notebooks* a "war of maneuver,"
and whose great historical example was of course the seizure of State
power in Russia, to a war of position. In contrast to the "lightning
speed" of the former, a war of position is a prolonged "siege" carried
out on every front against the complex ensemble of relations that
consolidates hegemony as "direction" and consent:

All this indicates that we have entered a culminating phase in the political-
historical situation, since in politics the "war of position," once won, is

decisive definitively. In politics, in other words, the war of maneuver subsists so long as it is a question of winning positions which are not decisive, so that all the resources of the State's hegemony cannot be mobilized. But when, for one reason or another, these positions have lost their value and only the decisive positions are at stake, then one passes over to siege warfare. (*SPN,* 239; *QC,* 802)[2]

Gramsci was not unaware of the conclusions that could be drawn from the privilege accorded here to a war of position, and his forebodings are more than justified for Anderson by the use of the *Notebooks* to support as a political "solution" in the West various forms of left-socialist democracy, where the "revolution" is to be accomplished relatively painlessly by an always-increasing popular participation in government. As a result, however, the *Notebooks* are far from consistent in their alignment of coercion and consent, domination and direction, State and civil society. In each case, Gramsci's attempts to rewrite his fundamental oppositions in more adequate form mark for Anderson a failure to understand two key "asymmetries." The first concerns the distribution of consent and coercion between the State and civil society. For whereas in the West consent is a feature of both, it is only the State that holds a monopoly on legalized violence, on all forms of direct coercion. Thus no matter how complicated, "the *relationship* between the two terms [consent and coercion] cannot be grasped by their mere conjunction or addition" (AAG, 41), since the location of each never emerges as an equal distribution.

The second and larger "asymmetry" returns to the primary opposition between East and West: "His whole *contrast* between Russia and Western Europe revolves on the difference in the relationship between State and civil society in the two zones: its unexamined premise is that the State is the same *type of object* in both" (AAG, 50; Anderson's emphasis). In fact, however, the czarist State was a feudal autocracy, in every way weaker than in Western democracies whose power rests "not only on the *consent of the masses,* but also on a *superior repressive apparatus*" (AAG, 55). However rewritten, then, Gramsci's failure to grasp these functional asymmetries drives the "objective logic" of his concepts toward a fatal overvaluation of a war of position as "decisive definitively." Despite his personal commitment, Gramsci takes his place for Anderson within that trajectory of Marxist thought limned in *Considerations on Western Marx-*

ism, determined ultimately by political defeat in the West. Indeed, a war of position itself comes to seem for Anderson less an original form of political praxis than an emblem of defeat, "a deadlock. In the final analysis, the function of this idea in Gramsci's thought seems to have been that of a kind of moral metaphor: it represented a sense of stoical adjustment to the loss of any immediate hope of victory in the West" (AAG, 71).

The norm of judgment throughout Anderson's argument is then a return to Lenin's "dual power" conception of the transition to socialism, where the State as the expression of bourgeois interests is gradually encircled by the organization of a new power in the hands of the masses, preparatory to the final, violent seizure of State power itself. For Anderson, the correct relationship between a war of position and a war of maneuver would recognize that the task of the former is merely preparatory, a process of building an ideological basis by winning the working classes to socialism. Thus Anderson traces the source of Gramsci's concept of a war of position directly to the United Front strategy adopted by the Comintern, at Lenin's insistence, after the disastrous "theory of the offensive" had virtually destroyed the KDP in March 1921. Terracini, speaking for the PCI, had in fact defended the theory of the offensive against Lenin at the Third World Congress in June 1921, but in the *Notebooks*, Anderson argues, it is Lenin's formulation of the United Front to which Gramsci returns as a model for a war of position.

Yet even the description Anderson provides of the central terminology in the *Notebooks* quite accurately registers, although Anderson doesn't emphasize the fact, that Gramsci's "promotion" of a war of position begins in a *critique* of "dual power." For unlike in Russia, it cannot be a centrally located "fortress" State that is gradually surrounded by the counterforce of the organized mass of workers:

In Russia the State was everything, civil society was primordial and gelatinous; in the West, there was a proper relation between State and civil society, and when the State trembled a sturdy structure of civil society was at once revealed. The State was only an outer ditch, behind which there stood a powerful system of fortresses and earthworks: more or less numerous from one State to the next, it goes without saying—but this precisely necessitated an accurate reconnaissance of each individual country. (*SPN*, 238; *QC*, 866)

Thus "Illitch," Gramsci continues, "did not have time to expand the formula" of the United Front because the "reconnaissance" of the particular situation in Russia had not demanded it.

However, there is good reason to argue that the implicit critique of Lenin is not based on a geographical distinction at all, and in current circumstances even more obviously than in the 1930's, Anderson's use of "East" and "West" is dubious to say the least. Such a contrast offers a convenient rationale for the concerted, Reagan-led ideological and material attack on people of color both inside and outside the borders of the United States—by explaining the conflicts as ultimately between "Eastern" communism and "Western" capitalism rather than involving the exploitation of races—but surely it has no real place in a left political argument. Gramsci's distinction in any case seems to me primarily historical rather than geographical: between Russia as a feudal society with power concentrated in a single site ("in Russia the State was everything"), and the "proper" (that is, modern, "proper" to the times as opposed to the "primordial" civil society in Russia) form of highly industrialized and capitalized nations where it is impossible to define a single location of power to be "encircled." Gramsci not only does not assume "that the State is the same *type of object*" (AAG, 50) in both "East" and "West," but he also recognizes that the historical development of capitalism in at least certain European nations and the United States results in the initially stupefying illusion that power is simultaneously everywhere and nowhere; no sooner is one "fortress" demolished than still another appears. The "war" then necessarily becomes a war *of position* rather than an encircling maneuver.

Gramsci's "reconnaissance" of such a "terrain" from the perspective of dual power adopted by Anderson will then inevitably seem like so many "conceptual slippages." For Gramsci, however, it yielded two critical conclusions. The first is that in modern and bourgeois-dominated nations, there is no place completely external to the organization of the State where some counter-hegemonic force could locate its own base of power. What Anderson describes as a third distinct and "final" attempt on Gramsci's part to elucidate the relation between State and civil society—one that merges the two "into a larger suzerain unity" (AAG, 33)—is nothing more than a process of working out the implications of this conclusion against attempts to posit various completely autonomous realms. The passages Anderson quotes are in fact culled from three widely separated critiques, with different dates of composition as well: of Daniel Halévy's argument that the major events of French history since 1870 arose from "private organizations" (*SPN*, 261; *QC*, 801); of the theory of laissez-faire economic practice as independent of the State (*SPN*, 160; *QC*, 1590); and of the idea that the State acts merely as a "neutral policeman" safeguarding the processes of an independent civil society (*SPN*, 261; *QC*, 2302). Even Gramsci's most categorical statement, "in actual reality civil society and the State are one and the same" (*SPN*, 160; *QC*, 1590), is perhaps a justifiable hyperbole given the specific argument it challenges, and he immediately qualifies his own assertion by admitting that the distinction nevertheless has a "methodological" importance. Thus taken in context, what these passages suggest is not some total fusion of State and civil society, which Anderson—I think rightly—criticizes in its fashionable Althusserian formulation, but rather how in modern and bourgeois-dominated democracies the State *in some way* is implicated in every form of social organization.

It is this conclusion that explains why for Gramsci a war of maneuver can never be completely "decisive." Only in a nation where "the State is everything," where power is concentrated in a single location, can such a strategy expect complete success. In other circumstances, however, and though a war of maneuver must always remain an alternative in specific instances, it will not result in "all the resources of the State's hegemony" being mobilized because it cannot possibly "attack" all the positions in which the State is implicated at once. In contrast, when fully underway a war of position "demands enormous sacrifices by infinite masses of the people" in all the activities of their lives. And as a result, the State must likewise bring all its resources of hegemony into the struggles:

So an unprecedented concentration of hegemony is necessary, and hence a more "interventionist" government, which will take the offensive more openly against the oppositionists and organize permanently the "impossibility" of internal disintegration—with controls of every kind, political, administrative, etc., reinforcement of the hegemonic "positions" of the dominant group, etc. . . . In politics, the siege is a reciprocal one, despite all appearances, and the mere fact that the ruler has to muster all his resources demonstrates how seriously he takes his adversary. (*SPN*, 238–39; *QC*, 802)

It is a measure of Anderson's confusion that he reads this passage as if the "enormous sacrifices" of the masses of people would be occasioned by a proletarian hegemony already in place—presumably a result of having achieved "dual power"?—and now organizing to protect itself (by "a more 'interventionist' government," "controls of every kind," and so forth) against internal dissension in the face of the bourgeois enemy.

Where Gramsci's first conclusion may be taken as "molar" in the sense that it examines the modern State as a whole and asks what strategy of political praxis could conceivably be "decisive" in an encounter with the State, the second conclusion in contrast is "molecular" insofar as it is concerned with the multiple forms a war of position must take. Thus the point of departure—what makes a war of position possible at all given the presence of the State in some way throughout society—is the realization that the State is not a monolithic instrument of ruling class interests:

It is true that the State is seen as the organ of one particular group, destined to create favorable conditions for the latter's maximum expansion. But the development and expansion of the particular group are conceived of, and presented, as being the motor force of a universal expansion, of a development of all the "national" energies. In other words, the dominant group is coordinated concretely with the general interests of the subordinate groups, and the life of the State is conceived of as a continuous process of formation and superseding of unstable equilibria (on the judicial plane) between the interests of the fundamental group and those of the subordinate groups—equilibria in which the interests of the dominant group prevail, but only up to a certain point, i.e. stopping short of narrowly corporate economic interest. (SPN, 182; QC, 1584)

The very expansiveness of the modern and bourgeois-dominated State, its involvement in some way in every facet of social life, on the one hand makes an ultimately decisive war of maneuver impossible, but at the same time it marks a limit to State power. For as a complex ensemble of relations rather than a homogeneous instrument of domination, it is vulnerable to pressures at countless different points. That is, the "molar" limits of its power remain the contradiction between capital and labor, the claim to universality and the fact that it can only subordinate rather than express working class interests. The "molecular" limits involve the heterogeneous intersections of ruling class interests and the interests of subordinate groups negotiated in each case with an often surprising degree of autonomy. The results are continual and local crises to be "resolved." It is then little wonder that through the second half of the *Notebooks* especially, Gramsci's attention ranges so widely, through the multiplicity of cultural practices usually associated in no direct way with political activity at all. The motive is not some attempt to provide a specifically Marxist interpretation of culture to supplement Marx's economic texts, but rather the result of working through an original understanding of what political praxis entails in very different circumstances than czarist Russia.

I I

I have suggested that the model of opposition by which Anderson arranges Gramsci's terminology fails to comprehend the fundamental critique Gramsci aims at the concept of dual power that sustains Anderson's own argument. Yet it is hard to deny "conceptual slippages" in the crucial definitions of terms and relationships throughout the *Notebooks*. Gramsci himself was under no illusion about the coherence of the *Notebooks*, and no one does him any service by the pretense. Indeed, without the concept of dual power as a single standard of judgment to measure Gramsci's "deviations," it is possible to recognize immediately that the ambiguities, shifting definitions, and "slippages" by no means have the same source in every case. This should be clear already in the distinction between a "molar" and a "molecular" significance to a war of position. For in the former, war of maneuver is superseded as the fundamental form of political praxis. In the latter, however, it exists as a strategic alternative available in specific circumstances, and as Anderson points out, Gramsci's "final direct counsel to the militants of the Italian working class" (AAG, 72) concerns the necessity of a military type of organization.

Nor do the difficulties end there. For Anderson's absorption of the concept of a war of position back into a version of the United Front strategy conveniently obscures the relation Gramsci's concept has to the theory of intellectuals so prominent in the *Notebooks*. What the latter demonstrates is that in developing a concept of a war of position, Gramsci had in fact not one but two antagonists. There was the "adventurism" of the ultraleft, a Communist International, as Anderson remarks, "plunged into an ultraleft frenzy that made the partisans of the March Action seem responsible and restrained by comparison" (AAG, 60). Against what could only be self-destruction in these circumstances, a war of position emerges as a shift in emphasis necessary first of all for survival. However, it thereby redirects practical activity against another antagonist, not ultraleft theoreticians, but the "revisionism" of "leading" intellectuals like Benedetto Croce in Italy, whose defensive confrontation with historical materialism Gramsci always understood as a sign of a more pervasive ideological weakness. Once having recognized that Lenin's success in Russia had a double effect elsewhere, then a war of position concentrates attention on the effect felt most dramatically: the attitudes and values of leading intellectuals put on the defensive by Marxist thought. The struggle against these leading intellectuals is a necessary task for working class, socialist intellectuals, and one that can be carried out with confidence. Thus not only does a war of position emerge on the one hand as a primary strategy and on the other as a simple and symmetrical alternative to a war of maneuver dictated by "molecular" circumstances. It is also conceived as both a strategic political retreat and a confident program of ideological confrontation.

Now one way to resolve the larger tensions between the "molar" and "molecular" implications of a war of position is to recognize how in both cases the concept functions in the *Notebooks* as a critical and second-order operation that has, as it were, two different kinds of "content." In the former, it is predicated on a description of the modern and bourgeois-dominated State that involves, in addition to the themes I have already sketched, a critique of "economism" in all its various forms, including a mechanical cause-and-effect model of "base" and "superstructure"; an extension of Marx's distinction between "productive" and "unproductive" labor that could account for the ideological importance of specific roles played by intellectuals, a category itself radically altered by Gramsci; and finally, a historical argument that preserves a fundamental Marxian emphasis on changes in the modes of production, but at the same time coordinated with a necessarily less precise attempt to reconstruct a history of class consciousness that challenges the revisionist direction of Croce's "ethical-political" history. The latter, for example, can be made especially useful for feminist analysis. For while class is always Gramsci's immediate focus of attention, it is of course impossible to imagine such a history of class consciousness without recognizing the determining force of social constructions of both gender and race.

In the second sense of a war of position, however, this "content" (whose critical formulation of a concept of the State, Christine Buci-Glucksmann convincingly argues, remains the necessary point of departure for understanding the *Notebooks*)[3] is seemingly dissolved into a barrage of heterogeneous and often contradictory lines of development demanding less a tendentially correct "deduction" from some larger theory of the State, than a capacity to adjust critically to the specificity of the immediate situation. It should be emphasized that the distinction is not one between "theory" and "practice," nor even between "long-range" and "intermediate" goals. It is, again, a distinction between two kinds of "content" addressed by a war of position as a second-order theory and practice of revolutionary activity.

If from "beginning to end," as Anderson argues, "the laws of the capitalist State are reflected and refused in the rules of the socialist revolution" (AAG, 77), then the meaning of a war of position can be exhausted in this critical form, whose relation to two specific kinds of "content" thereby "reflects" and "refuses" what Gramsci had come to understand of "the laws of the capitalist State." Yet Anderson's terminology, like my own of "form" and "content," betrays the presence of an aesthetic metaphor, and one Marx had explicitly challenged in its own terms in *The Eighteenth Brumaire*:

> The social revolution of the nineteenth century cannot draw its poetry from the past, but only from the future. It cannot begin with itself before it has stripped off all superstition in regard to the past. Earlier revolutions required recollections of past world history in order to drug themselves concerning their own content. In order to arrive at its own content, the revolution of the nineteenth century must let the dead bury their dead. There the phrase went beyond the content; here the content goes beyond the phrase.[4]

Indeed, arguing in detail from the *Notebooks*, Buci-Glucksmann suggests that for a proletariat, a war of position must be conceived "disymmetrically."[5] It is in effect a "content" that exceeds the "phrase," which only begins in the refusal of "the laws of the capitalist State."

Thus at the point when it seems possible to coordinate the "molar" and "molecular" implications of a war of position as a critical operation, the further difficulty occasioned by the concept emerges in that enormous shift in perspective whereby we are asked to understand a war of position as "decisive definitively" only to the extent that it names simultaneously nothing less than the attempt to realize a new "content" that goes beyond this critical "phrase": the conditions of collective life in a communist society. For what is involved is the shift from a concept that in both previous meanings works on familiar material, critically reorders existing possibilities of action, to one forced to assume the utterly unfamiliar task of imagining the relation, in an evocative Marxian terminology, between "prehistory" and "history," or between the realm of "necessity" and the realm of "freedom" as it might come to exist in the present. To argue that Gramsci never "resolved" this final "slippage" in the concept of a war of position in one sense says no more than that Gramsci's thought remained an expression rather than a resolution of real contradictions, which don't disappear no matter how hard one takes thought. But we can expect rather more from Gramsci than a "clearer" expression of these contradictions if a war of position as a principle of knowledge must also become a "principle of action" (*SPN*, 405; *QC*, 1487), if it is to direct conscious struggle in the present and not relax into what could only be another and less disturbing form of "dual power" itself.

Indeed, from the outset it is necessary to retain a "contradiction" between what can be called a "utopian" version of struggle on the one hand, and a war of position as a critical term on the other. For in this enlarged sense, the critical "content" of the latter is precisely the politics of dual power as a temporal order, as first the war of position to prepare the ground and then the war of maneuver as the final overthrow of capitalism. That is, the critical content is a falsely utopian "choice" projected by the politics of dual power: between preparing for some indeterminate moment in the future when the working classes seize complete economic and political control, as if these were objects that could be passed around from one hand to another; and concrete if partial gains in the present, one of the effects of what Gramsci called a bourgeois "passive revolution," the counterrevolutionary response to a proletarian war of position.[6] Given such alternatives, it should not be surprising that the working classes "consent" to the latter. The "failure" of Marxism in the "West," which Anderson in *Considerations on Western Marxism* attributes to the isolation of theory through political defeat, is equally the result of a theoretical and practical failure to demonstrate the abstractness of this "choice."

Increasingly in the second half of the *Notebooks*, the relation between the critical and utopian vocations of a war of position comes to be expressed for Gramsci as a process of "education." The most direct formulation of the connection occurs appropriately enough toward the end of a passage where, against Croce, Gramsci has been at pains to emphasize the necessarily collective nature of practical activity: "This problem," he argues, the transformation of heterogeneous individuals and groups of the population into a "cultural-social" collective, "can and must be related to the modern way of considering educational doctrine and practice, according to which the relationship between teacher and pupil is active and reciprocal so that every teacher is always a pupil and every pupil a teacher" (*SPN*, 349–50; *QC*, 1331). The "modern way" of conceiving pedagogical practice of course has its source for Gramsci in Marx's third thesis on Feuerbach, and it is here made to express the logic of collective life as a dialectical development of reciprocal education.[7] In this properly utopian meaning, a war of position is then "decisive definitively" not as some future stasis, where the mechanisms of the State are now securely in the hands of the proletariat, but rather as the process that marks an end to "prehistory" and the inauguration of that great historical narrative where women and men learn the full extent of their lived relationships in the act of carrying them out.

As the passage continues, however, Gramsci turns immediately to consider how the critical terminology that articulates the relations of power in the existing bourgeois State can itself be understood in the terms of a pedagogical network:

But the educational relationship should not be restricted to the field of strictly "scholastic" relationships.... [It] exists throughout society as a whole and for every individual relative to other individuals. It exists between intellectual and non-intellectual sections of the population, between the rulers and the ruled, *élites* and their followers, leaders [*dirigenti*] and led, the vanguard and the body of the army. Every relationship of "hegemony" is necessarily an educational relationship and occurs not only within a nation, between the various forces of which the nation is composed, but in the international and world-wide field, between complexes of national and continental civilizations. (*SPN*, 350; *QC*, 1331)

At another point, he suggests that the State itself

must be conceived of as an "educator," in as much as it tends precisely to create a new type or level of civilization. Because one is acting essentially on economic forces, reorganizing and developing the apparatus of economic production, creating a new structure, the conclusion must not be drawn that superstructural factors should be left to themselves, to develop spontaneously, to a haphazard and sporadic germination. The State, in this field, too, is an instrument of "rationalization," of acceleration, and of Taylorisation. It operates according to a plan, urges, incites, solicits, and "punishes"; for, once the conditions are created in which a certain way of life is "possible," then "criminal action or omission" must have a punitive sanction, with moral implications, and not merely be judged generically as "dangerous." The Law is the repressive and negative aspect of the entire positive, civilizing activity undertaken by the State. (*SPN*, 247; *QC*, 1570)

Hegemony understood as an "educational relationship" helps explain the curious reversibility and interconnection of coercion and consent. For the building of consent is obviously an "educative" process, a directly productive way of convincing subordinate groups of the "universal" truth inherent in the interests of the dominant group and getting them to work for those interests, as opposed to the costly necessity of maintaining power by force and repression alone. Yet this process of consent, once understood as educative, can also then be recognized as a "discipline," with sanctions and punishments; it is also coercive. Likewise, coercion too can be understood as performing an educative function, for it involves at least three rather than two parties: those who exercise force, those who are violently subjugated, and a third and often much larger, "observing" group for whom coercion is a "lesson" in what happens to anyone who opposes the "common good" and the "common will" as embodied in the State. The importance of coercion is not underestimated by this focus. Instead, Gramsci's argument makes it possible to realize why coercion is not just a repressive force. It can be a positive and productive State apparatus, something that need not—even in "stable" democracies—be kept hidden.[8] Put on display from time to time, in carefully selected ways, it is not only a powerful "incentive" to consent, but also a sign of the magisterially "impartial" role of the State in inflicting punishment on those who disrupt the rights of its citizens. Consent, likewise, is necessary for any coercion to function, as even Anderson must finally admit: "Just as gold as a material substratum of paper is itself a convention that needs acceptance as a medium of exchange, so repression as a guarantor of ideology itself depends on the assent of those who are trained to exercise it" (AAG, 44).

The term "hegemony," however, did not originate in the *Notebooks*, and as Anderson argues, the danger in Gramsci's expansion of the Comintern formula to a theory of power that comprehends bourgeois social formations as well is "the unexamined premise that the structural positions of the bourgeoisie and the proletariat, in their respective revolutions and their successive states, were historically equivalent" (AAG, 20). It is a danger accentuated in at least two ways by the purely relational character of hegemony that emerges from an understanding of its operations as "educative." First, it seems to imply that any group or any class indifferently —aristocratic, bourgeois, or proletariat—can occupy the dominant and "educative" role in a hegemonic relationship without altering the formal similarity of the relationship itself. Second, the ascendancy of the bourgeoisie was marked culturally by an enormous development of a school system of mass education that, while abstractly acknowledged to be in the service of bourgeois class interests, in practice all too easily can be conceived as an apparatus to be converted into the training of the working classes in socialism. Thus that familiar liberal ideology privileging education as an autonomous realm mediating the conflict of classes is simply perpetuated in a disguised form.

To counter these difficulties, it is necessary to return for a moment to Gramsci's characterization of a war of position as "siege warfare" that "requires exceptional qualities of patience and inventiveness. In politics, the siege is a reciprocal one, despite all appearances, and the mere fact that the ruler has to muster all his resources demonstrates how seriously he takes his adversary" (*SPN*, 239; *QC*, 802). As I suggested, the "reciprocity" of the siege will take on a peculiarly charged resonance later in the *Notebooks*. In this critical form, however, it allows Gramsci to explain the *differential* force of hegemony as an educative relationship. For to the extent the siege is reciprocal, a continual process of pressures and counterpressures, each hegemonic relationship will differ depending on where and with what groups it occurs. That is, once understood as educative, the hegemonic relation of aristocrat to bourgeois is not at all the same as the relation of bourgeois to proletariat.

Gramsci's argument also makes clear that any attempt to "reform" the educational apparatus of the State poses the issue in the wrong terms to begin with. For the system of public education in Gramsci's conception is neither an instrument to serve ruling class interests (but which could equally well serve the interests of the working class) nor an autonomous realm mediating conflicts. It is not an instrument at all, but itself a complex ensemble of relations wherein the interests and values of the dominant class are shaped in their specific detail, in the context of a constant and reciprocal struggle, compromise, debate, and within certain limits direct force as well. Thus for Gramsci, the *riforma Gentile* was a disaster for the working class in Italy. A more democratic access to specialized vocational training offered the promise of better jobs and working conditions, but at the expense of further segregating groups of the population, making impossible the formation of alliances among subordinate groups and the training in "self-government" on which any real "democracy" depends:

The multiplication of types of vocational schools thus tends to perpetuate traditional social differences; but since, within these differences, it tends to encourage internal diversification, it gives the impression of being democratic in tendency. The labourer can become a skilled worker, for instance, the peasant a surveyor or petty agronomist. But democracy, by definition, cannot mean merely that an unskilled worker can become skilled. It must mean that every "citizen" can "govern" and that society places him, even if only abstractly, in a general condition to achieve this. (*SPN*, 40; *QC*, 1547)

The price exacted for a chance to become a skilled worker was isolation from effective political training: "Thus we are really going back to a division into juridically fixed and crystallised estates rather than moving towards the transcendence of class divisions" (*SPN*, 41; *QC*, 1548).[9]

Gramsci's description of the changes brought about by the *riforma Gentile* is an exemplary analysis of public education as a contested network of relations, where the pressures on the traditional school system from all directions resulted in a ruling class retreat on the one hand, but on the other a reorganization and specialization allowing dominant interests to be consolidated in a new form. Yet this "new form" was not present in embryo from the beginning, manipulating the multiplicity of pressures and counterpressures to ensure what the ruling class wanted all along. (Gentile in fact resigned after a year as Minister of Education, and his later disillusionment with Fascist education might have been anticipated by him well in advance; even before the March on Rome, the congress of the Fascist Party voted against the establishment of the *esame di Stato* as Gentile had conceived it.) Its precise instrumentality emerged only from within the complex process of change—and the extraordinary events of Fascist power—which cannot be separated from the entire organization of economic and social life in which the school participates. Indeed, we may take as the ultimate point of the critique of the *riforma Gentile*, which Gentile's own career ironically underscores, the impossibility of any liberal attempt to "reform" an educational system in isolation from this larger social organization.

The conceptual advantage to Gramsci's expanded formulation of education is that whether in its "critical" or its "utopian" version of a war of position, it is never an isolated and individual activity, even when engaged in "alone," as Gramsci makes strikingly clear when one returns yet again to that great passage meditating on the dialectical logic of collective life:

One could say therefore that the historical personality of an individual philosopher is also given by the active relationship which exists between him and the cultural environment he is proposing to modify. The environment reacts back on the philosopher and imposes on him a continual process of self-criticism. It is his "teacher." This is why one of the most important demands that the modern intelligentsias have made in the political field has been that of the so-called "freedom of thought and of the expression of thought" ("freedom of the press," "freedom of association"). [And against any sentimental reduction of these formulas, one has only to remember the conditions under which this passage itself was written.] For the relationship between master and disciple in the general sense referred to above is only realized where this political condition exists, and only then do we get the "historical" realization of a new type of philosopher, whom we could call a "democratic philosopher" in the sense that he is a philosopher convinced that his personality is not limited to himself as a physical individual but is an active social relationship of modification of the cultural environment. When the "thinker" is content with his own thought, when he is "subjectively," that is abstractly, free, that is when he nowadays becomes a joke. The unity of science and life is precisely an active unity, in which alone liberty of thought can be realized; it is a master-pupil relationship, one between the philosopher and the cultural environment in which he has to work and from which he can draw the necessary problems for formulation and resolution. In other words, it is the relationship between philosophy and history. (*SPN*, 350–51; *QC*, 1331–32)

It is here as well, where a "utopian" philosophy is rejoined to a "critical" history, that the contradictions inherent in the concept of a war of position once more forcefully intrude. For as a "philosophy of praxis" and the means of a "decisive" victory for communism, war of position names the collective logic of reciprocal education as the realm of "freedom." Yet as a critical and second-order mea-suring of the possibilities of action, it is tied to the historical neces-sity of conflicts, the battles *between* ruler and ruled, "master" and "pupil." Thus whatever temptation to "reformism" may be inherent in the educational "philosophy" of a war of position is countered by the historically critical emphasis of this second perspective. And in turn, the presence of the former means that a critical history is never allowed to relax into a mechanical progression toward some final and apocalyptic war. The result, however, is no single vision or coherent theory, for the outcome of the contradictory pressures of these possibilities in any situation cannot be predicted in advance. It is the peculiar centaur of "pessimism of the intellect, optimism of the will" that everywhere signs Gramsci's contribution to an under-standing of political praxis.

I I I

There are a number of discussions throughout the *Notebooks* of literature and literary study, and of the political roles of artist and critic as intellectuals. The acuteness of Gramsci's comments should really come as no surprise; it was not for nothing that he had studied Croce and De Sanctis, and had himself before his imprisonment participated through his reviewing in a number of major literary quarrels during that exciting period of early-twentieth-century mod-ernism in Italy. Yet two considerations should forestall any attempt to project a "Marxist aesthetics" from the conception of political praxis that dominates Gramsci's attention in the *Notebooks*. The first is simply Gramsci's own reluctance to cast himself in the role of literary critic. This was not false modesty; he knew the extent and quality of his literary education, and indeed, it might be supposed that one relatively easy way to circumvent the prison censor would have been to couch his political arguments in terms drawn from the literature with which he was so familiar. That this option is rarely taken seems to me an indication of a fundamental suspicion on his part of the too-casual homologies between politics and literature that, as I will suggest in a moment, he criticizes at length. Thus his exercises in literary analysis—the passage on canto 10 of the *Inferno* and his discussions of "form" and "content," for example —work skillfully within Crocean categories for the most part. His overriding interest in what might be called a "sociology" of literature is generally kept separate from these more "purely" literary arguments, a separation Gramsci himself would recall very sharply: "Therefore there are two series of facts, one of an aesthetic character, and the other political-cultural, which is to say political through and through" (*QC*, 1793). At another point, he warns that the "two series" cannot be confused without risking "the defeat or stagnation of rigorous concepts, that is, precisely the failure to attain the ends inherent in the cultural struggle" (*QC*, 2187).

Second, I think there is considerable hesitation in the *Notebooks* about the very possibility of a Marxist aesthetics. For the pressure toward such a position all too clearly derives from the coexistence of Marxism with other and competing forms of cultural analysis in modern and bourgeois-dominated states, with the result that Marxism must somehow come up with an "aesthetics" if it is to compete successfully. And for Gramsci, who staked so many of the arguments in the *Notebooks* on the premise that Marxist theory and practice decisively altered the character of bourgeois philosophy, and put the latter henceforth on the defensive in any intellectual confrontation, to acknowledge an obligation outside Marxism to produce an aesthetics would be to give up a significant advantage. Thus one of the tasks of a sociology of literature is a critical account of aesthetics. But the point when such critique must itself engage in some form of direct literary analysis could only come for Gramsci from within the logic of Marxism's own development, and that point—and how it makes itself felt—are rarely discussed directly.

The clearest suggestion occurs in the contrast between Croce and De Sanctis he makes late in the *Notebooks*: "It is pleasing to hear in him [De Sanctis] the passionate fervor of a man who takes sides, who has firm moral and political convictions and doesn't hide them or even attempt to hide them. Croce succeeds in dividing these diverse aspects of criticism which in De Sanctis were organically joined together and fused into one" (*QC*, 2188). And in the next paragraph: "In short, the type of literary critic peculiar to the philosophy of praxis is offered by De Sanctis, not by Croce or anyone else (even less by Carducci): in such criticism the struggle for a new culture (i.e. a new humanism) and the criticism of customs, feelings, and world views must be fused with aesthetic or purely artistic criticism in a passionate intensity, even if in the form of sarcasm" (*QC*, 2188). But it is difficult to understand how this "fusion" takes place, especially given Gramsci's own warnings about confusing "two series of facts."

What can be specified immediately from the *Notebooks* are the difficulties Gramsci finds inherent in two "resolutions" that have occupied the attention of Marxist and non-Marxist critics alike. The first, in simple terms, argues that a work of literature can be a genuine artistic achievement despite the presence in it of explicit "moral and political convictions" that strike us, for whatever reasons, as untenable, as "reactionary," or as just outdated. With the example of Engels's letter to Margaret Harkness in praise of Balzac's realism, this has proved an attractive possibility to Marxist criticism, since it allows an emphasis on literature *to be read* at least as representing the real complexity of a particular historical moment. Yet Engels's letter is not a little self-serving, for when Balzac is praised for having seen in the novels "the real men of the future," and this "in spite of" his own "opinions," the novels are being lauded for having an intuitive grasp of what Engels, in retrospect, clearly sees himself.[10] That is, the very form of the assertion that a literary work succeeds despite the opinions of the author in it remains at best curiously solipsistic, and at worst a familiar strategy of legitimation. For it is of course the authority of what the *critic* "sees" that is universalized by an appeal to how the author was "capable" of presenting the same complex of relationships even given her or his own tendencies in just the opposite direction.

The more formidable conceptual dilemma of the letter, however, lies in Engels's appropriation of what is finally a formula of liberal tolerance to perform a task of political argument for which it is uniquely unsuited. For the reason for separating the author's opinions from what the work of literature "presents" is the conviction that somehow the "real" process of living goes on "beneath" or "beyond" or in more private, intimate, complex, and intuitive ways than could ever be registered by such "abstract" things as moral and political convictions, of any kind. The latter are then "tolerated" for the sake of what the person qua artist was able to reveal despite the lamentable fact that s/he remains a person with moral and political convictions. And in the argument Engels wants to make for the political value of Balzac's work, any version of such a formula is a disaster.

Gramsci's own references to Engels's letter in the *Notebooks* are nevertheless generally approbatory, although there is the curious qualification that Balzac's "reactionary" opinions are never actually present in the genuinely "artistic" quality of the novels: "That 'politically and socially' he is a reactionary appears only from the extra-artistic parts of his work (digressions, prefaces, etc.)" (*QC*, 1699). Croce's influence is obvious here, but in a letter dated September 5, 1932, Gramsci indicates that ideologically dubious literature remains a real problem for him:

I can admire aesthetically Tolstoy's *War and Peace* and not share in the book's ideological essence; if the two facts were to coincide, Tolstoy would be my *vademecum, le livre de chevet.* The same could be said for Shakespeare, for Goethe, and also for Dante. It would not be exact to say the same for Leopardi, notwithstanding his pessimism. For in Leopardi one finds, in an extremely dramatic form, the crisis of transition toward modern man: the critical abandonment of older transcendental conceptions without at the same time having yet found an *ubi consistam* which is morally and intellectually new, which gives the same certitude as that which was abandoned.[11]

The possibility of a more sophisticated resolution than Engels's hinted in these passages is worked out in more detail in the argument from the *Notebooks* containing the statement about "two series of facts," and beginning with this question: "Is the concept that art is art and not willfully imposed political propaganda in itself an obstacle to the formation of determinate cultural currents which are the reflection of their time and that contribute to the strengthening of determinate political currents?" (*QC*, 1793). Gramsci's answer is that such a strict concept of art "poses the question in its most radical terms." For "once the principle has been established that all we are looking for in a work of art is its artistic character, this in no way excludes inquiry into what mass of feelings, what attitudes toward life circulate within the work itself." De Sanctis certainly, and even Croce, had admitted as much: "What is excluded is that a work of art should be beautiful because of its moral and political content rather than for the form in which the abstract content has fused and become one" (QC, 1793). At this point, the dilemma then seems to resolve itself into an argument that it is the unique quality of a new literary *form* that works a kind of sea change on whatever "opinions" or "abstract content" the writer brings to her or his work. Thus the reason Balzac's "reactionary" ideology, for example, is to be found only in the "extra-artistic" portions of his writing is because in the very making of the novels it was transformed into a unique network of artistic relations bearing little resemblance any more to the "opinions" of the author, or indeed to any immediately recognizable quality of his or her life.

As the passage continues, however, this likewise familiar resolution becomes questionable. Suppose, Gramsci argues, one were to say that "John Doe 'wishes' to express a determinate content and not to make a work of art. The artistic failure of the given work of art ... demonstrates that such content in Doe is hollow and obstinate material, that the enthusiasm of Doe is fictitious and imposed from the outside, that Doe in reality is not, in this determinate case, an artist but instead offers what gives pleasure to his patrons." Again, the debt to Croce's aesthetics should be obvious, but the point is that the two assertions are not homologous. They represent "two series of facts," the first aesthetic and the second political. The demonstration of artistic failure "can help the political critic," but the latter then denounces John Doe "not as artist but as 'political opportunist' " (QC, 1794). Thus the force of the whole passage is finally a negative one: the impossibility of claiming artistic success solely on the basis of political content, and the way in which artistic *failure* can indicate the presence of a political false consciousness as well. Neither argument offers a means of resolving the dilemma of artistic "success" that is ideologically questionable, nor do they indicate how that "fusion" Gramsci praises in De Sanctis might be accomplished.

The most sustained appeal to De Sanctis in the *Notebooks*, however, moves in quite a different direction, summed up in the slogan

andare al popolo and in the call for a "national-popular" literature. Here again, the problems posed by Gramsci are familiar from
other contexts, and it is necessary to recover as carefully as possible
how Gramsci's arguments function if they are not to be assimilated
into a debate that can now be represented with almost schematic
clarity. "Popular culture," it is asserted, touches the entire range
of the population in one way or another, and we may thereby expect to find articulated within it, in however disguised forms, the
authentic hopes and desires of the people, as opposed to "high" art
whose complexities, whose locus of production and consumption in
the university, and whose blatant disregard for what the "ordinary"
person could possibly understand mark it as an elitist defense of
intellectual privilege. Alternatively, "popular culture" is understood
to be a reflex of commodity structure, a reification of the aesthetic
such that the only "end" of cultural production becomes the endless consumption of images that drug the masses, a spectacle that
as "leisure time" at once reproduces and compensates for their exploited labor. "High" art in its very complexity resists assimilation
and is thereby able to maintain an authentic and subversive stance,
increasingly the sole remaining place of the "negative" to challenge
the positive and persuasive force of a culture industry.

Now there are certainly enough statements in the *Notebooks*
attacking Italy's detached and cosmopolitan intellectuals to align
Gramsci with the first position sketched above, to the extent that
Alberto Asor Rosa, for example, was led to argue in *Scrittori e
popolo* that at worst Gramsci's formulations meant

> once again the deferment of a productive, critical relationship between our
> culture and the larger culture of twentieth century Europe, in particular the
> revolutionary experiences of the avantgardes.... The Gramscian national-
> popular gave Italian populism the unitary ideology which it did not possess
> before. But at the same time it took away from it the opportunity ... to
> connect the particular social-political moment with a climate of general
> humanitarian protest.[12]

Yet even the terms of Asor Rosa's critique suggest a rather different
emphasis in Gramsci; his central category, after all, is not "popular culture" as the term is often used, but the "national-popular,"
which means an equal concern with those local and specific narratives popular among and most importantly *produced by* groups of
the population on the margins of social organization, and whose

cultural interests remain marginal in part at least because utterly ignored by leading intellectuals. Indeed, it is primarily as a critical category that "national-popular" functions in the *Notebooks*. Italy has no genuinely "national" and "popular" culture. For Gramsci's sense of "popular culture" does not involve what is circulated widely to the masses from centralized sites of cultural production, but rather what people make themselves in the circumstances of their lives.

Thus Gramsci's challenge to "high" art is not articulated through a contrast with "popular culture" understood as mass circulated material, but rather through a contrast with *politics*, in one of the most difficult passages in the *Notebooks*:

However, as regards the relation between literature and politics, one needs to keep in mind this criterion: the writer must have perspectives necessarily less precise and definite than the man of politics, he must be less "partisan," if one could speak like this, but in a "contradictory" way. For the man of politics, every image "fixed" a priori is reactionary: the politician considers all movement in its becoming. The artist instead must have images "fixed" and cast in their definitive form. The politician imagines man as he is and at the same time as he must be in order to reach a determinate end; his work therefore consists in urging men to stir themselves, to extricate themselves from their present nature in order to become collectively capable of achieving the required end, that is, to "conform themselves" to the end. The artist represents necessarily "that which is" in a certain moment—personally, in a non-conformist way, etc.—realistically. Therefore from a political point of view, the politician will never be content with the artist and could not possibly be: he will find him always behind the times, always anachronistic, always surpassed by real movements. (QC, 1820–21)

With its disturbing echo of Marx's statement in *The Eighteenth Brumaire*—"here the content goes beyond the phrase"—there is no attempt to slide around the issue of "reactionary" opinions. For what Gramsci argues is that from a political point of view, from the perspective of a determinate struggle for a "new culture" and a "new society," not only literature that contains embarrassing opinions, and not only literature that can be identified as performing a specific mission for the ruling class, but *all* literature must be considered as reactionary by virtue of its very success in achieving a "definitive" literary form, no matter how new or radical or innovative that form may be.

Gramsci's conception of "realism" thus has as its immediate target that peculiarly modernist ideology of the new, with its location of artistic authenticity in the struggle to create new *forms* that escape the mass of opinions, conventions, exhausted language, and ideological detritus of the past. He is not simply antimodernist, however, in a version of Georg Lukács's later and invidious distinctions in *The Meaning of Contemporary Realism*. Rather, it is an argument that this specific modernist ideology of the new has obscured its own vital relations to language and society. Thus as an aesthetic criterion, Gramsci's realism is disengaged from the binary value judgment of "reactionary/progressive" appropriated by Lukács, in order to recognize how modernism has been a profound and necessary *reaction* to the symptoms of cultural crisis. Indeed, it becomes possible to understand the division between "high" art and mass circulated material in this sense at least as a false problem projected by the privilege on the one hand accorded to the former as "progressive" because it refuses the terms of commodity organization and, alternatively, to the latter because it remains in touch with the mass of the population. In Gramsci's terms, both are "reactionary," and the very real differences that separate them emerge in part from competing strategies of "resolution."

For literature "must aim at elaborating that which already is, whether politically or in some other way does not matter. What does matter, though, is that it sink its roots in the *humus* of popular culture [as Gramsci understands it, not as mass circulated material] as it is, with its tastes and tendencies and with its moral and intellectual world, even if it may seem backward and conventional" (*QC*, 1822). Unlike an elitist avant-garde, the writer avoids that "parthenogenetic" prejudice that a "new literature must identify itself with an artistic school of intellectual origin, as the futurists did" (*QC*, 1822). But this is not a political command to *write* "popular" literature instead that "ordinary" people could understand immediately, which is of course far more elitist since it assumes that the masses, poor retarded souls that they are, couldn't possibly understand the complexity of the writer's "elaboration" if she or he really used their full intelligence. Realism is not a program for new literature at all, and elsewhere Gramsci argues that the "battleground for the creation of a new civilization is, instead, absolutely mysterious, absolutely characterized by the unforeseeable and the unexpected [*impensato*]." [13] Thus the laconic observation that "if the cultural world for which one struggles is a living and necessary fact, its expansiveness will be irresistible; it will find its artists" (QC, 1794) stands as a critical warning not only to the intellectual imposition of direction, but also to the revolutions of form that fuel the procession of still newer avant-gardes.

At the same time, however, and by the logic of his own argument that modernism is "reactionary," a modernist ideology of the new with its unrelenting emphasis on formal innovation cannot be dismissed as merely false consciousness. For within modernism itself there are at least two dominant and antithetical "resolutions" to the directive to "make it new" that suggest less a division into schools or traditions than a way of realizing how the same text even marks its own break with the past across a necessary indeterminacy of focus. Schematically, the first can be located conveniently in the ambition Eliot finds informing Joyce's Ulysses, where the use of myth is praised as "a way of controlling, of ordering, of giving a shape and a significance to the immense panorama of futility and anarchy which is contemporary history." [14] That is, the past is preserved in the form of myth in order to reconstitute the intractable, resistant, and opaque fragments of the present into a text. Hence the force of Eliot's earlier comment in the same essay that Joyce's use of myth has the value of a "scientific discovery." For it is a making new whose result is a collective "book," the world as text. Against Eliot's reading, however, there is the irreducibly comic momentum of continual misdirection on the part of the characters of Ulysses, the misconstruing of textual order as it is projected by other characters. The high point of this comic disruption occurs at the expense of none other than the omnipresent listening ear of the author of Ulysses himself, whose coding of the figure of Bloom across so many available refinements and elaborations of sign systems collapses on the instant that Molly, of all people, realizes that Bloom seems suddenly, inexplicably in touch with his own immediate desires: "Yes because he never did a thing like that before as ask to get his breakfast in bed." [15]

Ulysses thus stands at the threshold of that increasingly indispensable methodological hypothesis of textual materiality, before the latter spills over into the incoherent attempt to claim signification itself as material production, precisely the kind of static homology that Ulysses both courts and comically subverts. For rather than a "resolution," a completely new text, the material *effects* of textual elaboration emerge in *Ulysses* as *repetitions*—hence the compulsive iteration and continual working over of formulas and phrases throughout the novel—of some more fundamental lack in the ensemble of relations (and misrelations) that marks the discourses Dubliners hold about themselves. *Ulysses* will try the patience of anyone who comes to it expecting a determinate political direction, whether as that now almost unheard of belief in "proletarian literature" or as the currently more fashionable textual revolution. Yet this discontent is in another sense a judgment on ourselves rather than on the author of *Ulysses* for failing to invent a more adequate form of cultural production all by himself.

With such judgment, realism as an aesthetic criterion passes into "the criticism of customs, feelings, and world views" (*QC*, 2188) and thus unavoidably meets once again the dilemma of "reactionary" and "progressive," as "two series of facts," the aesthetic and the political. Yet as I argued earlier, such formulas of binary opposition are throughout the second half of the *Notebooks* redistributed "disymmetrically"—to borrow Buci-Glucksmann's phrase—by the collective logic of "educational" relationships. We may anticipate that in this case as well, collectivity projects both a "critical" and a "utopian" resolution. Indeed, the critical version is available already in the status of realism as an aesthetic criterion, which in this larger sense is precisely the denial of homology, the direct translation of literary form into a "reactionary" or "progressive" politics that vitiates Lukács's arguments in *The Meaning of Contemporary Realism*. For the artistic requirement of "*images* 'fixed' and cast in their definitive form" results in "*perspectives* necessarily less precise and definite than the man of politics" (*QC*, 1822; my emphasis).[16] The writer will be "less 'partisan,' if one can speak like this, but in a 'contradictory' way." That is, the writer in no way abandons her or his moral and political convictions in order to produce "fixed" images that merely "represent" or "reflect" or "express" indifferently the specificity of a given historical moment.[17] Rather, the writer's perspectives exist "in a 'contradictory' way," for both those perspectives *and others* must be "fused" in "definitive" images.

Thus the "message" that everywhere emerges from the achievement of "definitive" literary form is an "elaboration" of conflicts in "that which already is" and is now being "produced" as artistic image. We may then say, contrary to Engels, that the success of

Balzac's realism comes not despite his "reactionary" opinions, but because of them, because artistically "the real men of the future" can be glimpsed only from within the conflicts in which they participate. A far better explanation than Engels's is afforded by Judy Grahn's discussion of her sequence of poems *The Common Woman*:

> The Common Woman Poems have more than fulfilled my idealistic expectations of art as a useful subject—of art as a doer, rather than a passive object to be admired. All by themselves they went around the country. Spurred by the enthusiasm of women hungry for realistic pictures, they were reprinted hundreds of thousands of times, were put to music, danced, used to name various women's projects, quoted and then misquoted in a watered-down fashion for use on posters and T-shirts.[18]

For so far from complaining about "misquotation" and "watering down," Grahn realizes perfectly well that it is only as her poems circulate in all these permutations produced locally by others in the circumstances of their lives, that the poems assume a realist, material force for the real women of the future.

The "utopian"—or, in Grahn's terms, "idealistic"—vocation of political criticism is then easiest to grasp as a way of once more putting in motion what realism as a critical term has kept from collapsing into a static homology. For *educationally*, if it is necessary to recognize "two series of facts," it is equally clear that neither alone is adequate to "the type of critic peculiar to the philosophy of praxis" (*QC*, 2188). "Purely" aesthetic criticism mistakes the achievement of "fixed" images for the overcoming of real contradictions, as if social divisions, like artistic failures, were merely the result of some slippage between form and content to be resolved by editorial re-writing. A "purely" political perspective, on the other hand, remains detached, perpetually discontented at the powerfully seductive presence of "reactionary" positions that emerge from the insistence on asking what an entire world of complex relations would be like as artistic image. The "passionate intensity" Gramsci recommends in De Sanctis, where the political "criticism of customs, feelings, and world views" is "fused with artistic or purely aesthetic criticism" (*QC*, 2188) then becomes nothing less than the utopian realization that "the ends inherent in the cultural struggle" (*QC*, 2187) are not only "partisan" but also and necessarily collective, for which the particular and realistic achievement of artistic form across the conflicts of the present is at once a contradictory and "metaphorical" elaboration. Literature thereby takes its place for the political critic in that dialectical rhythm where "the cultural environment he is proposing to modify . . . reacts back on the philosopher and imposes on him a continual process of self-criticism. It is his 'teacher' " (*SPN*, 350; *QC*, 1331). And for the writer, indeed, "realism" itself becomes a process of political education, of learning one's own perspectives, feelings, "attitude toward life," and artistic power in the making of images in and through "popular culture as it is, with its tastes and tendencies and with its moral and intellectual world, even if it may seem backward and conventional" (*QC*, 1822). Realism is not an imitation of "popular culture," in Gramsci's sense of that term, but an education recognizing one's own participation in it.

I V

I have retained as much as possible Gramsci's terminology of "feeling," of "attitudes," of "form and content," of artistic "images 'fixed' and cast in definitive form," to emphasize how much these arguments depend on Croce's aesthetics. Yet it should be clear that this is finally a terminology turned back on itself, to yield an understanding of artistic struggle and contradiction, of the work of literature as an activity caught up in conflicts rather than an expression of the sublime "harmony" Croce finds characteristic of the highest art.[19] And it is here where the critique of Croce's aesthetics rejoins the critique of an "ethical-political history" with its revisionist force:

Is it fortuitous, or is it for a tendentious motive, that Croce begins his [historical] narratives from 1815 and 1871? I.e. that he excludes the moment of struggle; the moment in which the conflicting forces are formed, are assembled and take up their positions; the moment in which one ethical-political system dissolves and another is formed by fire and steel; the moment in which one system of social relations disintegrates and another rises and asserts itself? Is it fortuitous or not that he placidly takes as history the moment of cultural or ethical-political expansion? (*SPN*, 119; *QC*, 1227)

Earlier, Gramsci had made the connections explicit between "ethical-political history" and Croce's aesthetics:

It can be observed that ethical-political history is an arbitrary and mechanical hypostasis of the moment of hegemony, of political direction, of consensus, in the life and developing activity of the State and of civil society. This formulation which Croce has made of the historiographical problem reproduces his formulation of the aesthetic problem. The ethical-political moment is in history what the moment of "form" is in art. It is the "lyricity" of history, the "catharsis" of history. (QC, 1222)

In a brilliantly sustained analysis of Croce, Lukács, and della Volpe, Arcangelo Leone de Castris argues from this passage and others in Gramsci that the very project of a specifically "Marxist aesthetics" is thereby an impossible union. For Marxism, with its commitment to struggle and class conflict as decisive historical forces of change, must always stand in a critical relation to the promise of aesthetics, to "the value-function of art which, in three diverse philosophical accounts [that is, in Marxist critics like della Volpe and Lukács as well as in Croce], remains circumscribed within the terms of an essentialistic definition and thus explicitly withdrawn from the contradictions of history. Art is non-contradiction, and thereby the alternative of an ideal recomposition opposed to the practical world dominated by contradiction." It is then no accident for Leone de Castris that in all three thinkers aesthetics marks "the conclusion of a complex intellectual road," as "the sign of an ideally autonomous research which offers itself as a model of compensation for the repair of social crisis." [20] The aesthetic is the intellectuals' mode of redeeming the time, while maintaining one's own precarious freedom from the contradictory growth of "mass" society. I will have a great deal more to say in the next chapter about the notion of "compensation" as an informing ideal of educational policy in the growth of a "mass," public education in the United States in this century. But at this point at least, Leone de Castris identifies in neatly summary form a certain visible congruence between aesthetic and educational directions informing the work of leading intellectuals.

Thus in contrast, the achievement of the *Notebooks* for Leone de Castris, which allows Gramsci to think a Marxist critical practice —if hardly a Marxist "aesthetics"—is the recovery of literature as, precisely, "reactionary." Literature is a contested activity caught up in the conflicts and contradictions of "that which is" throughout its elaboration. Yet there remains for me a distinction to be made between Leone de Castris's arguments and Gramsci's, the more subtle perhaps because Leone de Castris, unlike so much that is fashionable in the current projects of ideological demystification, speaks as someone committed to a political party and a specific political praxis. His reading of Croce, nevertheless, suggests a covert utopian promise on the far side of all that carefully tuned and demystifying analysis of aesthetics. It is the belief that once the networks of disguised interests and relations of power stand revealed in all their complexity for what they are, we would be obligated immediately to praxis, that liberated now "from any unilateral and fanatical ideological elements" (*SPN*, 405; *QC*, 1487), as Gramsci might put it; we would act immediately on what we know. That is, the careful, slow uncovering of political interests in the ideological practices of leading intellectuals suddenly stands revealed as already itself the sufficient and unequivocal motive for action.

Gramsci's argument is finally no less utopian perhaps, but in a rather different way. For what one "knows" concretely from an analysis of Croce's aesthetics are not so many formulations to be shed like an old skin at an apocalyptic dawn. It is the recognition instead of a struggle *just underway*, still caught up in contradictions, a "position"—in a long war of position—to be won from the very terms of Croce's philosophy. So it is that shortly after the critique of Croce's "ethical-political" moment as the "catharsis" of history, Gramsci returns to the formula reinvested now with all the force of his own "reciprocal" dialectic of a war of position: "To establish the 'cathartic' moment becomes therefore, it seems to me, the starting point for all the philosophy of praxis, and the cathartic process coincides with the chain of syntheses which have resulted from the evolution of the dialectic" (*SPN*, 367; *QC*, 1244). "Demystification" is then at best a misnomer for Gramsci's anti-Croce, a way of isolating a single critical moment in what he understood as a larger process of understanding. For Gramsci, such understanding can become a principle of knowledge that reveals the terms of conflict only because it is also a principle of action directed toward a position to be won in the struggles of the present.

In the terms of Gramsci's own ideological analysis, the critique of revisionism, of an "ethical-political history" and the aesthetics of intuition, the delineation of the roles of traditional intellectuals and the links to "senators Agnelli and Benni," and not least of all the "return to De Sanctis" with all it implied, could be joined together in the single project of an anti-Croce. For he understood the relationships of class struggle and cultural practices to be mediated everywhere by the unique and central position of Croce himself in Italian culture. The force of the argument, however, lies in its specificity. And once that is clear, the impossibility of trying to identify a single figure like Croce in contemporary culture in the United States should be obvious. For Gramsci did not begin, as it were, with Croce; he arrived at Croce out of an understanding of what possibilities of political praxis existed in the social formation of Italy as he saw it.

If there is no Croce in our culture, there is a powerfully centralizing literary "tradition" that in its own way might also occupy a vital zone of conflict and matrix of education for the future. Indeed, recent cultural history, where again and again formerly marginal, repressed, or censored texts are "incorporated" into a "tradition," indicates that a conflict is at least being fought on one side. It is perhaps only a kind of nostalgia that would attempt to appropriate directly from Gramsci's anti-Croce the means to change that history in the future. But I can think of no better example with which to challenge the isolation of ideological analysis from concrete cultural struggles. The conditions will be different, very different indeed, I will argue in the next chapter. For literature and literary study not only have a particular organization in the United States, but a particular location of work as well that itself occupies positions in the cultural economy involving a great many functions besides the study of literature. My argument will be a *use* of Gramsci's analysis as a point of departure, if also I think an exemplary point.

THREE

Literary Criticism: Work as Evaluation

The increasingly frequent appearance of "production" and its variants to describe the making of literature, and "ideology" or some determinate relation to ideological discourse to describe what results from that making, are indications of a number of conceptual changes in the practices of literary study generally in the university. Perhaps the easiest way to focus these changes is to recognize how they involve another range of questions than those posed by an older terminology of "creation" and of "aesthetic objects." For where the latter lead to issues of definition (what exactly is the *literary* quality of "literature"?), of differentiation and of origin, the new terms redirect attention to function, use, and the structures of exchange in circulation. Thus "how does it work," for example, replaces the search for an origin that could authorize a proper name, as it were. Likewise, questions involving "audience" and "audience appeal" turn into questions about the legitimation of cultural authority. Antinomies such as how a poem can simultaneously be a system of shared generic conventions and a unique, creative form turn into a scrutiny of how specific texts might be understood as normalizing or, alternatively, challenging dominant cultural values. Different questions then mean different practices of critical analysis, and as my examples suggest, an altered sense of the very relation between text and analysis.

Underlying these changes in terminology and in critical practices, there is of course a shift in what might be called for convenience analogical perspective. If since the Romantics it was an "organic" analogy that lent itself to descriptions of both a process of creation and the aesthetic object that results, here instead it is the material production of commodities that supplies the analogical force. Now Romantic poets knew well enough that poems weren't really trees, and it should be equally obvious that ideologies are not quite the same thing as commodities. They are not produced in the same way as material goods; they do not circulate in the same way; nor are terms like "use," "exchange," and "circulation" in relation to literary values the same as the "use-value," "exchange-value," and "circulation" of commodities that occupy Marx's analysis of material production in the first three chapters of *Capital*. *Books* may indeed be commodities in modern capitalist societies, but "literature" and its peculiar complex of ideological relations are no more simply commodities than poems are trees. Thus when Marx arrives at that best-known and most widely quoted passage early in *Capital*—about how a commodity may appear a trivial thing while "abounding in metaphysical subtleties and theological niceties" when looked at more closely—the similarity to how recent theorizing will describe the "mysteries" of literary discourse and its ideological relations is, precisely, a similarity and not a homology.[1]

The analogy can and has been attacked in many ways; I'm more immediately interested, however, in pursuing it a bit further, to see what directions it might yet be made to yield. For the passage I alluded to above does come very early in *Capital*, and Marx is quite emphatic about what happens next in his analysis. Commodities may be strange things, but he didn't propose to spend the next several hundred pages in elucidating their peculiarities. The point of that early remark is that one of the characteristics of commodities and commodity circulation, examined in and of themselves, is the multiplication of innumerable mysteries. And rather than pursue those mysteries on their own terms, Marx turns instead to a study of the transformation of labor under capitalism. What happened to the "craft skills" of work when carried out under the new conditions of the factory? How was the very process of work redesigned to conform to the conditions of this new workplace? What complex of social relations emerged between "workers" and "capitalists" across this workplace? What are the differences between these social relations of production and the material effort of work? How are the terms of the working day set? What specifically about the organization of work enabled the actual production of surplus value to be realized as capital? The list of such questions is a long one indeed, because for Marx understanding not only the "secret" of commodity form, but also the position of the proletariat as a revolutionary class begins in an understanding of these transformations of labor under capitalism.

Ideological production is not the same as material production, and thus there may well exist good reasons to focus an analysis of the former far more closely on the mysteries involved in the use, exchange, and circulation of ideological discourse, including of course that peculiar complex of literature and literary study. Certainly Gramsci's proposed anti-Croce in the *Notebooks* both delivers a considerable detail and suggests a cogent explanation for such scrutiny. (And though in volume 1 Marx rarely directly pursues an analysis of the "metaphysical subtleties and theological niceties" of the commodity form, he certainly attends to their effects in the writing of other economists.) At the same time, however, Gramsci's discussions of Croce were part of a projected history of Italian intellectuals. Indeed, the amount of material in the *Notebooks* dealing with what especially to a non-Italian reader may seem an almost tedious tracing of various groups, alignments, and tactical decisions is far greater than the electrifying few pages about the general social functions of intellectuals, or even of ideological analysis of "Croce's philosophy." For the material about Italian intellectuals is also at least a tentative outline of the transformation of *intellectual work*.

The questions appropriate to this history are not identical to those posed about capitalist material production by Marx, but clearly it made sense to Gramsci to ask about the work of ideological production as carried out by those socially designated as intellectuals. What is it like? Where does it take place? Who does it, and have those groups changed significantly in composition? How is the work organized? Who or what determines that organization? What relations does it have to the work of material production? How are people trained to do it? How is that training organized and legitimized? That is, Gramsci, like Marx, finally is not interested in "demystification." His anti-Croce wasn't just out to expose—beneath the "metaphysical subtleties and theological niceties"—how Croce's philosophy functioned *as* ideology, any more than Marx's interest was just to expose how material production under capitalism functioned as commodity structure.

I argued in the previous chapter that there is no single figure like Croce in contemporary culture in the United States, and there is no single discourse that commands the cultural field in quite the same way. Thus an "anti-Eliot" or an "anti-Dewey" or some such thing would be a sort of exercise in reverse hyperbole rather than a program of political praxis such as Gramsci assumed his anti-Croce might become in Italy. Nevertheless, there does exist a large, complex, organized, and multiple process of intellectual work carried out in English departments throughout the country. For literary circulation involves not only a range of often mystifying ideological practices, but also the organization of a *workplace*. Of course all university English departments are not the same. But before any celebration of the "diversity" or "pluralism" or "heterogeneity" or whatever generated by this unremarkable assumption begins, it is worth remembering that all university English departments *are* organized workplaces; that organized workplaces where literary study takes place on such a scale involve a relatively very new social formation; and that the presence of this formation signals a profound transformation of intellectual work.

Simply, then, rather than abandoning as suspect logic any analogy between "material production" and "ideological production," I think it worth pursuing the analogy further. For if in Marx's analysis, the mysteries of commodity form suggested a necessity to examine the transformation of labor under capitalism, then perhaps the mysteries of ideologies might likewise suggest an inquiry into the transformation of intellectual work. English departments are not the only and hardly the most important location of intellectual work. But they are such a location, and for reasons not altogether clear (at least if you take as evidence of "reasons" the typical "mission" statement of a university English department) a pervasive location. Gramsci's arguments can provide a point of departure for my inquiry, not only because he paid close attention to the enormous expansion of categories of intellectuals in relation to an educational system, but also because he recognized that unlike "traditional" intellectuals these newer categories of intellectuals are also often wage laborers who work somewhere with a lot of other people doing similar work. It may not be organized in quite the same way as factory work in Turin, and what is produced doesn't circulate like Fiats. Yet Gramsci at least thought it important enough to devote a great deal of the *Notebooks* to a history of intellectuals.

It's certainly true that thinking about the organization of work in English departments hardly installs you at some more "primary" level of concreteness, "beneath" the mysteries of ideologies. Anyone who thinks the allocation of work time in a university, for example, a "concrete" reality might likewise suspect that Hamburger Helper has a natural relation to cows. The point, however, is not still another new way to "demystify" ideological discourse from somewhere else; it's to stay there long enough to understand the work of ideological production and what it might explain about the social functions of intellectuals who work in English.

I

In what I assume is not an atypical exercise, the university where I work asks all faculty at the end of each quarter to submit a form indicating average number of hours spent each week during the quarter in various activities—for example, in class, class preparation, advising, research, travel, departmental and college administration, and so forth. I'd always assumed the exercise was a singularly silly one, but while average hours were hard to come by, I took it seriously enough a few terms back to discover that I could account with depressing ease for how I spent most of my time. I taught two undergraduate classes, requiring then two sets of decisions about what texts to order, what to read, what written work to assign. I read 211 student papers from those classes, assigning a grade to each one and a final grade to each of the total of 64 students who finished the quarter. I directed 2 graduate students in independent reading courses, helped write and evaluate 9 Ph.D. examinations, and directed 1 M.A. thesis. I wrote 18 letters of recommendation for students, to various ends, and 2 letters of recommendation for faculty. I read and wrote evaluations of 2 essays submitted to journals for publication. As a member of the department's executive committee, to whom the search committees for hiring new positions reported, I read dossiers for 28 job candidates and attended 4 lectures by visiting candidates. As secretary of the executive committee, I prepared minutes for all the committee meetings for distribution to the department. I was a member of a university committee assigned to write a review—in cooperation with one member from outside the university—of another department for the College Council; the review involved interviewing 26 people at length before beginning to write. I'm not sure how many, or how much time exactly, was spent "advising" former, current, and prospective students; in retrospect it seems considerable, in actuality probably less. I finished 2 essays I had presented earlier at conferences, for publication in journals.

I may have left out some things in this inventory (most obviously typing, preparing ditto masters and running them off, writing letters, and so forth); for others, similarly hired in the "area" of criticism and theory by an English department in a university, the relative emphasis among these activities may vary, as it will for me, from one term to another. For those in other "areas," it may vary more or vary less. But however variable the details, at least *grosso modo* such an inventory provides one kind of answer to the question of what "literary critics" do. It is not a very satisfactory answer if one is looking for conceptual definition, or for explanations of what functions "literary criticism" performs within a general complex of social relations. Nevertheless, it helps make clear three closely related points that bear on these more high-powered versions of the question.

First, literary criticism as practiced in an English department in the university is multiple. Which is not quite the same as "pluralistic" or "heterogeneous." It is multiple because the actual labor time is necessarily split among a lot of different activities. No critic in the university does nothing but write about literature and theory. The process of training "to be" a critic assumes writing about literature and theory as the essential job of work to be performed, and accordingly very little attention is given even to teaching, let alone writing departmental reviews or committee minutes. Training, that is, organizes a hierarchy of work activities around the primacy of conceptual definition (although there may be little enough agreement about *what* conceptual definition is primary). Labor time, however, tells another story. It would be unlikely to find a definition of "literary criticism" that begins by focusing on the construction of letters of recommendation attesting to a candidate's verbal and conceptual skills, but in the flat terms of labor time, it is no more unlikely than most definitions with which I am familiar. The temporal allocation of work imposes a multiplicity that has little respect for the primacy of intrinsic definitions.

The second point, however, while recognizing this multiplicity of activities, recognizes also that every one of them is located in the same workplace. The dramatic conceptual changes in literary criticism make it all too easy to overlook how relatively recent and *complete* this development is. For all the conceptual differences, Samuel Johnson wrote literary criticism over 200 years ago. He wrote essays, poems, a dictionary, prefaces, introductions, dedications, biographies, scholarly editions, and so forth, many dealing with the "same" texts still circulating. And as the *Norton Anthology of English Literature* proudly reminds us, he even earned a living writing. But he didn't go to work anywhere. He didn't go someplace where there were a lot of other people hired to do the same sorts of things he did in a building designed and constructed to house a lot of people doing the same sorts of things. Nor did he spend much time, as my inventory suggests I do, in "training" people to do that work in the same kind of place, or "screening" people who want to work in the same "department" of people, or deciding the "merit" or "tenurability" of those who already work in the same department. It's not just that literary criticism has changed conceptually since Johnson. What one does, where, for whom, and with whom have changed perhaps even more dramatically.

Finally, although this may not be as immediately obvious, my inventory indicates that though literary criticism is multiple, not only are those multiple activities located in the same workplace, but they have the same abstract labor form. Briefly, that form is the following: A accomplishes a task of speaking or writing; B evaluates the performance of that task; and B reports the evaluation to A and/or C. Each of the activities I listed in one way or another can be reassembled in this form, for it permits considerable variation and complication. B may directly assign a task to A; or it may be that A might not even think of her or his work as a "task" exactly, and a potential B and/or C remain an unknown; sometimes C will intervene directly, to the point of assigning not only the task but the person of A and B; sometimes C will be invisible, sometimes a distinct group; A may have lived hundreds of years ago, or A may be a contemporary. There is a very long list of possible combinations, and any single person will likely rotate through each of the three positions at some time or another. The *abstract form* of the process, however, remains the same. It doesn't directly define any specific conceptual content; it is the form through which such content circulates, in which it is passed on.

Now Samuel Johnson of course evaluated, and it is not entirely fanciful to see the Preface to his edition of Shakespeare, for example, as the "report" of B on the work of Shakespeare, on A. Johnson himself seems sensible of some such implication, and suggests that in writing about Shakespeare at least, the terms of the relation might have to become reversible; that is, Shakespeare is also and everywhere a measure, a B, of anyone who presumes to evaluate his plays. But if one then asks *why* Johnson felt it necessary to pronounce on the "excellencies" and "defects" of the plays in his Preface—given this potentially damaging reciprocity of judgment—the answer is not an easy one. Even "vulgar" economic considerations are not inappropriate; certainly they weren't to Johnson. (James Boswell records for example a letter to Charles Burney in December 1757, eight years before the edition was finally published, where Johnson worries that "the subscription has not been very successful."[2] Hence in part the eight years.) The reasons why Johnson expected his potential audience to expect evaluations of Shakespeare's plays are complicated indeed. Nevertheless, one possibility need not be explored at all. He didn't evaluate Shakespeare's plays because it was required by his *place* of work. He didn't have one.

It is impossible for literary criticism not to deal with values, however differently "values" and the relation of work to values may be construed. It is, in this very broad sense, "ideological work." Unlike Johnson, however, many literary critics today can recognize this involvement with values and still be offended at the suggestion that they *evaluate*. Johnson evaluated; Arnold evaluated; Leavis evaluated. We do research, scholarship, interpretation, editing, theory, history, literacy training, cultural criticism, ideological analysis, deconstruction, etc., etc. And when we do, we then produce a "paper" or "book manuscript," usually with both length and deadline—as well as a host of more nebulous factors—at least roughly determined. The paper or book manuscript is then submitted to a journal or a university press, where it is "read" and either approved for publication or returned. If the former, it is likely "reviewed" by still more readers, and certainly by promotion, tenure, and raise committees within departments. The similarity to the submission and evaluation of student "papers" is, perhaps painfully, obvious. But the student-teacher relation is hardly the "basis" of this process. It is not because, unlike Johnson, we are also teachers that we evaluate "literary criticism" in this way. After all, it is possible to imagine all sorts of relations between students and teachers, all kinds of conceptions of what it might mean for one person to "teach" another. There seems nothing natural, essential, or inherent in the relationship such that it must eventuate in the form of my A/B/C. Rather than its basis, the relation of student to teacher, like "research" and a myriad of other relations, has been *conformed* to this particular process.

As an abstract labor form, work in English involves multiple activities engaged in by a number of people concentrated at the same workplace. What results from that abstract labor form, what abstract labor "produces" and passes on, are evaluations. The details I've listed for my survey of labor time in my particular "area" of English, in order to arrive at this generalization, are by no means unfamiliar. They are, if anything, all too familiar. Nevertheless, they are not ordinarily what is implied by "work" in English. If someone asks you at a conference, for example, "what are you working on now?," the expected answer will hardly be "evaluations." Nor will it be "the minutes for the last executive committee meeting," "letters of recommendation," or even "my nineteenth-century American literature seminar next term." The expected answer will be a brief summary of the current article or book manuscript. Neither kind of answer is necessarily inaccurate, but the difference between them suggests what Richard Ohmann, in *English in America*, observes as one of the "peculiarities" of work in English. Indeed, a great many such "peculiarities of English departments," Ohmann argues, "and of the way teachers act through them, can best be understood as the result of a clash between the professional claims of the faculty and the externally imposed conditions of our working lives."[3] The argument is worth following, because *English in America* is one of very few available points of departure for an inquiry into the organization of work in English. That is, Ohmann's interest in the history of English departments, like Gramsci's in the history of Italian intellectuals, is also an interest in the transformation of ideological work.

There is much to support the sense Ohmann's comment registers of "external" imposition. Because English professors were first students, we have been habituated from preteen years to a regimen of approximately 50-minute segments of "learning time" in class-

rooms, to the routine of assignments, due dates, written work, and
so forth, and to a New Year that begins in September. However,
the graduation from student to teacher is hardly an escape, but a
reconfirmation that all these things constitute a physical as well as
a mental discipline. As Gramsci remarks: "Many people have to be
persuaded that studying too is a job, and a very tiring one, with
its own particular apprenticeship—involving muscles and nerves as
well as intellect. It is a process of adaptation, a habit acquired with
effort, tedium and even suffering." A more or less rapid process of
"adaptation," he goes on to add, has a great deal to do with "success" in school: "Undoubtedly the child of a traditional intellectual
family acquires this psycho-physical adaptation more easily. Before
he ever enters the classroom he has numerous advantages over his
comrades, and is already in possession of attitudes learned from his
family environment, he concentrates more easily, since he is used to
'sitting still' etc."[4]

The change from student to teacher, if anything, heightens an
awareness of the long process of adaptation. For it is not the end
of gradations and hierarchies, but the beginning of a whole new set
as rigid in its own way as the march from kindergarten to Ph.D.,
if often more refined. Its refinement necessitates an almost hyper-
awareness that learns to fasten, like Puritanism, on the smallest
details of behavior to wrench from them their allegorical significance. Faculty meetings always afford exquisite examples of this
Puritan tenacity. In any case, "everyone knows" all the time that you
don't teach best, or learn best, the importance of reading *Huck Finn*
in a class of 40 or 50 students during a prescribed interval of time
by means of assignments necessarily tailored for rapid evaluation
and recording, and that it is even harder to get at that importance
when one is also expected to "transmit" the "basic skills" of writing.
The organization of work seems determined elsewhere, for other
reasons altogether. Since the internal hierarchies of the profession
rarely reward quality of instruction anyway, the imposition becomes
a double one; already an alien routine itself, it is then perceived
as interposed between the time available for work and the satisfaction of "career" goals. It looks like an organization that continually
threatens to engulf a professional identity, a "real self" as it were, to
be maintained against these "externally imposed conditions."

With some obvious exceptions, English professors on the whole, no matter how "productive," don't make a whole lot of money either. Thus it is often a shock to find ourselves a target of sometimes very intense antagonism. I remember a conversation with my cousin, who began 25 years ago as a lineman for Southwest Bell, regarding his son who had just taken a job in a Southwest Bell office. His son had lost a chance at a gymnastics scholarship to the university, quitting school and getting married. His wife—a straight-A student in high school who lost a chance at an academic scholarship—was now at home taking care of a baby and hoping to get secretarial work in the near future. Nevertheless, my cousin was encouraged at the prospects, because at the job interview his son had been told that within five years he could still "make management" if he did well. I thought my response had been properly enthusiastic (although not "management," my cousin now earns more money than I do), but something in my tone must have given me away. "That can't mean anything to you," my cousin said, "but it means everything to me." It meant that unlike him, his son might yet have a "career," might yet be perceived as a professional, might yet acquire everything I seemed to have but without breaking from family, class, and home city ties to attend the university as I had done. It was a vindication of all these things against my defection to the enemy. So far from an "external" routine imposed on those who perform it, from my cousin's perspective the work of an English professor, as a professional, doesn't look like "real," productive work at all. It looks instead like a bonus derived from an educational system that belittled and defeated the efforts of a great many people like him subjected to its control, that distinguishes a qualitatively different form of life forever just above, virtually unattainable, and with a continually insidious power to appropriate the productive labor of others, by means of everything from laws to taxes.[5]

Clearly the terms I have borrowed and used very loosely to designate work as "abstract," "productive" or "unproductive," and so forth involve more than a material, technical effort of making a product. As Marx's analysis emphasizes, they describe a specific *social* organization of labor. Thus for example a woman baking bread on a farm, for the use of the family, was certainly working and certainly making a useful product. But she was not engaged in "productive" labor since the making and use of the bread yielded no *surplus* value. That same woman, working in a bakery with a can of sesame seeds sprinkling them on balls of dough moving through a machine, which are later baked into hamburger buns and sold to Safeway, is now laboring "productively." That her labor is also "abstract" is no descriptive abstraction either, but an account of how her work fits into a redesigned mechanism of efficient production. Because work is always a specific complex of social relations as well as a certain kind of effort, it can also involve sharply antagonistic perceptions of how it is organized. Thus another of the "peculiarities of English departments," to borrow Ohmann's phrase, is an organization of work that seems on the one hand to be *designed* somewhere else and imposed on the professional identities of those who perform it, and yet on the other seems itself part of a process of *designing* a system of expectations, controls, and appropriations to be exacted from someone else.

I have suggested in effect three different directions of inquiry into work in English. The first one turns on the distinction between the multiplicity of actual, concrete activities in which those who work in English are engaged, and what I have called the "abstract form" of these multiple activities, a process of evaluation. The second, following Ohmann, involves the many different conflicts that emerge between "the professional claims of the faculty" on the one hand, and "the externally imposed conditions of our working lives" on the other. The third distinguishes between how work in English often appears an organization designed somewhere else and imposed on those who do it, and at the same time an organization generated by those *in* English and imposed on others. These three directions coalesce at the point where an English department becomes a contact between a system of education and the society to which it belongs. That is, they coalesce at the *workplace*. I don't intend to imply that finally "ideological production" and "material production" then really are homologous, and certainly not that the labor process of the former is just like clerical work, work on an assembly line, on a Southwest Bell truck, or in a warehouse. Much of my argument will be taken up with showing why it isn't. Nevertheless, it does seem to me that one of the characteristics of "ideology" under the capitalism of our society is that it is "produced" in a workplace that concentrates a lot of other people engaged in similar work. An English department is such a place.

If one begins with the internal priorities of work in an English department, it is immediately clear why the shift in emphasis signaled by a terminology of ideological production finds literature and literary criticism obvious material. Analysis among other things denaturalizes the priorities of work centered in literature, by playing the exposure of ideological function against the value claims constructed to justify priority. But if instead one begins with English as a workplace in an educational system, one of many contacts between education and society, then it is no longer quite as clear why the privilege is accorded literature and literary criticism, nor exactly what end is served by denaturalizing it. For insofar as the social function of *education* is construed to be the training of people in job skills, for example, the contribution English makes is "peculiar" indeed. Many jobs in our society require a capacity to read, some a capacity to write as well. But neither the direct training of students nor the training of students to teach reading and writing rank very highly in the priorities of an English department. The work that is privileged, the study of English and American literature and literary criticism, is systematically carried out nowhere but in English departments, and nobody but English departments hires people to engage specifically in this work.

Alternatively, insofar as the social function of education itself can be construed as ideological, as a "socialization" of the young, the contribution of English appears more substantial. Yet whether that contribution is assumed to be an indispensable "humanistic perspective," or a kind of central propaganda office for disseminating the values of a dominant culture, exaggeration is easy. All things are relative, but English has become on the whole a large and expensive department to maintain, usually by far the largest and most influential of the humanities. And I find it difficult to believe it *is* maintained because a "humanistic perspective" is everywhere understood as socially indispensable. If it were, other departments in the humanities would likely have exhibited at least something of the same growth as English; rather, philosophy most obviously has declined into a tiny enclave of isolated specialists. Conversely, a culture that can sell Cabbage Patch dolls to the point of physical violence among consumers probably has rather more efficient ways of disseminating dominant cultural values than by means of "reactionary" readings of *Huck Finn* in English classrooms. Doubtless education in general does train at least some people in job skills, especially those who will have a role in the major technologies of knowledge that organize and distribute social power. It also functions to normalize dominant cultural values. Neither function, however, is especially helpful in explaining why English in particular has become a relatively important part of the educational system, and they are even less helpful in understanding the "peculiarities" of work in English I have sketched as directions of inquiry.

The multiple activities of work in English are all in one way or another involved with "value": aesthetic, moral, political, social, critical, or whatever. Work in English, in this broad sense again, is ideological work. What is *circulated directly* as a result of work in English, however, are not values but evaluations. To take perhaps the simplest example, what is passed on directly from an instructor in English in the form of a final grade for a student on a transcript is not the aesthetic value of *Paradise Lost*, the distantiation of ideology in *Middlemarch*, the aporias of sensuous imagery in a Keats ode, or the gender consciousness of a Rich poem. What is passed on is a grade evaluating student achievement in comparison to other students. The evaluation may be "based on" any or all of the above, and any or all of the above may then be circulated indirectly. What the workplace of education requires from the English instructor, however, is the evaluation of the student. The "concrete labor" of instruction may—*or it may not*—reflect dominant cultural values, may or may not "produce" new values, may or may not attempt a massive critical "destruction" of the "very notion" of value, but it *will be* passed on as an evaluation. It will circulate directly as abstract labor. In this sense evaluations represent a kind of surplus value of ideological work. That is, the organization of work in English as living, abstract labor generates evaluations as a surplus value that exceeds the ideological direction and force available from the work process itself. Thus the relation between value and evaluation in ideological work is not identical to the relation between value and surplus value in material production. But the analogy affords a way to emphasize that a structurally similar distinction exists in the organization of education.

For to some extent of course the distinction holds for *any* department, any contact between education and society. Education at every level generates evaluations. The distinction holds more visibly for English insofar as (1) the direct contribution of English to the technologies of knowledge is proportionally more difficult to demonstrate, and what contribution it does make is hardly reflected in the internal priorities of work in English; (2) the relation between the assignment of a grade and the "mastery" of specific skills, especially in literature and theory classes, is rarely passed on as such "outside" the university; it is passed on as a determinate relation, if at all, as it is recirculated back into the labor force of English; (3) English is proportionally larger and more influential within the university than other departments whose work, like English, involves primarily "values" in one way or another (involves, that is, ideological work). Thus the surplus value of evaluations appears more obviously and visibly the result of work in education the more obviously *indirect*, as in English, the social functions education performs for society. Education generally performs a number of social functions. But the specific function of education that can help explain the relative importance of English and the "peculiarities" of work in English must then evidence as a crucially constitutive element a conception of education as in some sense discontinuous with the larger social organization. It must evidence a conception of education that *stresses a surplus*, something education provides for the society over and above its strictly functional use value.

The conception of education I want to pursue has had a long history in the United States, at least as far back as Horace Mann. Briefly, it is a conception that vests in a general, public system of education a power to *compensate* for the problems projected by the structure and organization of society as a whole. As I will argue, what exactly that system is expected to compensate for has taken many different forms. The point to emphasize is that in all its forms, it is a conception that begins in an assertion of discontinuity, of indirection. Education does *not* simply reproduce existing social relations; it is not only functional. In one way or another, it adjusts and compensates for those social relations by adding something to them.[6] Given my premise that what English as abstract labor produces are evaluations, we can then anticipate that insofar as an educational system is organized as compensatory, that organization will be designed to supply a means of distinguishing and sorting out degrees of "achievement," of "individual capacity," and so forth, *unavailable in other ways from the structure of society*. Education compensates for that unavailability, and the different forms compensation has taken will pass through a common nexus of "sorting." In turn, insofar as it is possible to specify more exactly why this differentiation is socially important, what surplus it adds, and why education has been designated to supply it, then it should also be possible to understand in considerably more detail both the social organization of work in English—work as abstract labor—and the growth and importance of English departments within a system of education.

In capitalist production, Marx argued, concrete labor increasingly is redesigned to conform to the calculation of abstract labor-power. Thus factory machinery, for example, figures largely in Marx's analysis of the transformation of labor, not because—like later bourgeois economists—Marx was a determinist, but because he wasn't. Machinery was an *instrument* that enabled the owners of production to redesign, organize, and gain control over the very processes of work. I have appropriated the terms "concrete labor" and "abstract labor" to describe ideological work as well; here, too, they distinguish between the effort of work, the transformation of whatever "material" is worked on, and the social organization of work whose "abstract" form generates surplus value. In ideological work, however, not only is the material different; so is the relation between concrete and abstract labor. In English, the results of what one does circulate in a new form, as an evaluation. But *how* one works does not have to conform completely to the requirements of abstract labor. Unlike concrete labor in production, the work process itself is not completely redesigned in every detail. One must grade students in class, for example, but within certain limits it is not necessary to teach this text rather than another; it is not necessary to assign X number of papers, spend X number of hours grading; it is not even necessary to be scrupulously careful that students hear from you only "proper" and "right" social values. Likewise, if one wants to publish in recognized professional journals in English, what one writes will undergo a process of evaluation. But again, within certain limits, it is possible to exercise some considerable control over the work of writing. Indeed, "the professional claims of the faculty," to return to Ohmann's phrase, involve among other things precisely that control. It is not absolute by any means; hence in part the continual conflicts Ohmann adduces. But neither is it an illusion. Unlike concrete labor in a capitalist production of goods, concrete labor in English is relatively free.

Insofar as education is organized as compensatory, that organization should then help make it possible to understand why a relative freedom is permitted to concrete labor, and something more about its precise limitations. For as compensatory, work in education is also partially dissociated from the structure of work elsewhere in society. If it is to compensate for what is unavailable elsewhere, education as a whole must then be relatively free to construct its own distinctive *internal* organization of work. Other "professions" likewise evidence such an internal organization. Other professions, however, sell specific services to a clientele, and thus the internal organization will develop to define an area of expertise, to maximize control over that area, and to facilitate the sale of expertise. As compensatory, education does not provide services in quite the same way, nor does it have a specifically targeted clientele in the same way (although because education also provides professional training, the relations often become very complicated indeed). Further, specific units within education can generate their own intradepartmental organization of work; in English, this organization can even privilege an expertise in the study of literature that, MLA fantasies to the contrary, cannot be sold anywhere other than in English departments.

Thus one of the costs of dissociation, of an internal organization of work, emerges at the point where the work that goes on in education seems to have less and less direct contact, where it is likely to seem *to others* as not "real work" at all. This is, again, especially true of English, whose importance I will argue is primarily intraeducational, a function of the internal organization of education and not of a professional expertise that could be sold elsewhere. It should not really be surprising that students are often less than thrilled that somebody is being paid to exercise control over their job prospects by, of all things, evaluating how well they reconstruct the nature imagery in some poem written by some English guy 300 years ago.

In this chapter, I will focus primarily on the social organization of work in English, on work as abstract labor, and on evaluations as the surplus value that results. On the one hand, this involves, I think, a great many of the most familiar and routine details of labor time in English. But on the other, as I suggested, it is not a discussion of what most of us mean most of the time when we talk about "our work," nor will I have much to say here of what we often anticipate as the consequences of "our work." For my immediate purposes in this chapter, the most explosively radical theoretical essay and the most banal repetition of plot summary to a bored intro class on Friday afternoon have one "consequence" in common. In one way or another, they are converted to and circulate as abstract labor. The argument will develop, as it already has, by sometimes impossibly large generalizations; work in English as a "contact" between a system of education and the society to which it belongs covers a lot of territory. However, I think some understanding of this social organization of work necessary before going any further. For concrete labor in English is relatively free, and that has made possible not only a rather rapid and astonishing process of change in work skills and knowledges, but also a certain control over the directions of change. What I called in my first chapter an "ideology of the new" is in these terms a reflection of the power to control and direct changes in concrete labor. *But that is not the same as a power to control and direct the consequences of concrete labor.* Changing the values by which one reads recent poetry is not simply a matter of reading poems differently, in a new way. It is a matter of changing what happens to *whatever way* poems are read.

If it is to have consequences in the cultural circulation of ideas and values, if it is to intervene in the conflicts of social values as in any sense an effective part of a war of position, then we must find how concrete labor in English can be realized in some other terms than as a conversion to the abstract labor form of work in English. A praxis of cultural politics, I will argue, thus begins in the conditions of work. Cultural politics in this sense remains of course ideological work; the consequences possible to concrete labor in English involve the cultural circulation of ideas and values, not some utopian praxis "beyond" all such things. But if you do work in English, consequences at all—let alone "beyonds"—require dealing with the circumstances and location of work, with the social organization of English.

I I

Because of its recent use to designate, for example, specific programs of "compensatory education" for "culturally disadvantaged children," the connection between education and attempts to compensate for social inequalities is perhaps more obvious and visible than what has remained for some time a far more diffusely elaborated expectation. It is that education can provide a basis for a structure of social authority congruent with the principles of a democratic society. These are pretty much the terms in which Charles William Eliot in his inaugural lecture at Harvard in 1869 announced the mission of the university to be the training of an elite who could assume the direction of society. Thinking of the individual privileges that accrue to the educated professional, Ohmann remarks that "a profession is in many ways the nearest approximation offered by bourgeois society to title and rank" (*EA*, 236). But nobility was also of course the source of social authority, and that analogy cuts deeper if one thinks in terms of authority as well as privilege. For Eliot at least, that some stable structure was necessary to control the chaos of the times seemed self-evident. And in a democracy the source of that structure could only lie in the impartial use of knowledge by men who had earned the right on the basis of merit and training. Education by merit compensated for the absence of a stable, hereditary class structure. If in a democratic society, for Eliot, the potential danger was always the lack of a central and coordinating structure to establish purpose and direction, the inestimable advantage was that democracies by means of rigorous academic training could generate a far more competent and disciplined form of social authority. Education quite literally would take the place of title and rank, only it would do so "democratically," sorting out people by merit rather than birth; and it would do so more efficiently, by means of specific training and knowledge.

Among other things, this meant for Eliot that all disciplines of learning were to be treated equally in the structure of the university; the lecture begins by dismissing as affording "no practical lesson for us to-day" the old controversies about what subject "supplies the best mental training."[7] But it emphatically did not mean that all students would engage every subject equally: "As a people, we do not apply to mental activities the principle of division of labor; and we have but a halting faith in special training for high professional employments. The vulgar conceit that a Yankee can turn his hand to anything we insensibly carry into high places, where it is preposterous and criminal" (*IA*, 11). For what is at stake in academic training is the social authority of professional competence in the State, whose efficiency, like the efficiency of production, demands a division of labor: "As tools multiply, each is more ingeniously adapted to its own exclusive purpose. So with the men that make the State. For the individual, concentration, and the highest development of his own peculiar faculty, is the only prudence. But for the State, it is variety, not uniformity, of intellectual product, which is needful" (IA, 13).

Eliot knew very well that whatever the professed ideals of democracy or appeal of intellectual efficiency, his particular audience on that particular day might not take very well to any sign that a Harvard education would no longer be a mark of gentlemanly privilege and class solidarity. Thus he makes very clear that it is still a form of "aristocracy" he had in mind, but one based on achievement rather than wealth and birth: "If by aristocracy be meant a stupid and pretentious caste, founded on wealth, and birth, and an affectation of European manners, no charge could be more preposterous: the College is intensely American in affection, and intensely democratic in temper. But there is an aristocracy to which the sons of Harvard have belonged, and, let us hope, will ever aspire to belong—the aristocracy which excels in manly sports, carries off the honors and prizes of the learned professions, and bears itself with distinction in all fields of intellectual labor and combat" (IA, 22). The variety of training will serve the diverse needs of the State, but that variety will have a common background in the process of selection and training at Harvard. The university will continue to be open, to whole new groups of the population in fact, but if they succeed at Harvard they will be fit to rule, and fit for inclusion in a new aristocracy. The appeal is a doubly shrewd one, for it offered both a vital form of aristocracy that could be justified in democratic terms, and the means to organize and control the ascension to its ranks.

The extent to which social authority is at issue in this selection process is evident enough in Eliot's explanation of why women were not to be included "as students into the College proper" (IA, 22). Briefly, no one could yet know if women in fact could be trained to occupy positions of power in the State: "The world knows next to nothing about the natural mental capacities of the female sex. Only after generations of civil freedom and social equality will it be possible to obtain the data necessary for an adequate discussion of woman's natural tendencies, tastes and capabilities" (IA, 23). By the "experiment" in extension classes in effect, the university will help find out: "In these courses the University offers to young women who have been to good schools as many years as they wish of liberal culture *in studies which have no direct professional value, to be sure*, but which enrich and enlarge both intellect and character" (IA, 23–24; my emphasis).

Almost from the beginning, then, the idea that education could compensate for the potential lack of authority and direction in a democratic society rested on a claim not only to provide the knowledge necessary to the proper functioning of the social system, but also to generate the selection mechanisms whereby the best people would be sorted out to assume the authority of that knowledge. Much later, facing not an "internal" social crisis but the "external" threat of the Soviet Union after World War II, James Conant (one of the most influential educators of the twentieth century, and like Eliot a president of Harvard) provides in *Education in a Divided World* in 1948 a good illustration of just how compact the congruence of professional authority and democratic principles had become:

Of one thing we can be sure—not everyone should have a professional training, even using this word in the broad American sense. This proposition requires no documentation. A second premise, almost equally obvious to those who are convinced of the validity of our American ideals, is that those who do obtain a professional education should be chosen on the basis of pure merit. This follows as a consequence of the doctrine of equality of educational opportunity which has been emphasized so frequently throughout this book. But it may be supported on entirely different grounds on the basis of the welfare of the nation. A modern industrialized, highly urbanized country can prosper only if the professions are full of capable, imaginative, and forward-looking men. We must have extremely able lawyers, doctors, teachers, scientists, and public servants. There is no place for nepotism in the recruitment of this corps of specialists. To the extent that we now fail to educate the potential of each generation, we are wasting one of the country's greatest assets.[8]

In contrast to Eliot, Conant doesn't find it necessary to convince anyone that a "corps of specialists" is a kind of democratic equivalent to an aristocracy, that education must compensate for the absence of a hereditary class structure by producing professionals. Indeed, the power wielded by "lawyers, doctors, teachers, scientists, and public servants" over millions of lives is not discussed in terms of authority at all, but *economy*. It is indispensable to the proper, prosperous functioning of society to everyone's benefit, an outgrowth of democratic ideals, and a national "asset" like natural resources. In the coming struggle, the problem will be to capitalize as much as possible on that asset and reduce waste. In this sense at least, education no longer intervenes in democratic society to compensate for the absence of a hereditary class structure. It is instead a direct contribution to "the welfare of the nation." It's not as if democratic social organization projects no particular problems for Conant, but the locus of those problems is changed considerably in his argument.

Democratic equality as Conant understood it meant that in a very literal sense one started over with every generation. Because no professional position could be inherited, the transmission of a progressive body of knowledge built up across generations depended on a large, complex, and well-organized system of public education, not only in the universities but also in the secondary schools that became Conant's special concern. That is, once the compensatory function of the university to generate an aristocracy of merit has been naturalized, educators can emerge as professionals in their own right, the institution they serve a vital adjunct to the State insofar as it assures the continuity of knowledge on which professional authority depends. Hence the inclusion of "teachers" in Conant's list of specialists in a way that goes well beyond Eliot's premises. For Eliot in fact had acknowledged that teaching was "the one learned profession to which women have already acquired a clear title" (IA, 24), but then clearly that warrant could not carry the same privilege Eliot accords other professions in the direction of the State, nor would teachers belong to a "corps of specialists" as they do for Conant.

However, there was another dilemma posed by the discontinuity of generations to which education also had to address itself. For in a democracy, where one started over with every generation, it was not only the progressive structure of knowledge that was threatened. The more nebulous, internal, affective quality of life that could be passed along through the stable conduits of a "traditional," class-structured society was likewise in jeopardy. Thus when the idea of "compensation" appears in Conant's argument, it is in terms of finding some democratic equivalent to these conduits. And as in Eliot's assertion of an aristocracy of achievement, the equivalent is something even better. Education could allow access for more people than ever before to the cultural heritage available in the arts. That of course was the role of the "humanities" in Conant's educational design:

The study of literature is a means by which a man may live a rich life; it may so "accumulate years to him as though he had lived even from the beginning of time." Surely it is easy to convince anyone of the wisdom that comes from a long life lived with understanding. Good literature can compensate to some degree for the limits which time and space put on each individual's knowledge of human nature. In order to achieve his or her place in the sort of society here envisaged, each adult should be as free from frustration as possible. We can hope to neutralize the emotional strains of a mechanized civilization by cultivating enduring satisfactions. And for many men and women continued acquaintance with literature and the fine arts provides just such satisfactions. (*EDW*, 84)

Although himself a chemist and no humanist scholar, as he admits, this is not a bad description of what a second generation of New Critics, by now—1948—very visible indeed in the university, had extracted from I. A. Richards, T. S. Eliot, and others as an informing ideal of the social mission of literature. (Richards's help in fact is credited in the preface to *Education in a Divided World*.) Modern, urban, industrialized, democratic society had provoked in Eliot, as in the early work of Tate and Ransom most obviously, a bitter and often overtly political counterattack. But not so in their students. The "emotional strains of a mechanized civilization" for them, as for Conant, were simply part of the price paid for modern democracy. Literature is unlikely to change that situation, nor is it by any means clear that they would want it to any more than Conant does. But it can compensate for the worst side effects, as it were, by providing the "enduring satisfactions" that come with a profound awareness of the depth and complexities of human nature, transmitted across the generational discontinuities of a democracy. And it could do so, again, in a way congruent with the most valuable principles of that society, by developing methodologies of literary study not dependent on inherited social position and a highly refined "taste" or "sensibility," but simply on the talent and application of the individual.

I've suggested in my first chapter how this rather benignly optimistic understanding of the profession of literary study as a process of cultural democratization was at the same time continually on the defensive, beset with a pervasive sense of "crisis." For whenever education is expected to compensate for social problems in some way, the question of authority unavoidably becomes an issue. Though on the one hand a literary education by merit mimed well enough the pattern of other professions, on the other it was by no means clear why the specific form of compensation offered should lay claim to being better than any other form. Conant's advice, typically, is intended as a bracing imperative to face up to the challenge rather than "shudder" at the "barbaric question" (*EDW*, 83) of why reading Shakespeare was better compensation than reading comic books:

The equivalent of the social pressure of the ruling class tradition that once made many a reluctant youth study the classics may be at hand in the evident bewilderment of so many people about the nature of the society in which we live. By appealing to the curiosity of *all* youth about the origins of an obviously complex and unintelligible technological society, we may evoke willingness to learn about the past. (*EDW*, 91–92)

Modern humanists, unlike "traditional intellectuals," have no ground of authority in a hereditary class structure. Like every other professional, they would have to find an "equivalent," a form of socially useful knowledge of the same sort that made it possible to justify the indispensability of other professions. Conant's suggestion is that they find that equivalent in an understanding of the history of a bewilderingly complex modern civilization. People not only need to understand that history, as it might be made intimately available to more people through literature. They want to. Like every other profession, literary study would then serve a clientele, would provide answers to the questions that clientele was most desperate to have answered.[9] Had Conant been more aware of what was actually going on in literary study, he might perhaps have realized that throughout the first decades of the century literary versions of such a history in fact were everywhere. The trouble was that one of the villains of the story, usually under the code name of "science," was more often than not the very professional specialization Conant saw as a "natural" social asset. Echoes could still be heard in those bitter essays of Tate, Ransom, and Blackmur in the late 1940's, and much more virulently even later in Leavis's counterblast to C. P. Snow's Richmond lecture. But in the professional environment of the university such echoes were becoming fewer. And there seemed nothing much to replace their source.

Like Ohmann's observation about a professional nobility, Burton Bledstein's account of the rise of a "culture of professionalism" in the nineteenth century is more directly concerned with the privileges that accrued to professionals as the term itself began to take a definite shape. However, he does often comment at length on how professional knowledge could establish itself as a ground of social authority: "Professionals not only lived in an irrational world, they cultivated that irrationality by uncovering abnormality and perversity everywhere: in diseased bodies, criminal minds, political conspiracies, threats to the national security. An irrational world, an amoral one in a state of constant crisis, made the professional person who possessed his special knowledge indispensable to the victimized client, who was reduced to a condition of desperate trust." [10] Much of the modernist literature now part of the university curriculum fit well enough and even intensified such a description of an "irrational world." The authority of the professional, however, lay in mastery, the capacity to act on the "disorder" once isolated, to provide the kind of "answers" Conant asks for as indispensable to "clients." Literary study in English found such answers hard to come by.

Nevertheless, English prospered among professionals in the university. That is, *English* indeed became indispensable, which is not quite the same as saying that literary study was recognized as a profession. In "Where Do English Departments Come From?," William Riley Parker had argued that the growth of English departments depended in large part on how training in composition was linked to literary study.[11] The connection had a kind of "natural" antecedent, of course, in the long history of cultural accomplishment assumed to be a civilizing mark of a gentleman. And that antecedent explains much about the union of composition and literary study in English in the nineteenth century. By the late nineteenth and early twentieth centuries in the United States, however, the "natural" relation appeared already an anachronism. Thus in terms of specific training, literary study and composition in the same department no longer made much sense, and in his influential *Principles of Secondary Education*, published in 1918, Alexander Inglis was dismayed at the hodgepodge of functions English departments were expected to perform.[12] He thought composition study and literary study important, but the notion that one department should be responsible for both seemed to him, as to many other educators, a conceptual confusion. Despite such criticism, the union became even stronger rather than dissolving, because the compensatory task of education was from the beginning twofold: both the training of future professionals and the sorting out of students by merit. However little the specific *training* involved in composition and literary study might resemble each other, in terms of *selection*, of assessing the capabilities of students in the educational system, the linkage worked. For what it began to answer to was no longer the civilizing of a gentleman, but the far more complicated process of sorting made necessary by the extension of "cultural skills" to a larger and more diverse group of the population, itself a result of the dramatic changes in the very forms of work in the first decades of the twentieth century.

Here again Conant is useful, as in his Inglis Lecture at Harvard in 1959 he reviews the statistical evidence for "the revolution in American secondary education which has taken place in my lifetime":

In 1905 something like a third of the children who first enrolled in grade one entered a high school (grade nine). Only about nine percent of an age group graduated from high school, only four or five percent of an age group entered college. In 1930, instead of only a third of the youth entering high school, well over three-quarters were registered in the ninth grade; instead of nine percent graduating, almost forty-five percent of an age group finished high school; and the college entries had risen from five percent of an age group to about fifteen percent.[13]

It was in the midst of these changes, as Conant points out, that the NEA Commission on the Reorganization of Secondary Education, on which Inglis served in 1918, recommended lengthening the time students remained in school: "Consequently this Commission holds that education should be so organized that every normal boy and girl will be encouraged to remain in school to the age of 18 on full time if possible, other wise on part time" (quoted in *RT*, 17–18).

During roughly the same period Conant is discussing, from 1905 to 1930, statistical studies began to classify the occupational status of workers by skill for the first time. Using data obtained from the census, William C. Hunt in 1897 had developed four categories to differentiate among groups of nonfarm workers: proprietors, clerical employees, skilled workers, and laborers. But by the end of the period, Alba Edwards had developed a more complicated scheme that, among other things, introduced the term "operative" to distinguish "laborers" whose work involved using or attending machines.[14] His reconstruction of earlier data then maintained this distinction as one of "skill." The result was that there seemed new and massive statistical evidence to support the earlier NEA claim that a more highly skilled work force required a longer period of education, and to support the development of vocational education in the schools, which had been opened to federal funding by the Smith-Hughes Act of 1917. Inglis himself, in *Principles of Secondary Education*, had argued powerfully for vocational education on the grounds that not only was the apprentice system of training for more skilled jobs disappearing, but that employers couldn't be expected to go to the expense of training more highly skilled workers who, given an "increased mobility of labor" (*PSE*, 595), might then take their skills somewhere else.

More children in school, for a longer period of time, from far more diverse backgrounds than previously; a perception of a more "mobile" and more highly skilled work force made necessary by the technological advances in production; the still-growing prestige of the professions: all these things combined to put intense pressure on the acquisition of *cultural skills*. Bledstein describes how in the 1870's aggressive college presidents were already using the threat that lack of such skills might permanently foreclose an individual's chance of success (*CP*, 278). By two decades into the new century, cultural skills were becoming a prerequisite of "skilled" labor as well as the professions, and by the time of Conant's lecture in 1959, he could argue that anyone "at all familiar with the employment picture in the United States" could be presumed to understand that "a constant increase in the ratio of skilled to unskilled jobs" (*RT*, 10) had made irreversible the trend toward longer—and more diverse —education for more people. "Skilled" labor, that is, had come to designate more than just what one did on the job. It also comprehended a wide range of cultural skills, including of course a certain demonstrated verbal mastery, learned in the process of a longer education. What had been almost exclusively a property of professionals throughout the period Bledstein traces seemed rapidly being extended to whole new groups of the population.

As Wallace Douglas argues, university composition courses, at least from the time of Eliot's tenure at Harvard, were not just in the business of training basic literacy.[15] Eliot, as Douglas makes clear, saw composition as necessary to the task of training his aristocracy of achievement. For it too inculcated a disciplined habit of thought and reflection, in Eliot's words (which Conant echoes later in his exhortation to humanists in *Education in a Divided World*), a capacity "to observe keenly, to reason soundly, and to imagine vividly" (IA, 1). It was a training distinguished from mere reading and writing by its connection to the building of "character."[16] Eliot, however, had directly linked composition training to an *aristocracy* of merit, and as cultural skills, the distinguishing features of that merit, began to appear not only in the population in other universities throughout the country but in secondary schools as well, it became increasingly necessary to develop still more precise ways of assessment. Literary study in the university afforded the means to do so. Thus from an administrative viewpoint at least, so far from being arbitrary, as both Ohmann and Parker at times suggest, the union of composition and literary study in the same department acquired a new "naturalness," as it were, with the latter perceived as a refinement and extension of the skills assessed on a lower frequency in composition classes. This administrative logic was then preserved in the distribution of work in English, where as departments grew larger, teaching composition was increasingly assigned to junior faculty and to graduate students.

Ohmann and Douglas both note the antipathy of English faculty to the union, which of course continued well into the 1930's and 1940's in much the same terms, as literary training became more assertive, and still continues today. But this too should be obvious enough. Genuine professionals were understood to work at the very frontiers of knowledge, at the edge of a "heart of darkness" where expertise was tested in the most demanding situations. Teaching composition looked instead like a "service," a favor to others that increasingly distracted from the exploration of that most arduous of all verbal terrains, the literary text. It might help sort out those students capable of becoming future professionals, but that was just the point. It was a task of "compensation" in a rather different sense than either literary scholars themselves or someone like Conant had envisioned for the humanities. Instead of training people for an indispensable profession, it was an intraeducational chore of *sorting* for which others reaped the benefits. It looked like a reversal of the merit/talent ladder, having reached a certain point on it only to be told to reconstruct the beginning steps for *someone else's* clientele. That it also paid for the exercise of literary scholarship, made the English department almost everywhere the largest and most powerful in the humanities (while other departments, like philosophy, for example, were busy finessing themselves almost out of existence), only exacerbated the frustration of being a kind of high school extension service in the midst of the university.

However, as Conant's own influential and Carnegie-funded study *The American High School Today* (also published in 1959) suggested, the reorganization of secondary education in the United States had proceeded well beyond the history reviewed in the Inglis lecture. The key recommendation in *The American High School Today* would push that reorganization still further. Like so many others who grew up in the heady world of "progressive" educational ideas, Conant had always been concerned about how to strike a balance between the imperative to offer everyone an education commensurate with her or his abilities, and the (to him) obvious fact that the talent of certain individuals made possible a much more rapid advancement. Theoretically there may seem no necessary conflict here, but in the practical terms of *cost* at least, there was a conflict indeed. The answer proposed by *The American High School Today* is larger high schools:

The truth of this statement is evident if one considers the distribution of academic talent in the school which serves all the youth of the community. It will be a rare district where more than 25 per cent of a high school class can study with profit twelfth-grade mathematics, physics, and a foreign language for four years (assuming that standards are maintained). If a school has a twelfth grade of only forty and if indeed only a quarter of the group can handle the advanced subjects effectively, instruction in mathematics, science, and foreign languages would have to be provided for a maximum of ten students. If the girls shy away from the mathematics and science as they do in most of the schools I visited, the twelfth-grade mathematics classes may be as small as six or seven. To provide adequate teachers for specialized subjects is extremely expensive. Furthermore, to maintain an interest in academic subjects among a small number is not always easy.[17]

Later, he concludes: "The prevalence of such high schools—those with graduating classes of less than one hundred students—constitutes one of the serious obstacles to good secondary education throughout most of the United States" (*AHS*, 77).

I'll return in the next section to the matter of "academic talent" and "standards," but the obvious question here is "good secondary education" for whom? Clearly for those, primarily male, who would go on to even more advanced subjects in the university and eventually take their place in that indispensable "corps of specialists." Secondary education for Conant was obligated to educate everyone up to what their abilities permitted, but it made sense as *cost effective*, an asset to the "welfare of the nation," only if organized toward the top. For in the logic of his calculations, the 75 percent for whom advanced subjects were beyond their abilities (or, in the case of "girls," outside their "interests") would be just as well off if the high schools were not reorganized as larger. The cost of reorganization would be at the expense of the 75 percent.

Of course no one could know with certainty, in advance, how academically talented any individual student might be, and in the larger high schools Conant was recommending, the difficulty of finding out became proportionally greater. The *social* risks involved were greater as well. Thus many of the specific recommendations in his study concern the necessarily more delicate task not only of "fitting" each student to a program commensurate with his/her abilities, but also of convincing both the student and her/his parents of the fit and making sure no stigma attached to "less advanced" programs. The very first recommendation then stresses the general importance of "counseling"; recommendation 2 the desirability of avoiding "clearly defined and labeled programs or tracks such as 'college preparatory,' 'vocational,' 'commercial' " (*AHS*, 46); recommendation 4 grouping students by abilities *in each subject* (reflecting here Eliot's emphasis on a mental "division of labor"); and so forth. Recommendation 19 is especially revealing of the process. In recommending a required course for everyone in the physical sciences, he indicates that besides "the physics course given in the twelfth grade with mathematics as a prerequisite (recommendation 13) another course in physics should be offered with some such designation as 'practical physics' " (*AHS*, 73), presumably so that no one would think it was just physics for dummies.

He has almost no suggestions for the specific content of any of the courses he recommends, with the major exception of English in recommendation 6, which is worth quoting in full:

The time devoted to English composition during the four years should occupy about half the total time devoted to the study of English. Each student should be required to write an average of one theme a week. Themes should be corrected by the teacher. In order that teachers of English have adequate time for handling these themes, no English teacher should be responsible for more than one hundred students.

To test the ability of each student in English composition, a schoolwide composition test should be given in every grade; in the ninth and eleventh grade, these composition tests should be graded not only by the teacher but by a committee of the entire school. Those students who do not obtain a grade on the eleventh-grade composition test commensurate with their ability as measured by an aptitude test should be required to take a special course in English composition in the twelfth grade. (*AHS*, 50–51)

Besides the fact that it is almost the only recommendation that deals in any way with course content, it is remarkable for other reasons. Composition is the one subject directly linked to aptitude tests where the academic abilities of students are measured *in general terms*; everyone takes the tests in every grade, and in the ninth and eleventh grades the results are determined by a committee of the entire school. I know of no research that indicates to what extent, if ever, this specific recommendation was implemented, but it's possible, of course, to recognize versions of it throughout the educational system. The necessary delicacy of sorting out academic ability could be buttressed by the authority of "objective" tests to be sure, but it's as if only the kind of extended performance available for scrutiny in a composition test could fine-tune a teacher's perceptions of that ability. This form of evaluation is perhaps "softer," more susceptible to "subjective" error even if the whole faculty of the school is involved. But it might also reveal much more than standardized aptitude tests.

Correspondingly, however, the time involved for such evaluation is greater. Thus the person in the field (perhaps not quite a "specialist" in the same sense as other teachers, for everyone on the faculty is presumed competent to grade composition), the English teacher who corrects a theme a week from each student, occasions the only mention of a specific *upper* limit on the number of students. Obviously more English teachers would then be necessary, and would in turn feed enrollments in English in the university. The crucial point, however, is the reason for the increase. It would not only—or even primarily—be for the purpose of training students more effectively; rather, it would occur as a result of the set of problems projected by the reorganization toward larger secondary schools. English would become even more indispensable, but insofar as it was also more closely linked to composition teaching, itself more closely linked to the intraeducational dilemmas of sorting out student abilities.

III

In my quick sketch I have indicated a complex of ways in which education was expected to play a vital, compensatory role in society, and within that complex the positions English came to occupy. In the most general terms, given the social values and ideals of a democracy, authority was perceived to belong properly to a "meritocracy" rather than a ruling class, a corps of trained professionals whose expert knowledge isolated problems within specific areas where solutions could be generated. In a democracy, that is, the university compensated for the absence of a hereditary class structure by sorting out and training those in each generation with the ability to succeed to professional service. However, as secondary schools expanded to accommodate what seemed an always larger and more highly skilled work force, as "merit" itself then became a larger and more diverse category in response to more diverse social "needs," the problems created by the discontinuity of generations projected by this logic of merit became more acute as well. Against these discontinuities, the system of education provided both an institutional home for the progressive construction of the specialized knowledges of the professions, and the mechanisms for the transmission of cultural values, attitudes, beliefs, and practices.

The growth of English within the educational system locates the point where these two means of establishing continuity coalesce to transform the tasks of sorting and training students into a single process. For the possibility of student access to the body of specialized knowledges increasingly was mediated across the general field of "cultural skills" dominated by English. Within English itself, the linkage of sorting and training emerged as a confused ensemble of tensions between, on the one hand, the attempts to organize literary study as also a professional discipline in its own right, and on the other the demands for composition courses and teacher training. But in terms of the educational system as a whole, English functioned as a kind of differential gearbox whereby the motor forces of sorting and training could be applied uniformly to a student's progress through the system. Whatever the "higher ideals" and "internal requirements" of the subject, English grew in importance because of its intraeducational utility.

I think this helps explain why in an argument concerned with English in the university it is necessary to spend so much time discussing secondary schools. The presence of composition as it came to be understood in the curriculum of the university not only connects the actual functions of English departments much more closely to the high schools than most other disciplines in the humanities, but also specifies that connection in a way that conditions a curriculum of literary study. Curricula could develop however an English faculty saw fit to train future specialists in literature—so long as the development also continued the process of sorting "essential" at the high school level as well as in the university. Ohmann observes how "given its head," the English department typically planned a curriculum "by filling the catalogue with courses matching professionally designated special fields" (*EA*, 221). But that is perhaps not as "curious" as he suggests, since as a process of distinguishing more and more specialized levels of difficulty, it accords very nicely—or at least doesn't interfere—with this crucial task of sorting.

I have as yet said very little about what is perhaps now the most familiar understanding of education as "compensatory," even though it is obviously very much a part of the complex of assumptions I have sketched. That is, in a society committed to equal opportunity but where manifest inequalities exist, education must compensate by providing the means for individuals to escape the circumstances of those inequalities. The full force of the relation is hard to see, however, if one assumes that from the beginning the whole notion of social authority resting on the demonstrated merit of professionals was merely an illusion, a more or less conscious duplicity disguising something else. I think that Conant and others like him believed beyond a shadow of a doubt that a *society* itself really was "disadvantaged" if in perpetuating racial, gender, and geographical discrimination by means of economic hierarchies, it cut itself off from the potential abilities of the individuals thus segregated.

"Equal opportunity" was not just a moral and political phrase; it expressed a fundamental conviction that the "merit" of society in every sense mirrored the merits of those individuals within it, and that whatever blocks to the full development of those merits existed had to be dealt with. These are commonplaces of civics textbooks, to be sure, but that doesn't mean that like good professionals we must get bored with them immediately and start looking for something deeper and more exciting to test our skills on. "Boring" after all is also "familiar," to a great many minds indeed—the point Marx emphasized where ideas become a material force, worth following out to see where they go and what problems they generate.

As Conant at least realized, ideally "merit" could be translated as it were into economic terms, where it involved a "continuation of the highly competitive economic system with its wide divergence of pecuniary rewards" (*EDW*, 6). This doesn't necessarily mean that the higher the individual merit, the higher the pecuniary reward, but it does imply a kind of structural equivalency. "Merit" is the ideal form of an educational system whereby all individuals are encouraged to develop and exercise their abilities to the fullest extent, as "competition" is the ideal form of an economic system whereby more and better products are produced to become available to more and more people. However, even if taken in this ideal sense of structural equivalency, the very necessity for education as "compensatory" made sense only if one also assumed that the educational system on the whole was progressing much faster toward an ideal than the economic system. Otherwise, obviously, there would be no need to "compensate." As Bledstein remarks, business has been for a long time the "traditional villain" of educators (even though, as he goes on to point out, the "professional image" of business "is largely a product of business schools in American universities" [*CP*, 289]). The sources of the hostility, however, involve not only competing professional claims, but also a long series of practices negotiating the connections between the transformation of work on the one hand, and on the other the "revolution" Conant describes in secondary education from 1905 to 1930.

Though as I suggested earlier, degrees of skilled labor became a new focus of attention during this period, Harry Braverman's *Labor and Monopoly Capital* is a massive documentation of how the majority of actual jobs performed in factories, warehouses, and offices were designed to involve less and less of what by even the greatest stretch of imaginative word usage could be called "skill." I think anyone who has worked such jobs would find Braverman's account immediately convincing. The point, however, is that this "degradation" of work Braverman describes did not take place in isolation. Because of the correlative growth of secondary education, the very terms and definitions of "skill" were altered to mean not only what one *did* on the job, but what qualities one *had* in doing it. What I have called "cultural skills," that is, were increasingly made to appear interdependent with job skills.

Like a number of others, Inglis had argued that the disappearance of the apprentice system meant that the schools must provide some kind of vocational training. What had disappeared with apprenticeship, however, involved a process of education extending well beyond the work itself. Braverman cites Robert Hoxie, one of the early advocates of "scientific management" techniques and writing at about the same time as Inglis's *Principles*, to the effect that the disappearance of apprenticeship had occasioned for employers "poor and lawless material from which they must recruit their workers, compared with the efficient and self-respecting craftsman who applied for employment twenty years ago." [18] For Hoxie, as he goes on to explain in *Scientific Management and Labor*, any program of vocational education should have as its primary mission the inculcation of these lost virtues. In perhaps the most dramatic example to "resolve" the problem, Henry Ford in 1914 had increased the wages of at least some of his workers to five dollars a day, on the premise that such money would attract the best people and make a lot more of them a lot more attentive to their work. But such flamboyance aside, for Hoxie, Inglis, and others the long-term resolution had to be the development of an educational equivalent to the apprentice system, something uniquely suited to the modern age as apprenticeship had been to the past.

For if there was very little about the jobs becoming available that could be used to "restore" a sense of pride and achievement in work, there were other incentives besides Ford's. Mobility was one, and mobility coupled with advancement up a ladder of skill as well as pay was even better. Mobility, a chance for advancement, and increased social prestige was best of all. These were values already deeply a part of the educational system, and thus by an extension of that system to "vocational" education it could be counted on to reinforce whatever steps possible to take in the organization of work itself. And indeed, with the fracturing of the labor process into smaller and smaller units throughout any number of industries, the potential existed to transform these divisions into elaborate hierarchies of distinction. That real difference in job skills might be small or even nonexistent mattered relatively little. For with the help of the schools, increasingly it was other skills that were at issue.

Instead of a group of five workers to load sacks of flour onto boxcars, for example, one of the five could be designated as responsible for making sure the stacked tiers of a specific order were uniform, to facilitate unloading inventory at the destination. Still another could be designated to calculate a uniform arrangement of all the orders to be shipped in each boxcar. The first would still be involved in loading, but in a job where he was now distinguished from his fellow loaders, and could look forward to advancement to the next position where he might be relieved of much of the actual physical labor— loading sacks weighing anywhere from 50 to 100 pounds. The system as a whole was more "efficient" insofar as it permitted a more exact accounting and control of the loading process, and a chain of responsibility to assure both. And it provided for workers a kind of built-in incentive in prestige as well as pay to keep it functioning smoothly.

Needless to say, such divisions corresponded only abstractly to the set of divisions beginning to transform the organization of secondary schools. For none of the five jobs required more than a minimal working knowledge of simple arithmetic and "space relations," which in any case would be learned from practice on the job and not in school. But it meant before all that long in the process of change that even at the lowest level of "skill," the man hired simply to put sacks of flour where he was told to in a boxcar could be required to have a high school diploma on the grounds that he might be expected to move up eventually to more "skilled" positions. Further, that skilled position was also a more responsible position, overseeing the labor of others, and the diploma testified—however vaguely —to "character," to a capacity for self-discipline and the shouldering of responsibility. The requirement itself added to the prestige of the job. What happened, that is, was a process whereby both education and work developed along ostensibly parallel tracks of increasingly complicated distinctions. Nowhere did the two really correspond point by point, despite efforts in that direction. But it was understood that the educational system, by connecting skill training to the building of self-discipline, self-respect, and character (the things missing, in other words, from the job force as Hoxie saw it), would lay the foundation for preserving the connections on the job itself. Education, that is, did not train workers to do a specific job so much as it trained workers to think of skills of all kinds as indissolubly linked with personal qualities. To devalue the skill of the job would then mean in effect devaluing oneself as well.

For women, however, the development of these "parallel" tracks was especially vicious. In *Principles*, Inglis had relied on the data from the 1910 census to create a blueprint for a more comprehensive system of vocational education. One of his particular concerns for reform lay in the broad area of "clerical training," with its emphasis on office skills such as typewriting and stenography. For the census data indicated that of the roughly 1.7 million people engaged in clerical occupations, well over a million were bookkeepers, cashiers, accountants, and nonsales clerks. Further, another 3.6 million were employed in such nonclerical trade occupations as sales clerk, retail dealer, and so forth. Thus for the majority of actual clerical and commercial trade jobs, there were no programs of preparation at all in the schools other than general subjects and sporadic attempts at "business English" or "business math." "Stenography and typewriting," he noted, the skills that *were* trained in the schools, "are passing more and more into hands of women or girls and at present a relatively small proportion of clerical positions emphasizing these subjects are occupied by men or boys" (*PSE*, 584). His proposals for change (which would eventually become a kind of prebusiness curriculum) were then intended to reflect more accurately the diversity of commercial occupations, to make the "tracks" more nearly parallel, as it were. But the other effect of course was to segregate even further than it already was the training in "office skills" like typewriting and stenography, and to segregate the "audience" for those classes as exclusively women. Not only did women not benefit from more complicated and expansive programs of commercial vocational education. As these programs became themselves a prerequisite for hiring, according to the logic of "parallel tracks," they helped make it impossible for women who had begun in the office as secretaries or stenographers to advance to any higher positions. They helped lock in a vast army of women employees for low-paying and dead-end jobs that over the next three decades were to be by far the fastest-growing sector of clerical occupations.

The position of women clerical workers indicates one powerful reason for the looseness of correspondence between the two "tracks" of development. Commercial vocational education, as Inglis understood it, like the school system as a whole, was organized "toward the top." It emphasized the availability of more "skilled" occupations to those who had demonstrated the ability and hard work in the schools. The actual growth of clerical work at the *other* end, in the lowest-paying and most mechanically routine jobs reserved primarily for women, suggests a far different organization indeed in the economy. I'll return in a moment to the implications of this difference in organization. But the immediate point is how the organization of schools toward the top nevertheless provided one inestimable advantage to educators in the long story of hostilities between business and education. For while it was difficult to connect directly the hierarchies of job skills to a set of social ideals except through the obviously ambiguous terms of advancement and prestige, the hierarchies of education on the other hand seemed an unequivocally clear expression of precisely those ideals. However imperfect as yet in practice, educational hierarchies of distinction were understood as attempts at least to reflect nothing but the talent and abilities of students in the system. Job distribution, in contrast, seemed subject to all kinds of variables. Education could then be seen as a countervailing force, compensating for the inequality of job distribution and rewards by equalizing the variables, and in its devotion to "pure merit" eventually to win out over the forces of blind prejudice still operating more virulently in the economic sphere.

But exactly what "talent" and "ability" were to be assessed in the schools? Conant after all was writing *The American High School Today* right after the wave of hysteria generated by Sputnik, yet even his recommendations regarding mathematics and physics courses specify almost nothing about course content. Nor is his relative silence unique. Earlier, in one of many such meetings held toward the end of World War II to anticipate the problems of postwar education, the planning group for secondary education at the conference sponsored by the UCLA School of Education in 1944 proposed seven areas that needed special attention. Number 2 spoke to the problems generated by the "Carnegie-unit" definition; number 3 to the organization of required subjects, which left a relatively light load for twelfth grade; number 4 to the presence in most curricula of (unspecified) "courses and units whose present-day value is subject to question."[19] But typical of such conferences, none of the recommendations involved any real discussion of course content.

Whatever else can be said of Inglis, his *Principles* at least had been full of recommendations for what should actually be taught in the schools. The reason for the change I think was the belief that *content* had become a matter for professionals *in each field* to decide. As experts it was their business to know. The result, however, was that the organization of secondary schools toward the top meant not only a system programmed primarily to make more advanced subjects available to all students who could "handle" them, but increasingly the assumption that at least rudimentary forms—"practical physics" —of such knowledge were best for everyone in the schools. General education, that is, was neither very general in terms of comprehensive, integrated training, nor finally very educative. It became more and more an assemblage of low-level versions of what some students would find out more about later as they began to "specialize." The authority of professionals to determine course content thus meant in practice that the fields of acknowledged professional expertise constituted in the schools virtually the whole of worthwhile academic knowledge. It was not really a matter of where exactly in the curriculum more specialized work ought to begin; the entire curriculum became more specialized from top to bottom, with the difference in levels a matter of how much was made available at any one time.

"Training" and "sorting," as I have emphasized, formed a complicated symbiotic system, and it is possible here to see just how complete that symbiosis had become. To the extent that training involved gradually increasing mastery of specialized knowledges, it was as well a process of distributing the organization of knowledge in a field along the fault lines of grade level in school. Conversely, sorting out the merit of individual students by talent and ability was also a form of training, insofar as it determined what level of specificity one would be able to engage. (At least two of Conant's recommendations in *The American High School Today*, for example, suggest the desirability of grouping students by ability in each subject rather than across the board.) Equal opportunity to demonstrate merit meant an equal chance to show promise of becoming professionally competent in one subject.

The very tightness of the system, however, also helped make clear that so far from really starting over with every generation, certain students would inevitably begin with an advantage. Those coming from professional families, or with college-trained parents or siblings, would already possess the most "rudimentary" forms of knowledge from their home environment. The immediate question, in a curriculum organized around specialized fields of knowledge, was where to locate a chance to "catch up," afford "disadvantaged" students training in the skills that would give them an opportunity later to compete equally in the full range of courses. The growth of kindergartens—that is, lengthening the average time in school at the "front" end as well as at the upper level of high school—was part of the answer, and was eventually extended even further into various programs of federally funded "preschool" experience.

The other answer was English. For if anything seemed a common denominator in the curriculum it was verbal skills, necessary everywhere. (Conant's recommendation for an all-school composition test reflects this perception.) Hence "remedial" reading classes (Conant's eighth recommendation speaks to the point), and of course the training of people to staff those classes, became something of a growth industry, adding to the scope, diversity, and complexity of English. Yet the notion of a distinctively "verbal skill" afforded by training in English represents a curious equivocation. On the one hand, its shadow as it were remained a much more general range of *cultural* skills, trailing off into those nebulous qualities of "character," of "discipline," "reliability," "responsibility," and so forth. But on the other, it had come to mean something far more specific, something much more like a technical *skill*, a set of teachable operations, detached from any communicative context, that could be learned by students and applied *to any* context.

The equivocation was useful for two reasons. The issues surrounding the education of "disadvantaged" students of course put a great deal of pressure on a general sense of cultural skills. For what looks like "character" and "self-discipline" can also look like enforced conformity and a process of discrimination. Thus the shift in emphasis possible by focusing instead on the specifically verbal as a *technical* skill slid neatly away from the problem. It still carried a "shadow," but further and further in the background as the whole ensemble of relations was regrounded. Second, insofar as this technical skill could be applied to any communicative context, it could also function as precisely what was missing from an increasingly specialized curriculum, namely a general foundation for later work. Finally, as a skill rather than a "subject," that foundation could be carried along up the steps of specialization, offering not only a chance to "catch up" at the beginning, but also a process of refinement in skill corresponding to subsequent steps. In the process of the shift in emphasis, however, English had then to be denied any real authority over *content*, over cultural skills, cultural values, *ideas* at all. For as training in English approached such a content, it threatened to reaggravate the very problems the shift was to have left behind. The more purely technical the training of verbal skill in English, the more English could appear the appropriate place in a curriculum for "disadvantaged" students to catch up, and the better it could function as a primary vehicle of sorting throughout the curriculum. Thus the price for this new growth and importance of English was a *diminishment* of more general cultural importance. English became at once more and less crucial to the ends of education.

The logic of compensation, however, suggests another and more formidable problem altogether than the dilemma of where best for students to "catch up." For at the conjunction of the idea of a hierarchy based on merit and the idea that it is then necessary to start over with each generation to sort out people for their proper roles in that hierarchy, there exists a kind of zero point, a point where ideally, all other things being equal, each new generation could appear *already* sorted. "Of one thing we can be sure," Conant had argued, "not everyone should have a professional training, even using that word in the broad American sense. This proposition requires no demonstration" (*EDW*, 168). It requires no demonstration because at that zero point there already exists a differential— of *intelligence*. That is, the logic of compensation on the one hand has as its target all the multiple ways in which social and economic organization might be seen to impede the opportunity that ought to be available to everyone, but on the other it has as its goal the *recovery* and development of whatever capacity of intelligence exists in every individual. Actual achievement, demonstrated ability in school, obviously depends on a great many things besides intelligence, the motivation and so forth of the individual as well as the opportunities open to that individual. But intelligence nevertheless operates with a veto power; it marks again a zero point beyond which there is nothing the school can or should do. The second and far more difficult question then, to put it simply, was how to know when you had arrived at a perception of real intelligence. When was "compensation" in fact doing its job of removing obstacles to the opportunity of individuals, and when was it wasted effort?

Research in "intelligence" has had a longer history, indeed, but it began to be localized around the development of educational testing programs, especially "IQ" tests, coincident again with that "revolution" in secondary education from 1905 to 1930. Generally speaking, the earlier the results of such research the more farcical they are likely to seem to us. The studies of C. C. Brigham, H. H. Laughlin, and Lewis Terman in the 1920's, for example, were cited as "scientific" evidence for the inferiority of the Southern European "races" —who were the major targets of the immigration quotas imposed in 1924. As recently as 1960 the Stanford-Binet test administered to six-year-olds included a card picturing a Caucasian woman and a black woman and asked the question, "Which is prettier?"[20] That is, "intelligence" as a kind of zero point in the logic of compensation begins to appear also a point always receding further and further into the distance, each new claim to having arrived turning out to be merely a reflection of the very cultural variables it was supposed to have escaped. Hence in part the outrage that greeted A. R. Jensen's research in the late 1960's and 1970's, which claimed a close correlation between genetic inheritance and intelligence as measured in IQ tests. It was as if Jensen himself had simply regressed to a much earlier stage in the process. Yet in one sense Jensen was everywhere faithful to the logic of *merit itself*, with its polarities of "heredity" and "environment," and he admits with disarming casualness that the *definition* of intelligence was of course a cultural one: "Had the first IQ tests been devised in a hunting culture, 'general intelligence' might well have turned out to involve visual acuity and running speed rather than vocabulary and symbol manipulation."[21] Indeed, the controversy surrounding Jensen's research for the most part left intact the assumption that intelligence was an individual capacity, a zero point basis of merit. The issue, as always, was how—or whether —it could be measured accurately.

If inadvertently, however, Jensen's Robinsonade about "hunting cultures" suggests that one might well ask instead why *measurement* would become an issue at all. To the extent intelligence is culturally defined, it should be obvious to nearly anyone in the culture what intelligence involves. Presumably in a "hunting culture," the measurement of running speed wouldn't have to be debated; it would pay off every day, whether in bringing home food or in contests of skill. And few would have any doubt what running speed was. If intelligence as "vocabulary" and "symbol manipulation" likewise paid off in this culture, why in the world would there be such a high value on, such furious debates about, and such considerable difficulty in measuring it? One answer is that such intelligence is so crucial that its possessors must be identified as soon as possible, at a very early age in the school system, to ensure they get the best training possible, so that they can contribute to their full capacity when they become adults. The corollary of that answer, however, is the rather absurd premise that though high intelligence is absolutely indispensable to the very functioning of the culture, the culture at the same time furnishes no real way to specify what high intelligence *does*, what exactly it contributes. For if such ways existed, there would be no problem in identifying and measuring potential in the young. In a culture where running speed is important, four-year-olds run races. That culture doesn't create a profession whose task is to *construct* complicated definitions of running speed, and then construct equally complicated test situations to conform to those constructed definitions.

The less Ptolemaic explanation is that "intelligence" *does not* obviously pay off in this culture. That at least is the conclusion reached by Samuel Bowles and Herbert Gintis in "I.Q. in the U.S. Class Structure": "The available data [which they draw from Sewell, Jencks, Blau and Duncan, and others as well as their own research] point strongly to the unimportance of I.Q. in getting ahead economically."[22] Bowles and Gintis thus isolate what "pay off" means. In social terms, it means "getting ahead economically"; educationally, however, it means treating *intelligence*, as Conant suggests in *Education in a Divided World*, as an economic asset to the society. And the two don't mesh very well. Bowles and Gintis's arguments are then intended to challenge not only the assumptions held by those like Jensen and Richard Herrnstein that intelligence *is* highly rewarded by society because economically necessary to that society, but also those held by their more liberal opponents who argued that certain social groups are denied rewards because IQ tests discriminate against them. IQ tests indeed discriminate against them, but that isn't necessarily the reason they are denied social rewards.

I find Bowles and Gintis's analysis of the data convincing, yet whether or not that analysis is really exhaustive, the immediately relevant point is that the data could be construed as even ambiguous. For that means recognizing how "vocabulary" and "symbol manipulation" must answer very different *kinds* of social needs than what "visual acuity" and "running speed" might be assumed to answer in a "hunting culture." Indeed, they seem to duplicate on another level the relation I have already described between specifically "verbal skills" as taught in English, and "cultural skills." For whereas a notion of verbal skills attempts to isolate a purely "technical" component of a much larger and value-charged field of cultural skills, the specification of intelligence as vocabulary and symbol manipulation generalizes that distinction in order to isolate, as intelligence, the very elementary unit *of merit itself*, purified of every variable of cultural value.

In fact, Bowles and Gintis go on to argue "that the actual function of I.Q. testing and its associated ideology is that of legitimizing the stratification system, rather than generating it. The treatment of I.Q. in many strands of liberal sociology and economics merely reflects its actual function in social life: the legitimization and rationalization of the existing social relations of production" (IQ, 218). Thus the educational system as a whole plays the major role in legitimizing IQ tests themselves as a necessary measure of intelligence, by constructing a link between intelligence and economic success, and providing a much larger context of continuous evaluative procedures:

The linking of intelligence to economic success [what I have referred to earlier as linking personal qualities to job skills] indirectly via the educational system strengthens rather than weakens the legitimation process. First, the day-to-day contact of parents and children with the competitive, cognitively oriented school environment, with clear connections to the economy, buttresses in a very immediate and concrete way the technocratic perspective on economic organization, to a degree that a sporadic and impersonal testing process divorced from the school environment could not aspire. Second, by rendering the outcome (educational attainment) dependent not only on ability, but also on motivation, drive to achieve, perseverance, and sacrifice, the status allocation mechanism acquires heightened legitimacy. Moreover, personal attributes are tested and developed over a long period of time, thus enhancing the apparent objectivity and achievement orientation of the stratification system. Third, by gradually "cooling off" individuals at different educational levels, the student's aspirations are relatively painlessly brought into line with his probable occupational status. By the time most students terminate schooling they have validated for themselves their inability or unwillingness to be a success at the next level. Through competition, success, and defeat in the classroom, the individual is reconciled to his or her social position. (IQ, 229)

For reasons I'll try to make clear in a moment, however, I would prefer to state these conclusions in slightly different terms: the symbiotic system of "training" and "sorting" in the schools functions *outside* the schools primarily as "sorting" rather than "training." That is, with the obvious exception of certain professions, the actual performance of a majority of jobs in the economy depends relatively little on the cognitive abilities trained in the school. As I argued earlier, not only is the "fit" between hierarchies of distinction in education and hierarchies of skill at work a loose one, but the organization of schools "toward the top," unlike the economy, projects an almost exclusive focus on cognitive ability in sorting and training. Once put in these terms, however, it makes very little sense to then ask whether individuals acquire intelligence by "heredity" or "environment," since intelligence is not a "capacity" of individuals at all. Like work itself, *intelligence, too, is a specific social relation*, and like work as well, the distribution of that relation in any given context may or may not "carry over" anywhere else. "Intelligence" and "evaluation" are not two distinct things, one an individual capacity and the other a series of analytic attempts to measure that capacity. They are everywhere the *correlative* poles of an organized process from which individuals emerge as if they possessed certain attributes and capacities. One might add of course that if not always an antagonistic social relation, the process is at least one where the poles are never equal nor symmetrical. The inequality of the relation is more often than not obvious enough to blacks and other "minorities," to women, and to working class students who persist in the "perversity" of seeing IQ tests and the like as weapons being used against them rather than an opportunity to demonstrate their capacities or as a mildly boring deviation from normal classroom procedures.

My reason for pushing Bowles and Gintis's conclusions in this direction is to emphasize that though the educational system might well involve a process of "legitimization," *what* it legitimizes is not necessarily an existent social division of labor, as Bowles and Gintis assume. The difference I think can be put this way. The hierarchies of education function to sort out "meritorious" individuals. Hence as I've suggested, the basic unit of this organization of social relations is "intelligence" understood as a capacity possessed by the individual, to be demonstrated ideally at least in the acquisition of specific skills and knowledges. Unlike the hierarchies of education, however, the social division of labor sorts out *specific tasks in production* rather than individuals. Braverman cites this distinctive feature of a capitalist division of labor as "the Babbage principle," quoting from the 1832 edition of Charles Babbage's *On the Economy of Machinery and Manufactures*:

That the master manufacturer, by dividing the work to be executed into different processes, each requiring different degrees of skill or of force, can purchase exactly that precise quantity of both which is necessary for each process; whereas, if the whole work were executed by one workman, that person must possess sufficient skill to perform the most difficult, and sufficient strength to execute the most laborious, of the operations into which the art is divided. (quoted in *LMC*, 79–80)

Most if not all societies have some division of labor. What is distinctive about the Babbage principle is the division of *each work process itself* into separate and distinct tasks, rather than dividing society into groups of individuals each performing a specific process of work to produce different products. An employer pays for the performance of certain designated tasks. What "designates" the tasks, the basic unit in this organization, is then not really a "unit" at all like intelligence. It is instead a *ratio* of simple to complex tasks into which a specific process of work can be divided. The higher the ratio, the more cost-efficient the production. "Skill" and "force" are merely functions of this ratio and not of the individuals who "possess" them.

To return for a moment to my earlier example of loading sacks of flour into a boxcar, if all five workers were responsible for the loading and arrangement of tiers to fill an order, and the arrangement of orders in every car, then all five would be paid equally for the "skill" and "force" necessary to perform the whole process. However, once the process is broken down into its component parts, the total cost can be lowered. For only one person, rather than all five, must be paid for the responsibility for the arrangement of orders in a car; only one must be paid for calculating how the tiers of a specific order are to be stacked. The other three can be paid only for putting sacks of flour where they are told to put them. As Babbage has it, the employer "can purchase exactly that precise quantity of both ["skill" and "force"] which is necessary" for each separate task of the loading. A single process is reorganized to maximize the ratio of simple to complex tasks, which in turn projects a "precise quantity" of skill and force involved in each. Thinking in terms of individual *workers*, the differences among the tasks may seem minimal indeed, but thinking in terms of a ratio of simple to complex *tasks*, the differences pay off in cost-effectiveness.

The "problem" in the Babbage principle is that obviously an employer cannot hire a ratio of simple to complex task performance; what must be hired are individual workers to perform each task. And that "worker" with respect to the calculation of an economy of tasks is indeterminate. In my example above, any of the five workers might perform all of the tasks. Relatively more complex tasks might specify further degrees of "skill," but after all *what* degree of skill exactly is derived not from a comparison among indeterminate workers, but from a determinate calculation of simple to complex. Nevertheless, the slippage from determinate to indeterminate, from task to worker, is so easy as to seem almost automatic. Hence Herrnstein, justifying higher pay for more skilled professional workers: " 'If virtually anyone is smart enough to be a ditch digger, and only half the people are smart enough to be engineers, then society is, in effect, husbanding its intellectual resources by holding engineers in greater esteem and paying them more' " (quoted in IQ, 228). However, the social division of labor across society, as it proceeds by the Babbage principle, does not require an engineer or a ditch digger. It requires a *task* of engineering and a *task* of ditch digging. Further, to the extent that division of labor permeates a society, the ratio of calculation dictates on the whole more of "simple" tasks like ditch digging and less of "complex" tasks like engineering. At this point at least, the process has nothing whatsoever to do with "husbanding intellectual resources" and a great deal to do with maximizing the ratio of simple to complex. "Engineer" and "ditch digger" remain indeterminate categories.

It is primarily the system of education that then specifies these indeterminate categories as involving a "unit" of individual capacity, of "intelligence" coupled with training and demonstrated ability. It provides a "worker" to be hired. That is, education is indispensable less because it legitimizes the social division of labor, conditioning workers to accept their lots (although it may also, of course, do both), than because it *compensates* for the indeterminate factor in a calculation of tasks in that division of labor by generating categories of workers in the first place. It *extends* an organization of tasks based in a ratio of simple to complex into a surplus stratification of "intellectual resources" in individuals. The difference in emphasis from Bowles and Gintis's argument is important, for what must be accounted for is *both* the necessity of a system of education *and* the continual tensions that exist at the points where the systems cross, as it were. When that crossing works smoothly, it is possible from one side to see an organization of tasks loading flour as a more economically efficient system, and from the other side an organization of workers in a system that continues to reward responsibility and skill, with more prestigious and better-paid positions. Needless to say, however, the crossing isn't always smooth, and as Bowles and Gintis's own focus of analysis on the lack of correlation between IQ intelligence and job rewards helps demonstrate, there is no intrinsic reason it should be. Education doesn't simply "legitimize" and "reinforce," it compensates for a problem projected by the very mechanisms of a division of labor. And in that sense, *the division of labor itself cannot dictate exactly what form that compensation will take*.

I have tried to indicate what forms it *has* taken in my discussion of a logic of merit. Education of course works to "legitimize" that internal logic, and just as clearly—as I have indicated also—there are powerful connections at every point to the division of labor in the economy. Yet in one sense perhaps the greatest sleight of hand is the pervasive belief that despite the manifold tensions that exist, these connections really do form mutually congruent systems, whether the result from a perspective like Bowles and Gintis's then looks like an invidious perpetuation of class inequality, or whether from a perspective like Conant's it looks like gradual progress toward an ideal of democratic classlessness. A logic of merit, however, must eventuate in meritorious individuals in sufficient numbers to justify the organization of the whole system *toward the top*, around the ideals of merit. Consequently, the criteria for what constitutes merit to some extent at least are generated internally, within that system. IQ testing among other things suggests "vocabulary" and "symbol manipulation" are highly rewarded as signs of merit. But the fact that they aren't necessarily economically rewarded is one indication of the functioning of internal criteria. For in contrast, though unavoidably complex tasks requiring highly skilled individuals to perform them still exist, the logic of a social division of labor works everywhere to maximize the ratio of simple to complex tasks. Unlike the merit system, this organization is functioning "well" when it *diminishes* the necessity for the performance of highly skilled tasks. My earlier example of women in clerical work makes the point neatly. As commercial vocational education was "reformed," the curriculum was expanded to emphasize the skills "necessary" for more prestigious jobs. The greatest economic expansion of jobs, however, occurred in typewriting, stenography, and so forth, as almost exclusively low-paid women's work.

"Tensions" between these different organizations are not merely local "crises," but inherent in the very different ends involved. The tensions have been ameliorated from both sides, by means of "upgrading" the skill requirements of jobs that as practiced require very little skill at all; by enhancing the prestige and indispensability of the "expert"; by generating a sense of always more "experts" being in high demand; by positioning English itself within the educational system as a crucial component designed to supply "skill training" that refines the range of "vocabulary" and "symbol manipulation" in verbal skills. Since it would be virtually impossible for either system to exist without the other, these steps appear in "everyone's" interest. But they have had a diminishing rate of success, which in turn necessitates one final way in which education can be understood as "compensatory," and correspondingly one more reason for the intraeducational utility of English.

I V

In the first chapter of his *On the Economy of Machinery and Manufactures*, Babbage notes with approval that while "the general population" of England had increased by roughly 15 percent in each of the three ten-year periods from 1801 to 1831, the population of Manchester, Glasgow, Liverpool, Nottingham, and Birmingham had increased by 123 percent during the thirty-year period, with the greatest increase in every case but Glasgow coming in the third ten-year period.[23] These facts were important to him, first because they made clear "the vast importance to the well-being of this country, of making the interests of its manufacturers well understood and attended to" (*EMM*, 18), and second, in more specific terms, because they attested to the massive transformation of "unproductive" to "productive" labor increasingly located in the cities he surveys. This concentrated productivity and efficiency meant, among other things, that cotton grown in India was purchased as cloth "by the lords of the soil which gave it birth" at a cheaper price in England. And he adds in a footnote: "At Calicut, in the East Indies, (whence the cotton cloth called calico derives its name,) the price of labour is *one-seventh* of that in England, yet the market is supplied from British looms" (*EMM*, 17n; Babbage's emphasis). The rapid advance in machine technology of production in England had resulted simultaneously in much higher wages for workers and a much cheaper product.

Marx, however, saw still another transformation involved in the process of increasing the available supply of productive labor in the cities and improving machine efficiency of manufacturing: "The technical conditions of the production process—machinery, means of transport, etc.—themselves now make possible a very rapid transformation of masses of surplus product into additional means of production. The mass of social wealth, overflowing with the advance of accumulation and capable of being transformed into additional capital, thrusts itself frantically into old branches of production, whose market suddenly expands, or into newly formed branches, such as railways, etc., which now become necessary as a result of the further development of the old branches. In all such cases, there must be the possibility of suddenly throwing great masses of men into the decisive areas without doing any damage to the scale of production in other spheres." The pace and direction of change, that is, as manufacturing itself expands, depends on the further transformation of at least some portion of the newly available productive labor force into a "reserve army" of labor: "Modern industry's whole form of motion therefore depends on the constant transformation of a part of the working population into unemployed or semi-employed 'hands' " (*C*, 785–86). The unprecedented "success" of the transformation of unproductive to productive labor at the same time made possible this "reserve army" available to each new process of production as it began to industrialize, thus feeding the development of industry.

What Babbage had been intent to impress on his audience, however, was that no industry "develops" very far by hiring more and more workers. The superiority of "British looms" was possible because the machinery of production permitted more goods from *fewer* workers. His lesson was given convenient illustration recently by General Motors's announcement of their "revolutionary" Saturn plant, which is projected to turn out twice as many cars as any existing GM plant, but will employ hardly more workers than even their most recent operation in Wentzville, Missouri. We might then draw as the corollary of Marx's analysis that though "modern industry's whole form of motion therefore depends" indeed on the presence of a reserve army of labor, the necessity that such a reserve army be kept from growing so large that it threatens the very stability of society *depends on the continued motion of modern industry*. The workers no longer needed at one point must have somewhere else to go—industry must be in motion—or swell the ranks of the unemployed. Where they go most often is into as yet *less* mechanized forms of production, and into jobs with less pay. As Braverman observes after quoting Marx at length on the reserve army of labor, "we see in capitalist industry a secular trend to accumulate labor in those portions of industry and trade which are least affected by the scientific-technical revolution: service work, sales and other forms of marketing, clerical work insofar as it has not yet been mechanized, etc. The paradox that the most rapidly growing mass occupations in an era of scientific-technical revolution are those which have least to do with science and technology need not surprise us. The purpose of machinery is not to increase but to decrease the number of workers attached to it" (*LMC*, 384), something Babbage had understood very well.

For a long time industry moved fast indeed. So long as it moved fast enough, and so long as those employed in the primarily "service" sector Braverman describes (as well as those who were unemployed or semiemployed) were perceived to be women, "minorities,"

immigrants, and workers whose skills had been made "obsolete,"
it was possible to rationalize the potential problem of a huge reserve army by claiming that such people weren't sufficiently well
trained to perform the jobs required by an always more rapidly
changing technology of production. (And incidentally as well, by
continually changing the definition of "employment" and pushing
upward the level of what constitutes "acceptable" unemployment,
things the Reagan administration practiced, and in fact refined to
an art form.) Throughout this long process, the refrain was that
first "industrialization" and then "automation" didn't destroy jobs;
they merely changed their location and the skills involved. That is,
insofar as there was any admission of a "problem," the "answer"
lay, as always, in education that could compensate by training more
and more people for the new jobs available. Eventually, however, it
began to be clear even in government statements that the evidence
was cutting dangerously close to this rationalization:

> In the past, jobholders had more education than did jobseekers—in 1959,
> for example, the median education of the employed was 12.0 years, while
> that of the unemployed was only 9.9 years. ["Only" itself is something
> of a euphemism here; by ninth grade most people would already possess
> all the actual skills needed for the majority of jobs available.] Since then,
> the average education of unemployed workers has risen so that by 1971
> the difference between the median education of employed and unemployed
> workers, 12.4 and 12.2 years respectively, is no longer statistically signifi-
> cant. (*LMC*, 441–42, quoting Walter Deutermann's 1971 study done for the
> Bureau of Labor Statistics)

Two closely related "explanations" for such evidence became
fashionable, both at the expense of education. The first was that
in concentrating so much attention on professional training coupled
with the greater emphasis on equal opportunity for more people, the
schools had produced a vast overabundance of professionals and encouraged far too many students to think they could become professionals. Merit was all right, of course, but it required high standards
being compromised everywhere in deference to the complaints of
overambitious suburbia as well as the complaints of "minorities"
about unequal treatment, and of course the radicalism of the 1960's.
The result was the demise of "excellence" and a whole group of the
population having accumulated a great many years in school while
still being unfit for the jobs that actually needed doing. The under-

current to this argument is the logic of a social division of labor to *restrict* as much as possible the number of complex tasks requiring highly skilled workers. Yet it could hardly be voiced in those terms, because just as clearly such an argument runs directly counter to the claim that technological change doesn't destroy jobs, etc., it merely requires workers with more skills.

The second argument was that the curriculum of the schools had departed too far from basic, *general* training. The contradiction here is only apparent, for while the first argument is directed at job skills, the second is directed at "cultural skills." In pursuing all kinds of marginal interests (on the basis of the values of educators, not the clientele they supposedly served), and proliferating more of them all the time, schools were turning out students who could, for example, "express themselves" in things by a species of courtesy called "poems" or "songs," but could hardly read or spell correctly. Twelve or thirteen years of education might not mean one actually knew much of anything. Further, the justification of these marginal interests on the grounds of "individual enrichment" led to a student population so enriched they couldn't condescend to taking a job that might do someone some good. The spectacular growth and visibility of the "service industries" Braverman refers to had put a lot more people in direct contact with "such" workers, with the result that on a lower frequency the argument reduced itself to the reiterated complaint that "you just can't get good help these days." That is, like Robert Hoxie's complaints in the second decade of the century, it is an argument about the "poor and lawless material" in the work force.

Both arguments assume education should compensate for the dilemmas of employment and unemployment in the economy by providing more basic, disciplined, necessary training rather than frittering away school time on inessentials. That is, both assume the congruence of an educational system and an economic system, and fault the schools when the discontinuities become obvious. What they overlook is how all these "inessentials" in the schools were in fact compensating for the dilemmas of employment and unemployment at the point where the dilemmas became most critical: by occupying the time of what otherwise would be a continually growing reserve army of labor. What would unemployment be like if the time spent in school had *not* been increasingly lengthened, if the schools had *not* generated internal reasons for keeping students, if departments like English had not diversified to provide *something else* for students to do in school? As Braverman points out, in 1971 again nearly 90 percent of the population between the ages of 17 and 24 were in the armed forces, unemployed, or in school. Take out school from that triad and the unemployment figures would be astronomical, no matter what kind of job training people had. For "minority" populations, typically leaving school at an earlier age, the unemployment figures *are* astronomical. "The postponement of school leaving age to an average age of eighteen," Braverman argues, "has become indispensable for keeping unemployment within reasonable bounds" (*LMC*, 439).

Braverman himself tends to ignore the extent to which other things do go on in the schools, the way in which both students and teachers (often at personal sacrifice) have been able to take advantage of a certain freedom at least from the very logic of work he describes. The point remains, however, that having to compensate for the "success" of capitalism in creating a huge reserve army of young labor puts severe limits on the possibilities of educational "reform" in any direction, certainly one that might challenge the organization of work and the values rationalizing that organization. The report published in 1973 by the Kettering Foundation–supported National Commission on the Reform of Secondary Education marks a stunning contrast to the generally sanguine and for the most part uncontroversial proposals made by Conant in *The American High School Today*. Hindsight is unfair, and the authors had behind them in a way Conant did not a decade of turmoil and a mounting barrage of complaints about the failure of public education. Yet unlike Conant, they do try at least to face as squarely as possible the "disintegration" of mission in the schools. One major reason for that disintegration, as Braverman had noted, is "the custodial function" the schools have had to assume.[24] The report argues that compulsory attendance hasn't really worked in any case; absentee rates are huge, and the disruption of both classroom activities and school discipline is obvious. Their recommendations in this area, however, beginning with lowering the age of compulsory attendance to fourteen, focus almost entirely on "meaningful" career education. They do not go as far as the U.S. Office of Education and HEW recommendations, but the emphasis is clear enough. Schools can compensate, they can recover a sense of mission and purpose, by renewing attention to job training.

The report recognizes too, often very powerfully, that the schools must do much more to eliminate gender and racial discrimination in the process of such training. But the major problem with career education as it exists, they suggest, is one of psychology, seconding the 1969 statement by the National Advisory Council on Vocational Education that they quote:

At the very heart of our problem is a national attitude that says vocational education is designed for somebody else's children. This attitude is shared by businessmen, labor leaders, administrators, teachers, parents, and students. We are all guilty. We have promoted the idea that the only good education is an education capped by four years of college. This idea, transmitted by our values, our aspirations, and our silent support, is snobbish, undemocratic, and a revelation of why schools fail so many students. (quoted in *RSE*, 51)

As I have argued, secondary schools are organized toward the top. This kind of statement, however, has all the eye-opening insight of those Hollywood melodramas where city slickers learned the clean, manly virtues of slopping hogs or driving a combine for 15 hours in 100° weather. The trick of course is that the 15 hours a day every day of every harvest appeared on screen as a montage of 30 seconds, just as here a life appears in a paragraph montage of quiet, dignified labor that ought to be respected by everyone.

"Phase three of career education," the report continues, "includes extensive opportunities for students in grades 11 and 12 to concentrate on the acquisition of specific skills related to occupations they have chosen. Career counselors must be certain that these occupations are in demand, important to society and fulfilling for the individuals who choose them" (*RSE*, 58). Two paragraphs later, they quote a "tiny sample" from the 1972–73 edition of the *Occupational Outlook Handbook* of such fulfilling and socially useful occupations, available to those with a high school diploma: "business machine servicemen, construction machinery operators, stewardesses, hospital attendants, receptionists, electronic computer operators, and cashiers" (quoted in *RSE*, 59). Here is my "tiny sample" of some typical duties for a "receptionist" during the work day: answering telephones; greeting clients or prospective clients or whoever happens to walk in the door accidentally and making them feel "comfortable"; answering telephones; locating client files; answering telephones; making coffee (often *written into* the job description); answering telephones; collecting, sorting, and distributing mail; answering telephones; typing letters; answering telephones. With respect to "locating client files," Braverman quotes (*LMC*, 321) from a 1960 manual published by the Systems and Procedures Association of America, *A Guide to Office Clerical Time Standards: A Compilation of Standard Data Used by Large American Companies*, whose title gives it away. It is intended to provide among other things standard time values for each work operation in an office as an aid to improving employee efficiency:

Open and Close	Minutes
File Drawer, open and close, no selection	.04
Folder, open or close flaps	.04
Desk drawer, open side drawer of standard desk	.014
Open center drawer	.026
Close side	.015
Close center	.027

Chair Activity	
Get up from chair	.033
Sit down in chair	.033
Turn in swivel chair	.009
Move in chair to adjoining desk or file (4 ft. maximum)	.050

You can see right away the disadvantages if the file cabinet is more than four feet away from the receptionist. In any case, if all this doesn't make for fulfilling work, it's hard to know what does. The chance to do it is worth staying in school at least until twelfth grade in order to acquire the necessary skills through career education. For life.

Despite its criticism of existing vocational education, then, the report follows a familiar pattern of "compensatory" education for social inequalities. First, the problem is perceived to lie in the *psychology* of the situation. Second, the necessity to change the psychological attitudes involved is hammered home. Finally, specific programs are devised so that those *victimized* by the situation will be enabled to change their attitudes. (The Kerner report, for example, a few years previously, followed the same pattern. It demonstrated the

racism of white society, and then lectured the schools on the necessity to provide black and other "minority" children with the resources to cope with racism.) There is hardly any suggestion in
the commission's report that something might be seriously wrong
with the organization of work itself. The problem is "our" attitude
toward work, and the answer is to change the attitudes of the students soon going to work.

I assume the effects on English departments of the complex of
events that surfaced in the debates over the failures of the school
system (and that led to the report itself among other things) will
be familiar enough. In a situation where pressure is being put on
education to train job skills more directly, those disciplines like English whose importance is primarily intraeducational will become
obvious targets. One can in any case refer to yet another report,
this published in 1982 by the PMLA Commission on the Future of
the Profession, for a litany of the woes English departments experienced during the "crisis" I've been describing. That report returns
my argument nicely to Ohmann's formulation about "the peculiarities of English departments." MLA "in *society*," the report argues,
must dedicate itself "to improve the stature of the humanities, in
influence and rewards, within the educational system and the larger
community."[25] That is, the most important social mission of MLA is
not to change the values that rationalize the organization of work,
but to change the *attitude* of society toward *our* work.

v

Where for Marx abstract labor names the social organization of
work, relationships among people, concrete labor instead describes
the relations between people and the "material" on which work is
engaged. It names the effort, both "physical" and "mental," that
transforms the material of work. In capitalist production, however,
concrete labor typically loses its internal integrity and coherence to
the extent that any given work process will be broken down into
the smallest component units, which are then reassembled and redesigned to maximize "efficiency" and to ensure that control over
the process is in the hands of management rather than labor. The
actual effort of work becomes completely subordinate to this social
organization; the tasks performed are determined not by the skill

of the worker or the properties of the material on which she or he works, but instead by the requirements of abstract labor. Apologists for the values rationalizing work, work very hard to disguise the process of redesigning. But it's hard to disguise. Time-motion studies of clerical work, for example, such as the brief table I quoted above about locating client files, result in an arrangement of everything from office furniture to efficiency standards, to which the concrete labor of the receptionist must conform. That is, not only the results of what the receptionist does, but the very processes of work itself are determined by the criteria of abstract labor. The physical motion of a body from desk to file cabinet has been plotted in advance. Bodies that don't conform to these physical motions will "betray" themselves in a lowered productivity. The recent business fetish for "excellence" offers any number of examples of how refined the process has become. Employees are to be given more "freedom" in their movements, not because this is desirable in itself, but because— surprise—the resulting increase in time duration is minimal, and is more than offset by a reduction in the necessity for *redoing* certain operations.

For some time now the mode of calculation has been similar for "mental motions," as it were. In presenting the "therblig" classification system, the 1948 edition of the *Production Handbook*, edited by L. P. Alford and John Bangs, emphasizes that in micromotion analysis—where film frames can document the duration of each therblig —the "mental reactions" of the worker become especially evident.[26] The therblig symbol for "search," for example, is ⟨◔⟩, that is, an "eye turned as if searching," and for "find" is ⟨◉⟩, an "eye straight as if focused on object" (*PH*, 578). In the micromotion study of filmed work operations, a high ratio of ⟨◔⟩ marks to ⟨◉⟩ marks can reveal one of several things. Possibly the objects of work need to be rearranged in a more uniform pattern so that the worker can more rapidly grasp the needed object and reduce search operations; possibly the whole process must be redesigned so that fewer objects of search are presented to the worker; but possibly the *worker's mind* is simply wandering in between work operations, in which case production standards, for everybody, must be set higher.

The social organization of labor in education does not of course generate surplus value in the same way as production work. As I have argued, its contribution is indirect; education generates a stratification system of "intellectual resources" where individuals are sorted out by talent and ability as then available to fill designated jobs. There are in fact many other occupations that, like work in education, are only indirectly related to the creation of surplus value. Most obviously, those employed in the vast marketing apparatuses of corporations contribute primarily to the *realization* of surplus value, by expanding the consumption of manufactured products. It is the complex of compensatory functions education is expected to perform, however, that has the most immediate effect on the relations between abstract and concrete labor in education. For it not only marks work in education as having an indirect relation to production, but it also and more importantly permits a distinct, internal organization. This organization resembles abstract labor in production insofar as the results, the constant series of evaluations of student skills being trained, are appropriated for use elsewhere. Students enter the work force trailing clouds of evaluative reports from the schools, just as in more subtle ways they enter into all kinds of social relations with their place in the stratification system of the schools as one major factor (marriage and friendship, for example, tend to fall within roughly equal educational parameters). These evaluations then function in education something like surplus value in production; they are generated by the social organization of labor in education, and they result in a kind of sociocultural capital.

The organization differs from abstract labor in production most strikingly in that it does not determine every element of the concrete labor tasks carried on in the schools. Within certain boundary conditions, control over concrete labor in education is exercised less by designing the work process itself than by targeting certain aspects of its *results*. This is not to suggest that these boundary conditions are irrelevant, but the practices ranging from "accountability" to amount of research published that directly affect concrete labor typically do so by focusing on its results. Indeed, the relative autonomy of concrete labor in education has long been recognized as a powerful recruiting incentive, itself a kind of "compensation" for the lower pay, multiple responsibilities, and so forth, that teachers face.

The actual work carried on in university departments of English comprehends a curious amalgam of tasks. Though any individual faculty member will have an "area" of specialization, she or he will be involved in any number of ways with other tasks as well, and not only because teaching quite often occurs "outside" one's areas. Tenure and promotion decisions are obvious examples of crossing areas. Conceptually, it seems to me very difficult to identify why the particular range of tasks falls within one department, which is perhaps one reason why most statements of the "mission" of the English department descend within half a sentence to vaporous rhetoric. A history of English departments would undoubtedly suggest as an answer that English departments did not emerge and develop in accordance with a clear, conceptual direction. I have been arguing that development was not entirely haphazard, however, but occurred in relation to a specific social organization of work derived in large part from the complex of compensatory functions education is expected to perform. As a department, that is, English is primarily an intraeducational phenomenon, an ensemble of roles created in response to a set of pressure points emerging in the modern history of education itself in the United States.

Thus conceptual definition, like a sense of "mission," must operate to some extent after the fact, stitching together as much as possible roles whose connections have their source in how education sorts and evaluates a student population. For while education as compensatory projects a variety of different functions for society, from the training of a professional elite to a holding tank for a reserve army of young labor, each of these functions projected inward, into the system of education itself, necessitates complicated sequences of evaluative hierarchies. English is a major collection point of these inward projections, a point where the compensatory social functions turn into their educational form as evaluation. Thus, for example, insofar as education is expected to compensate for an absence of a hereditary class structure by training professionals, it must generate internal criteria for selecting those students with the abilities to become professionals. English then occurs at the point where the social function of training professionals turns into the educational task of evaluating general student ability to proceed to professional training. Likewise, insofar as education is expected to compensate for the "home environment" of "culturally disadvantaged" students so that they can compete equally for jobs, it must also generate internal ways of evaluating the verbal skills perceived as necessary for that competition. And English, again, occurs at the point where this social function turns into an internal educational task of evaluation.

The result of such positioning as a collection point is that English is almost invariably the largest, most influential, and most diverse of the departments in the humanities. Philosophy in contrast, once the "queen" discipline of knowledge, has become a tiny enclave of specialists. Richard Rorty sees this as having happened because where philosophy retreated into recondite technical exercises, English managed to avoid such specialization and is now busy exporting its methodologies of "textualism" across the board of professional knowledges.[27] But though philosophy—and history and foreign language—professors may feel that "critical theory" is now the most exciting place to go for ideas, theory is after all only one relatively minor (in terms of numbers of people involved and labor time) activity within English departments. It is a benefit derived from how English has emerged as *intraeducationally* indispensable, a benefit that is made possible not directly by the wonders of "textualism," but by the relative freedom of direction that accrues to English departments by virtue of their size, influence, and diversity.

"The peculiarities of English departments" arise largely because the conflicts between the social organization of work I have sketched in this chapter and the concrete labor that I want to discuss in the next chapter are peculiarly acute in English. For its size, influence, and diversity are less the results of an internal coherence of any specific concrete labor recognized elsewhere as important enough to warrant that size, than of the social organization of work in education and how English is positioned within that organization. The more English departments perform intraeducational functions, the larger and more influential they become, with more opportunities for multiple directions and more power to control those directions internally. But the larger and more influential they become, the more the concrete labor engaged becomes dependent on the social organization of work that determines those intraeducational functions.

To some extent the economy of education, like the economy of production, seeks to maximize a ratio of "simple" to "complex" tasks. More total labor hours in English are occupied in "simple" tasks like teaching freshman composition than in "complex" tasks like writing a study of Jane Austen's novels. In production work, however, the designation of simple and complex typically reflects the relative emphasis of "physical" and "mental" effort in the task. Thus the mental calculation of tiers of flour sacks in a boxcar is more "complex" than the physical effort of putting flour sacks where one is told to, and so on. In education, on the other hand, where (however mistakenly) almost all the tasks teachers perform are construed as purely mental anyway, such distinctions are far more powerfully influenced by the degree of individual control over the work. That is, it's by no means clear that writing a study of Jane Austen's novels is really more "complex" than teaching freshman composition, but it is pretty clear most of the time that the former permits more individual control over the work. Likewise, university teaching is more "complex" than secondary teaching, since again it permits more individual control over the concrete labor involved.

Among the multiple tasks performed in English, "literary study" —in all its versions, from editing to theory—emerges as the most desirable concrete labor, in part again because it is the most "complex," permitting the most individual control over the work. As such, it also makes possible much more conceptual coherence and clarity of definition. This statement may seem odd in the face of the virulent controversies within literary study, and the continuing laments about its "fragmentation," but one has only to compare such things to statements about the "mission" of English departments to recognize a degree of internal coherence and substance in the former that the latter attains if at all only by virtually eliminating most of what goes on in English to concentrate on literary study. Thus it is primarily literary study that, in Ohmann's terms, is most clearly aligned with professional identity and the "professional claims of the faculty," and thus most visibly in conflict with "the externally imposed conditions of our working lives," with the social organization of work in English.

A shift in focus from this abstract labor to literary study as concrete labor, from work as the production of evaluations to "our work" and the potential consequences of "our work," seems then to cross an almost incommensurable divide. For despite how the details are (often confusingly) mingled, in the development of work skills and knowledges in literary study in the United States in the twentieth century, the most important weapon in the struggles against "externally imposed conditions" has had to involve a whole series of claims that attempt to *dislocate* concrete labor from the organization of the workplace. As I have argued elsewhere, "apology" has provided the major impetus of critical theory at least since early New Criticism.[28] Literary study and literature as the conceptual center of concrete labor in English have been defended, justified, "apologized" for, in ways that inevitably begin by converting the location of work into an accidental quality. Even increasingly visible challenges to literary study as "traditionally" understood must first imagine literature as somehow a vital element of ideological control, over and beyond the mere study of literature in a particular workplace. Work happens to take place just here, in these forms, but its real effectivity is potentially anywhere and everywhere in the society.

However, as apology thereby attempts to neutralize an "imposed" organization of work, by freeing concrete labor from the workplace, another series of conflicts altogether emerges. For after all, there is a whole vast array of products and services, including "reading material," of course, already available in what *does* seem far more anywhere and everywhere than literary study, namely a consumer marketplace. Conant thought it a "barbaric" question why reading Shakespeare gave more "enduring satisfactions" than reading comic books, but he also thought it a necessary question for literary criticism to answer. Thus just as it is difficult to inquire very far into the social organization of work in English as abstract labor without also inquiring into the connections to abstract labor in production, likewise it is difficult to think of specifically literary study as concrete labor without considering its relations to the processes of consumption in society.

The signs of the conflicts that result appear in a long series of distinctions: between "literature" and "popular culture"; between the "intrinsic value" of literature and the "extrinsic" relations of other forms of discourse in society; between the "creative work" of writing literature and the "persuasive manipulation" of advertising and propaganda; between the "work" of scholarship itself and the "leisure" of merely reading (the material of the latter of course can become the material of literary study as well, but then the "reading" is no longer "mere"; it, too, is "work"); between literature as somehow independent of, or a critique of, or a "distantiation" of ideology, and discourses that instead "reflect" or "reinforce" dominant values of the culture; between what I called in my first chapter an "ideology of the new" as a force for cultural change and renewal, and "fashion" as the ceaseless reproduction in new forms of existing cultural relations; between literature as an ongoing "process," and literature reduced to a "commodity"; and so forth. Many of these distinctions have a history much longer than that of the modern English department, but the educational location of literary study in English departments has altered their form considerably.

In the next chapter, I want to concentrate on the development of the concrete work skills and knowledges of literary study as they have been shaped by a marketplace competition for an audience, and for influence on an audience. Here again, because of its educational location, the relations and conflicts are no more direct than the relations between the social organization of work in education and in production. Literary study does not any longer, if it ever really did, compete *directly* against consumer goods for a public, but rather tends increasingly "to find itself" in competition, as in large part a result of the conflicts between abstract and concrete labor *in* education. In this next chapter as well, I will rely on sometimes impossibly large generalizations in constructing my argument, in the hope that a focus on work will establish at least a direction for them. The distinctions between "literature" and "popular culture," for example, comprehend a great many ideas and values. My interest will be in the perceptions of how each is understood to involve a series of concrete work skills and knowledges.

As I suggested in my first chapter, however, "popular culture" is perhaps only a curious name for what is rarely thought about or studied as if it involved specific processes and organizations of work at all. Since in terms of the work of production and the ownership of the material means of production at least, it should be clear that when you refer to widely circulated material like TV shows or films, you can't really be referring to something that is "popular." Yet of course TV shows and films do *circulate* widely indeed, and whatever the apparatuses of production involved, the networks of circulation are intrinsicated in complex ways in an enormous range of people's "everyday experience." In concentrating on the relations between cultural consumption and the concrete labor of literary study then, it will not be "popular culture" that supplies my focus, but rather, and much more specifically, the organization of *advertising*. For on the one hand, advertising is a singularly appropriate paradigm of how mass circulation of any kind occurs in our modern social formation. On the other hand, however, and no less than literary study, advertising work takes place at a particular location, with its own internal organization, division of labor, and so forth, and its own internal history. Advertising, that is, permits my argument a consideration of the process of cultural circulation generally, and at the same time an inquiry into specific forms of cultural work. The double emphasis is important, for reasons I'll try to make clear at the beginning of the next chapter, because the way advertising work has reconstituted cultural circulation has had perhaps the decisive influence on how concrete labor is perceived and carried out in English.

Work and Value

People *will* read: what practically all people will do they must be trained how best to do. Assuming that people will read, the question becomes important as to what they will read and how they will read.... It must be constantly in the mind of the teacher of literature that the values of utilization and appreciation are dominant in that subject and that high-school pupils are to be trained to utilize and appreciate literature, not to produce it, to become intelligent consumers of literature, not producers nor yet even literary critics. The former function is general and universal: the latter is extremely limited and restricted.[1]

Men who are not constantly in close touch with publicity and its problems often look upon advertising as nothing more or less than so many written words. That is why so many literary men, and reporters out of a job, think they can write advertisements. On the contrary, advertising has nothing at all to do with literature. It is salesmanship—but in advertising the salesman stands behind a printed page instead of a counter.[2]

To a remarkable extent these two sets of comments—the first from Inglis's *Principles of Secondary Education* and the second from *The 1909 J. Walter Thompson Blue Book on Advertising*— move in the same world, where more people have available more time and money, and where they will read and will buy. In the mid-nineteenth century in the United States, as newspapers and magazines proliferated and the population who read them grew larger, a number of individuals began to establish themselves as performing an increasingly useful function of selling advertising space in these media to manufacturers eager for access to potential consumers on a scale never possible before. The service was valuable to the owners of magazines and newspapers, for it meant that the cost of their product to consumers could be lowered considerably; revenues were made up from the sale of advertising space. The first advertising agents, that is, had as a clientele the print media and were an important factor in the cheap availability of new reading material. Advertising also influenced the nature of that reading material, however, since advertisers were if anything even more interested in circulation figures than the owners of magazines and newspapers were. Agents thus found it easier to sell space in some publications than in others; those publications with large amounts of advertising could be sold more cheaply than their competitors; and their circulation accelerated accordingly. What people read and what they bought became an interconnected process fairly quickly.

Of course neither *Principles of Secondary Education* nor the *Blue Book* is unique in the recognition of the importance their respective fields would have to this process in the immediate future. To some extent, however, both benefited uniquely from the newly emergent patterns of circulation that occupy their attention in the comments above. Inglis was not only an influential educator and a respected authority. As a member of the NEA Commission that produced a massive report on the reorganization of secondary schools, at least some of Inglis's ideas explained in *Principles* took shape as well in a form that over the next decades would become perhaps the most visible emblem of education as a *national* priority, a focal point of national concern: precisely that of the "report," issued by an officially sanctioned body of recognized experts drawn together for just that purpose. Retrospective familiarity with the content of such reports as rarely justifying anything like the drum roll of importance that usually accompanies the formation of the commission, the publication of the report, and so on, should not obscure the function they perform in circulation. Marx reminds us accurately enough that ideas can become a material force, and it is necessary to add how in a modern cultural economy it is the materiality of a process of circulation that makes the transformation possible. Inglis's *Principles* is worth attention in large part because of its positioning through the NEA Report within the changing terms of cultural circulation. Likewise, and though the *Blue Book* certainly owes something to the prestige of the Thompson agency, it also exploits new possibilities of circulation in ways similar to the NEA Report. For the *Blue Book* after all is advertising advertising; that is, it converts Thompson prestige into a certain authority to speak for the importance of advertising generally, at the same time that it finds in the extended circulation possible to this general discourse still another way to extend the territory of Thompson. Like reports in the field of education, such strategies are by now familiar indeed in advertising. It is the *Blue Book*, however, that makes visible this quantum leap in the effective advertising use of the potential of circulation.

In one important sense nevertheless, *Principles* and the *Blue Book* intervene at opposite poles in the situation they describe of increasingly interconnected literacy and consumption. By 1909, the Thompson agency was already a large and successful example of the transformation of advertising agents: from brokers who were paid by print media to sell advertising space, to a firm responsible for the market analysis, creation, design, and distribution of ads, an entire "advertising campaign," as it was already called. The *Blue Book* marks the change as the arrival of a new "economic force," something "that would effect a revolution in selling in the same way that Watt's steam engine revolutionized manufacturing.... Advertising was not invented like a patented clock—nor is it a scheme, like a plan to raise money for a college or a church. It is the permanent result of an economic revolution which brought it to the surface after centuries of ferment."[3] Agencies such as Thompson thus represented themselves as a new field of work expertise. Like the manufacturer, the advertising agent must have "a knowledge of the goods" (*BB*, 19); like earlier broker-agents, must know media (the *Blue Book* points out that Thompson maintains separate departments for magazines, newspapers, and "bill-posting"); and like sales personnel must be adept at the actual skills of getting people to buy, including a knowledge of various markets and their potential. But the whole, as it were, is greater than the sum of these parts. The advertising agent in this sense represents an expertise that redefines the very nature of the business: "Why did this method of selling goods, unknown to our fathers, grow to such gigantic proportions in a single generation? The answer is this: *Advertising draws a straight line from the manufacturer to the consumer.* These are the two points that limit the problem of production and consumption, and advertising is the shortest line between them. It has made the hit-or-miss selling methods of sixty years ago as obsolete as the Edict of Nantes" (*BB*, 18).

Inglis is also concerned with consumption, and with a "line" from producer to consumer. But "assuming that people will read," that "lines" in this sense exist, the question that interests him is not only "what they will read" but perhaps even more important, "how they will read."[4] His intervention, that is, occurs at the point of how to train *intelligent* consumers." For while not as sudden or dramatic as the "revolution" in selling described by the *Blue Book*, Inglis nevertheless felt himself in the midst of a crucial moment in the formation of public education in the United States. The entire new population entering the schools was also entering into the cultural, social, economic, and political life of the country in unprecedented ways, and thus what went on in the schools would perhaps have the decisive impact on the future directions of the society. Within the schools, English seemed to him the field affording the best opportunity to shape the standards and values of that new population: "At the present time English is probably the only study universally required of all pupils in the secondary school at some stage or stages within the course. Probably one sixth of the total time of the high-school course is devoted by most pupils to the study of the mother tongue and its literature" (*PSE*, 421). Where the *Blue Book* imagines the advertising expert as drawing a straight line from producer to consumer, Inglis thinks of the secondary school literature teacher instead as an expert whose job of work is to understand which *cultural* "lines," as they contact consumers, are of the most real social value, and who will be trained for that work in a university English department, whose faculty will then represent an even higher form of the *same* expertise.

Given this pivotal location, however, the collection of activities carried on in English (everything from the study of syntax and spelling to acting out scenes from Shakespeare) struck Inglis in something of the same way as "the hit-or-miss selling methods" of sixty years before struck the authors of the *Blue Book*. Thus much of his argument is intended to sort out and restructure the field in accordance with the new tasks made necessary by a much larger and more diverse student population. Teaching the English language is unquestionably crucial, but it shouldn't be confused with teaching literature. The literature teacher Inglis wanted would know a great deal about the intricacies of "the mother tongue," about the "production" of literature, about the "elaborately formal study of the techniques of literary composition" (*PSE*, 445) that is the province of the "literary critic," about the standards of aesthetic judgment and taste addressed by the "public critic," and so forth. But while her or his expertise draws on a number of sources, like the advertising agent's expertise it has a different and ultimately more inclusive end: training consumer skills. Because for Inglis, such culturally acquired knowledge is everywhere directly linked with the central function of education itself, the shaping of sociocultural values. Thus while his intervention occurs at a different point, like the *Blue Book* Inglis is intent on fashioning a role for a new kind of expert, a role commensurate with the expansion of culture just as the role of the advertising agent is commensurate with the expansion of the marketplace.

The emergence of an advertising agency like Thompson involved a fundamental shift in client relationships. So long as the advertiser was also the maker of the product, or the individual or firm offering "services," the clientele was of course also the consumer. A hat maker in Connecticut, to borrow the *Blue Book* example, had as a clientele those people living in the vicinity who went to the hat maker for their hats, which could be advertised variously by the hat maker through sales representatives, signs, word of mouth, and so forth. As the hat maker became a manufacturing firm, however, a rather different problem presented itself: "What was the use of manufacturing a hundred thousand hats every year in a village that could not afford to buy more than three thousand? ... How was a hat manufacturer in Connecticut going to tell the people of Ohio that his hats were the best for the money? What miracle of communication could span a thousand miles?" (*BB*, 17). The answer, of course, was advertising on a scale that demanded the new expert, the agency like Thompson who could draw a "straight line" from Connecticut to Ohio. But the *Blue Book* is not selling Thompson's expertise to Ohio consumers, nor even to newspapers and magazines distributed in Ohio, like earlier broker-agents. It is a prospectus drawn up for the new clientele for this expertise, the manufacturers who hire Thompson to run their advertising campaigns.

In contrast, while Inglis's secondary school literature teacher is also presented as possessing the expertise of a professional, it is by no means clear who or what exactly is the clientele for that new expertise. Obviously it is not the "producer" of literature. (Although as Inglis presents the daily practices of the job, this might seem the case to a casual observer. That is, the literature teacher may appear as if she or he were hired by the author of *King Lear* to promote his wisdom and knowledge of human nature as very unlike that of the author of *Cap'n Billy's Whiz Bang*.) In any direct sense, the clientele is not the student-consumer either. For what the student receives are the "social-civic values" and "individualistic-avocational values" (*PSE*, 441) *of literature*, where the teacher acts in effect as a kind of surrogate student, demonstrating how best to understand those values in literature until students can do it successfully on their own. And in a nice reversal of roles, the advertising agent—who actually *is* of course hired by a producer—is likely instead in the construction of the ad to adopt this role of the teacher, demonstrating for consumers the benefits of the product advertised.

Regardless of the mystification of client relationships, however, what is clear is that both experts are to act on potential consumers. "Reduced to its lowest terms," Inglis argues on the first page of *Principles*, "education is the process of producing, directing, and preventing changes in human beings." Many of Inglis's contemporaries would soften such a statement in the direction of encouraging individual development, and so forth, none of which Inglis denied. But the fundamental point—the "lowest terms"—remained for him that education *does something* to the individuals who are to be educated, in whatever complicated ways that "something" takes place. Teaching had in fact provided a model to advertisers in the skills of influence. *Printer's Ink*, in an October 1895 editorial, had made the suggestion directly: "Probably when we are a little more enlightened, the advertisement writer, like the teacher, will study psychology. For however diverse their occupations may at first appear, the advertising writer and the teacher have one great objective in common—to influence the human mind."[5] Neither expert, that is, is envisioned as merely offering certain professional services to a consumer-clientele. The *public* they address is not a clientele, and the ends they advance are "political" in the sense they are *directive*. Both experts intervene in "everyday behavior" to direct that behavior toward specific ends. Indeed, because of the subject, the directive work of the literature teacher especially, like that of the advertising agent, occurs in the midst of the most intimate details of everyday behavior: "With the thousand and one phases of everyday behavior history, sociology, and economics have little or nothing to do. Even civics in its broadest sense has relatively little to do with those phases of life's activities. On the other hand that is exactly the

field where literature, in its broadest and best sense, reigns supreme"
(*PSE*, 439)—or would, if there were not the work of the advertising
agent in precisely the same territory.

It is worth emphasizing, perhaps over and over, the points of congruence and exchange between the roles of literature teacher and
advertising agent in the new circumstances Inglis and the *Blue Book*
recount. For though the histories of these roles make them almost
contemporaries, their territories and audiences are virtually identical, and their position in business and education respectively was
a matter of continually growing importance in the first decades of
the century, they are rarely connected, the prescience of the *Printer's
Ink* editorial notwithstanding. Though advertising work is studied,
as it probably should be, in relation to the economy and the development of a "mass culture," reflection on the teaching of literature
remains haunted by the amusing fantasy that while its subject may
have been "popular" once—in Shakespeare's England inevitably—
it is now primarily a matter involving a tiny fraction of an elite.
But most of the population of sixteenth-century England had never
even been to London, let alone heard of Shakespeare. In contrast,
the percentage of people in the United States today who have read,
seen, heard about, or in some way at some time encountered Shakespeare's plays is enormous. Already by 1915, as Inglis points out,
nearly 60 percent of the students in secondary schools were taking
relatively advanced courses in English literature. They also read advertisements and "popular" literature to be sure; the point is that
a vast new population did both, with whatever varying degrees of
intensity and interest, and they did both in large part because teaching literature *circulates* literature every bit as surely as advertising
agents circulate products, services, and "reading material."

It should not really be surprising, then, that in their respective
definitions of work expertise, Inglis and the Thompson agency have
a wary eye on each other's field of expertise. Inglis's preoccupation
with "intelligent" consumption has as its obvious target the barrage of reading material and advertisements that students would face
throughout their lives, with the English classroom as the one place
where they might be trained in the necessary skills to think intelligently about that material. The *Blue Book* is equally emphatic in the
opposite direction; literary training by no means qualifies anyone to
write advertisements for the marketplace. What is involved are not

only competing work skills, but skills in part at least *defined against each other*, and what Inglis and the *Blue Book* make explicit continued to function in the subsequent development of both fields of expertise. Thus in literary study, the specifically *literary* quality of a text was differentiated not only from historical or philosophical discourse—as it had been for some time—but increasingly and even more insistently from "popular culture" circulating in the marketplace. The qualities of the latter were then marked ambiguously, as on the one hand read by, and "in touch with," a large mass of people, but on the other, and like advertising itself, "manipulative," sentimental, commodified, and so forth. Likewise, as advertising agencies such as Thompson grew in complexity and importance, there was a similar rift growing between market analysis "research" and "creative" copywriting. Thus even a recent school text, like *Advertising* in the McGraw-Hill marketing series, can lecture advertising students about "creative" writing skills with something of the same ambivalence that literature teachers approached "popular culture": "Creativity in advertising most assuredly draws on 'pure' writing talents, but, as should be obvious by now, the nature of the business [like, in corresponding warnings, the "nature" of literature] demands a certain kind of discipline not found in creative writing circles."[6] And by the conclusion to the argument, just as one is likely to discover that "popular culture" and "literature" are really opposites, *Advertising* asserts that "creativity" in advertising "is really the opposite of pure freedom of imagination" (*A*, 396).

To anyone trained now in literary study, such a description of literary creativity as a kind of "pure" freedom of self-expression is at best comically anachronistic. But perhaps it is no more so than the preconceptions that emerge in literary judgments of what advertising and advertising work is all about. Those who work in advertising certainly claim as much. The 1973 *Advertising Age* definition of advertising, for example, echoes a common theme of astonishment at how advertising is perceived elsewhere:

This is not the monster or the irresistible force so often portrayed in fiction. Most serious students of advertising are astounded at the image of advertising that seems to exist so widely in non-advertising minds. When they hear authors and legislators and educators and economists discoursing on the awesome all-embracing power of advertising to hypnotize America's millions, to mesmerize the dollars out of their pockets, and to turn them from the road of economic virtue and sobriety into the primrose paths of overspending for useless, unneeded products, they shake their heads in wonderment. They know that advertising is not that good, not that powerful, not that influential.[7]

It's all too easy to dismiss this disclaimer, but without knowing anything at all about the conditions of work that are its referent.

Yet even if one were to accept it provisionally, there is of course a rider. Advertising pays. In 1975, two years after the *Advertising Age* statement, total expenditures for advertising reached $30 billion in the United States alone, well over 2 percent of the GNP (*A*, 713). More immediately important for my purposes, this bottom line of dollar figures lends support to the assumption, for those who work in advertising, that whatever the extent of its influence, the expertise of the job and the history of development of work skills *can* be linked to the successful realization of the goals of advertising. Advertising performs an indispensable function for its clientele, and the advances in knowledge, sophistication, and technical control have contributed directly to making the services of an advertising agency even more valuable. Thus reading advertising experts on the history of advertising, for a person "in" English, is a curious exercise, to say the least.

What makes it curious, however, is not really this rhetoric of progressive work expertise in advertising history. For despite the often-repeated piety that neither literature nor the study of literature "improves," in fact almost any glance at any discussion in the last 50 years or so of either evidences a similar—and massively more detailed—emphasis on advances in knowledge, technique, sophistication, and so forth. Whoever the chosen author—for example, poet or novelist or critic—s/he inevitably displays a "greater" something than her or his predecessors, and one always leaves off reading a book on Wordsworth or Joyce or Paul de Man wondering why anyone would bother to read Pope or Dickens or Cleanth Brooks again *except* as "history" (or in the fascinating retrievals of this "history," where Pope leapfrogs Wordsworth to anticipate Pound, and so on). Classroom discussions just as inevitably manage to suggest to students how much more knowledge of literature is available now than they might have expected ten years—or even ten minutes—ago.

The difference from reading advertisers on the history of advertising is how in these discussions of literary "history"—especially the closer one gets to the present—work expertise is *disconnected* from the realization of functional ends, from consequences. I have yet to see a book on "imagism," for example, that makes any serious claim that public powers of "perception" are remarkably "cleaner" or more "precise" now than when imagism was launched. *Literature* may be different (and by the twists of literary "history," Dante no less than Robert Creeley), but that of course is the point. The more remarkable the claims for a development and refinement of work skills, the more dramatic the "decline" in general effects. Hence in part that persistent nostalgia for Shakespeare as a "popular" author, and for that oddly named nonprofessional arbiter of culture, the "public critic." (One wonders if literature teachers today then teach "in private.") In contrast to how those in advertising tell the history of work expertise, where the skills and knowledges of work are directly linked at every point to specific consequences, literary "history" emerges as a progression of expertise that nevertheless, at any given moment, is unable to realize the aims projected as a rationale for the necessity of work in the first place. Obviously neither version of self-history represents simply a "neutral" recounting of events, but the differences are so striking they are hard to ignore. Nor can they be accounted for by dismissing the comparison as dealing with incommensurable fields. Inglis's model of the secondary school literature teacher is most immediately useful as a reminder, whether one likes the reminder or not, of the ensemble of relations that connected the two fields as they developed in the early twentieth century.

Inglis's arguments, however, were educationally influential, and unlike a more typical literary history, they did project a functional model of teaching literature. For as Inglis understood it, the subject for the literature teacher is not literature per se, the "extremely limited and restricted" domain of the "literary critic." It is literature as *continuous* with a vast range of reading material available to both students and teachers, as it saturates everyday behavior. What can be distinguished in that reading material as literature "at its best" is what emerges as carrying the tale of the tribe, as it were— the complex of cultural values and traditions from the past—into the marketplace of the present via the mediation of the teacher. Its value is functional; literature "has value as instilling in the individual all that has gone to make a society what it is and of creating in him unconsciously its own ideals, thought, and aspirations" (*PSE*, 439). Thus the literature teacher for Inglis is located at a central point where students must be educated to become aware of those "unconscious" values. For in "modern literature," those values of course must encounter the forces and values of the present historical moment: "The tremendous influence of modern literature on the individual has created a problem which cannot safely be neglected by the secondary school. Some, perhaps much, of that literature is good and valuable. Much also is bad and harmful. Which of the two sorts will prove strong influences in the lives of secondary school pupils may be determined in part by the study of literature in the schools" (*PSE*, 441). The qualification is important, for "to expect such study wholly to determine" the outcome is "to expect the impossible." Nevertheless, what happens in the literature classroom can decisively influence students, and as a result can also influence the future directions of the society.

For Inglis, then, the "material" on which the literature teacher works—the occasion for the exercise of her or his concrete work skills at all—is twofold. On the one hand, as the first section of *Principles* declares, it is the same as for all teachers, "the raw material with which education deals" (*PSE*, 3), the newly heterogeneous student population entering the schools. On the other, it is the complex of sociocultural values as they emerge in everyday behavior. Literature *is* "at its best" when it functions as the connecting feature in this conception of the "material" of work, where as the primary carrier of the latter, it is also what continues to shape the former. For all that the literature teacher, like the advertising agent, is then assumed to act on consumers toward some end, occupying a new role of expertise in relation to a public, it should be clear why Inglis's discussion nevertheless specifies no readily identifiable "clientele" for that expertise, such as the manufacturers to whom the advertising agency offers its services. Literature teachers are of course hired as professionals by an educational administration, but they don't work for that administration in the same way as an advertising agency works for its client. The peculiar nature of the subject, the way literature connects everyday behavior and sociocultural values, means that in effect in teaching "about" literature one works for society "as a whole" as one's client. Unlike other fields of teaching even, where it is not only possible but necessary to mark out a "restricted" field of expertise, the function of literature and the teaching of literature must be "general and universal" (*PSE*, 442), not in the philosopher's sense of some universal "human nature," but because it must *circulate* across the whole range of the society.

Thus in Inglis's discussion, the actual work skills of the literature teacher do represent a progressive expertise linked to a functional end. First, the expertise of the job is involved with the "consumption" and not the "production" of literature. For though relatively few students will ever undertake the work of the literary critic— the "formal" study of how literature is produced—and still fewer evidence the interest and talent to become producers of literature themselves, almost everyone in the schools "will read," and continue to read when they leave school. The work of the literature teacher then realizes a progressively more detailed, conceptually exact, and sophisticated capacity to teach the skills of reading. Second, literature "at its best" is a primary carrier of sociocultural values, the point where both the individual opportunities of self-realization the culture affords and the ideals of the society as a whole emerge in the representation of everyday behavior. Here as well, the work of the literature teacher may then be expected to progress toward a more conscious and coherent understanding of sociocultural values as they are communicated, through literature, from one generation to another. However, "literature" in this ideal sense does not of course comprise all of what people read. They will read whatever literature becomes available. Thus the third and most important element of the teacher's work skills will be the capacity to put both areas of expertise to work in the battles over values that take place in the English classroom, "producing" as a result students who are themselves more skilled in recognizing and understanding the values in what they read. For it is in this sense, finally, as it circulates from one person to another, that literature can be realized as a potentially decisive social influence.

Inglis's model differs from the progressive work expertise detailed in literary "history," because that concrete labor is connected to social ends; it is a form of *cultural* politics. That is, he knows perfectly well that it is not "politics" in the sense of a visible, organized, institutional apparatus for reaching and implementing policy decisions, but he also knows that such institutional formations are not the only place where politics takes place. As a political activity, his conception of work in English hardly involves a denial of the individual satisfactions of literature. His point is simply that those satisfactions occur in a specific context and exist in a specific complex of relations with other people and other forms of activity, that no one will just "naturally" fall in with the "best" of what literature affords. Because concrete labor in English as he understands it meets by far the majority of students as consumers, his primary focus of concern is with literature *as it circulates*, not as it is made, and not as it is "in itself." And this means concerning himself also with *everything* that circulates as "reading material," for that is where the conflicts of sociocultural values in the society are fought out.

Inglis understood as clearly as anyone that the massive growth of public education would make the schools for the foreseeable future a site of conflicts. But he also understood as an immense advantage the relocating of what had been a diffuse and capillary network of conflicts within a single institutional formation directed at a specific group of the population, at school-age youth. Thus in the section of *Principles* on vocational education, for example, the problems occasioned by rapid changes in production, the composition and training of the labor force, the new demands of organized labor, and so forth are at once acknowledged and then localized in the schools, where the curriculum of vocational education he proposed could be seen as a resolution. What in the workplaces of production appeared an increasing proliferation of intransigent dilemmas could be managed by generating a particular curriculum of training in the schools designed to anticipate and forestall the diffusion of conflicts throughout the social structure.

For all his emphasis on literary study as a form of cultural politics, however, English as Inglis defined it remained the anomalous point in this process of relocation, the point where education as a containment of conflicts within a specific social institution was breached as it were by how teachers of literature perform a "general and universal" function for society. For the sociocultural values that emerge in the English classroom as a focus of contention are *not* localized by their appearance in that classroom. Unlike the problems of the job training of production workers, which can be reorganized and "resolved" when they are moved from the workplaces of production to a vocational education curriculum in the schools, the problems posed by the clash of values do not change when they cross from the marketplace, the home, the newspaper, and so forth to the English classroom. They remain, and must be dealt with, as "general and universal" across society.

What I have indicated already as an indeterminacy of client relations in Inglis's model of work for literature teachers is then also a sign of finally contradictory demands imposed on that work. The classroom is where teaching literature becomes a cultural politics insofar as the teacher intervenes in the *circulation* of sociocultural values: as Inglis saw it, determining which values ought to be passed on from one person to another, which ones ought then to become a basis of collective identity and social direction, and which values in contrast ought to be exposed as fraudulent. The classroom is a battleground, yet at the same time Inglis's arguments provide no real way for literature teachers to control the "ground" of the "battle." Work expertise must have as its end an intervention in the process of circulation, but it is condemned to intervene at a location defined and organized in ways by no means necessarily congruent with the practices of that work expertise. For teaching literature is not quite like any other field of study. Insofar as the subject matter must circulate generally and universally, its social function is very different. Nevertheless, as located in the schools, teaching literature must conform to the same professional standards of discipline, knowledge, accreditation of expertise, classroom size and duration, curricular design, administrative structure, and so forth as other fields. And there is nothing in how this *location* of work is organized that recognizes the differences Inglis emphasizes between literature and other fields.

Nor is there anything in Inglis's discussion of work expertise in teaching literature that suggests how such expertise might alter the location of work, design a "ground" more conducive to carrying out the battles over the circulation of sociocultural values. For the battles Inglis imagines taking place are not intraeducational, pitting literature against other fields of study. Teaching literature in the schools challenges the sociocultural values that circulate in a *marketplace* dominated by the influence of advertising. Teachers must attempt to win "intelligent" consumers for the values embodied in literature "at its best," as opposed to a marketplace that circulates *any* values conducive to selling goods and services. Advertising, that is, circulates not only goods and services, but cultural codes of behavior that facilitate the selling of goods and services as widely as possible. Like teaching literature, in fact, advertising work is "general and universal." The ground of such work, however, is defined by the interests of a specific clientele—the manufacturers who hire advertising agencies—and thus the location of work is organized to take advantage of that ground and to extend its territory as far as possible. Teaching literature must then compete against the massive resources of advertising without the benefit of either a specific clientele or a location of work to facilitate their intervention in the circulation of sociocultural values. Literature teachers are condemned by Inglis's model to the worst of both worlds. They have a function, which like the function of advertising is "general and universal"; they have a location of work, which like the location of other disciplines is very specific. But they have the advantages of neither advertising nor other disciplines of study. Function and location in the teaching of literature are incommensurable.

It should then be possible to see why, from very early in the century, the rhetoric of progressive work skills in the study of literature, unlike in advertising, has so often been disengaged from functional ends. The demands Inglis's model imposed on the practices of work in English emphasized the necessity to intervene in the circulation of sociocultural values, but without recognizing how work practices must also develop to reshape or redefine the grounds of circulation itself. As a result, values circulate by means of a workplace and a marketplace that are someone else's territories, governed by alien rules. Not only are battles hard to win under such circumstances; disengagement appears a *positive* necessity, a way to escape the incommensurable *intersection* of function and location in Inglis's model as it exercised its influence in the growth of public education. Thus the issue in focusing on the complex development of work skills and knowledges in English is not simply to expose an ideological rationalization for retreat, some set of underlying assumptions or pressures that reward practices of nonintervention. If this were the case, it would be a relatively straightforward matter to reverse those assumptions or organize a series of counterpressures on dominant values that circulate culturally. But if, instead, "disengagement" represents an escape from a contradiction, a history of efforts to *realign* function and location, then the issue, first, is to understand what consequences followed from those efforts, and second, to ask what, now, must be done to alter the terms of realignment in a way that preserves what was won in the process while at the same time also making possible a praxis of intervention in the circulation of sociocultural values.

In the previous chapter, I argued that work in English circulates as a kind of "surplus value" of evaluations. As living, abstract labor, work in English helps generate an elaborate stratification of "intellectual resources" in the student population in the schools. This cultural surplus value "compensates" in any number of ways for problems projected by the social organization of production: the identifying and training of a professional "meritocracy," the indeterminacy of "workers" who are to fill specific tasks in production, reserving an army of young labor from production tasks, and so forth. That is, the *location* of English enables the *use* of work in English, however that work is understood "in itself," to further these social functions of education. In this chapter, I want to turn instead to describe something of the changes in advertising work, the way in which advertising has developed to the point where it can influence the very design of production itself, and more immediately important for my purposes to the point where it can *also* take advantage of the cultural surplus value generated by education. The practices of advertising work, I will argue, shift their basis from the skilled "salesmanship" of the individual, heroized by the *Blue Book*, to agencies such as Thompson itself. As part of this shift, advertising *control* over the circulation of goods and services, and over cultural values and codes of behavior to facilitate the expansion of consumption, likewise shifts its basis, to make greater and greater use of the cultural training carried on in education. That is, abstract labor in the workplaces of education becomes as crucial to the *consumption* of goods and services as it is to the distribution of labor power in production. Thus a praxis of intervention cannot depend on an internal capacity to develop always more exacting, critical skills and knowledges of work in English. It must attempt to frustrate the circulation, in the form of cultural surplus value, of *whatever* work takes place, no matter how critical or exacting. Intervention begins in recognizing what political opportunities the organization of the workplace might afford, in order to frustrate what the workplace imposes as a conversion of concrete to abstract labor.

The history of concrete labor in English as, again, a series of efforts to realign function and location against the incommensurability projected by the institutionalization of Inglis's model, then represents both a resource to draw on and a source of difficulty to such praxis. Briefly and schematically, I will argue that the realignment involved three crucial changes: (1) rather than what is transferred from literary text to consumer, and from one consumer to another, through the mediation of the teacher in the classroom, value is understood to emerge "intrinsically" from the very process of work itself; (2) rather than a specific institutional workplace, location becomes a point of exchange where educational management as a clientele contracts for the self-defined professional expertise of the literary *critic* to act also as a *teacher*; (3) rather than "the raw material of education" that the teacher works on to "produce," "direct," or "prevent" their development in specific ways, students become another potential clientele, to whom the critic as teacher makes available work skills and knowledges that will enable them to avoid being manipulated by the shimmering, miragelike sheen of cultural messages engineered across the proliferating media of mass communication.

The first of these changes suspends the issue of social function as Inglis understood it by dissociating value "in itself" from value "in circulation." It doesn't redefine circulation; it redefines value in relation to work. As a result, it becomes possible to claim that literature —not "at its best," but *by its very nature as literature and not something else*—expresses, constructs, reveals, or discovers (depending on exactly how this "nature" of literature is conceived) potentially "general and universal" values *whether or not* such values indeed circulate generally throughout society. Thus the social function of literature is no longer contingent on how well value is transferred from text to consumer or from one consumer to another. Work as the source of intrinsic values is assessed in its own terms, not through a process of circulation, and whatever social function literature *might* perform is then contingent on work rather than the reverse. Likewise, work is no longer itself a battle, a series of conflicts over which values will circulate most widely in the culture. It is instead, loosely, a cognitive activity, a prebattle intellectual heuristic as it were, to identify what might be at stake. And however different, because of the subject matter, from the production of knowledge elsewhere, it shares a certain freedom from practical consequences.

Given the putative independence of work from circulation, the constraints of the workplace can be understood as a series of variables to be negotiated between professionals in English and their clientele of educational management, regarding such things as number and size of classes, size of faculty, standards of evaluating student achievement, degree requirements, curriculum, rates of pay for teachers, and so on. The workplace, that is, becomes after the fact a place not of "real" work, but of a kind of second-order accretion of work, where something already done is recapitulated in simpler form to be passed on, by a process whose rationale pertains to something other than work itself. "Battles" thus reemerge, but as Ohmann reminds us over and over in *English in America*, at the continually contested point of contact between "real" work and this second-order accretion.

However, within the classroom (that is, within the zone won from negotiation as to some extent under the individual teacher's control), students can be seen as a clientele in a rather different sense than educational management. On the one hand, they are a captive audience. They are constrained by the requirements of "getting an education" to submit to a determinant amount of time in English where their achievement will be assessed by English teachers, in contrast to the marketplace where instead they will be "free" to sell their labor power for wages, or to exchange their wages for consumer goods and services. On the other hand, however, work in English at least can be offered to students as an alternative "freedom," in effect. And once understood, work as itself this potential freedom of realizing individual possibility reveals how it is the *marketplace*, rather than the English classroom, that hides a complex system of constraints circumscribing their actions. Paradoxically, the period of apprenticeship, the forced *durée* of training in English, can be a vehicle for far greater freedoms than are available in the marketplace. Although a relatively late instance, Robert Scholes's remarks toward the beginning of *Textual Power* offer a succinct summary of a long-familiar claim: "What students need from us ... is the kind of knowledge and skill that will enable them to make sense of their worlds, to determine their own interests, both individual and collective, to see through the manipulations of all sorts of texts in all sorts of media, and to express themselves in some appropriate manner."[8] Students are a clientele, to whom we offer the services of a professional liberationist. Thus social function, suspended in the dissociation of value "in itself" from value "in circulation," re-emerges as utopian promise. For work is then both a source of value "in itself," and the sign of an as yet unrealized moment when, the devices of manipulation exposed for what they are, work practices at last come into their own, freely available to anyone and everyone to exercise as they will.

Many of the practices involved in the three changes I have out-lined here have a considerably older history in the study of litera-ture. Yet their form is altered as they are caught up in the concrete labor of English in the schools, with the felt necessity of realigning function and location. For as utopian promise, the social function of literature can now be identified with the "real" work of both literature and criticism existing at a point whose condition of pos-sibility is a "just beyond," a new and free-floating location, peril-ously close to but unfurrowed by the rivuleting flow channels of demands from the workplace and the marketplace threatening at its edges. Work practices and ideals carried over from the past must then be armored, as it were, to resist appropriation by the specific, institutional workplaces of education and the cruder social forces they serve. Self-conscious complexity becomes part of the value of work, complicating even the persistence of long-familiar practices. For such complexity is not only an index of the internal difficulty of work, which must continually assess its own constructions, but also an elaborate defense to ward off the easy *use* of work for other ends. It becomes a measure of the *freedom* of concrete labor.

That freedom is no illusion. Unlike concrete labor in production most obviously, concrete labor in English is not redesigned at every point to conform to the calculation of abstract labor power. In the conclusion to the chapter, I will argue that this relative freedom be-comes the source for the nexus of values named by "tradition" and "the new," which I described in my first chapter. As value terms, both depend not only on a set of political assumptions about social organization, as I argued, but also on *specific conceptions about the work of, and work on, literary texts*. That is, the power of literature to suspend the pressures of the present in order to reconnect culture to a past, to "tradition"—or alternatively, in order to project a dif-ferent future, "the new"—presupposes a free process of work. For it is a conception of work that supplies the missing element in a politi-

cal analysis intended to demonstrate how monolithically inclusive
social organization has become, offers a way to explain how it is that
literature of all things escapes the coordinates of power exercised
so implacably everywhere else in society. It escapes because it is a
different order of work, existing "just beyond" the reach of those coordinates. Nevertheless, this free-floating location, this "beyond," is
always precarious and hence must always be in motion. The precariousness is registered phenomenologically, in the immediacy of work,
as the constant fear of "appropriation," and the necessity of motion
by the dismal reminders of how the promise of new movement after
new movement in both literature and criticism seems ultimately to
dissipate into the general textures of business as usual.

Before reaching this conclusion, however, my argument will have
to account for a number of specific features about the development
of work in English. If indeed concrete labor has a relative freedom,
then my description of the organization of the workplace in the previous chapter, as the location of abstract labor generating a cultural
surplus value of education, must be extended to show how that organization accomplishes a process of *converting* concrete to abstract
labor. On the one hand, this will involve a structural description of
what is felt immediately as "appropriation." That is, I must provide
an account of the institutional process by which the results of concrete labor, rather than appropriated for what they are or as a way to
"defuse" potentially "radical" disruptions they might engender, are
instead converted to something else, to circulate as abstract labor.
On the other hand, however, it will be necessary as well to show
why an initial disjunction between concrete and abstract labor in the
workplace has been possible at all; why it is that the long battle for
at least a relative freedom of the former could be won; why, in sum,
ideological work as carried on in English departments does not evidence the same conformity between concrete and abstract labor as
production work. I suggested as part of the answer, in the previous
chapter, that the complex of compensatory functions education performs also permits a dissociation of work in education from work
in production, and a distinct internal organization of work. But it is
now a matter of determining why this dissociation takes the form of
a relative freedom of *concrete* labor.

Abstract labor as the source of a system of evaluative distinctions
suggests that education exercises a powerfully normalizing influ-

ence, acting as a single institution where normative values are both established and enforced in circulation. Inglis's understanding of the work of the literature teacher as a cultural politics certainly indicates the importance for him of controlling as much as possible within the schools the circulation of ideas and of sociocultural values. Yet the threat of disruption Inglis feared most was not how the diversity of a new population in the schools might alter irrevocably the dominant, normative values of the culture. To some extent at least, he even welcomed such change; social organization could not be responsive to the diverse needs of a diverse population unless dominant values changed. What worried him was the potential of advertising to feed on change itself, to shatter *any* "intelligent" consensus of values circulating by means of the schools, if in the process the consumption of goods and services could be expanded. The work of the literature teacher for Inglis had as its "raw material" a heterogeneous student population, but it had as its *target* the indiscriminate expansiveness of the marketplace whose motor force is the always-proliferating means of circulation afforded by advertising.

In however confused ways, Inglis thus arrived at how education is caught in a central contradiction of culture imposed by the development of modern capitalism. To the extent (as I argued) that education compensates for the indeterminacy of a division of labor in production, the schools are a normalizing apparatus. For in the distribution of labor power, production requires from the culture a uniform system of stratification. In this sense public education as a single institutional formation localizing the cultural training of the young is constituted as an efficient way to ensure that uniform system. However, as Inglis's fears of advertising suggest, the *consumption* of what is produced instead requires of the culture a constant proliferation of differences. As production expands by means of more products, more services, a more and more rapid turnover of products, and so forth, culture in effect must itself "produce" new markets, a population whose "norms," so far from being uniform and static, encourage rapid change and adaptation. The process is then doubly complicated by a kind of reverse movement, as the pressure of expanding consumption dictates continual changes in production and production work, and as the scale of production possible dictates a massive, if temporary, normalizing of markets to purchase identical products. One rather obvious consequence of these complicated interchanges is that social values—those discriminating against "minorities," for example—do not remain uniform; they change and continue to change, but the result is not necessarily "progress."

Throughout, however, culture must act as *both* normalizing and productive. Within a system of education as, again, an attempt to localize the functions of culture within a single institution, this dual obligation emerges as a disjunction between abstract and concrete labor. Insofar as education normalizes social relationships, whatever concrete labor is carried on in the schools must be converted to abstract labor. But insofar as education must also be culturally productive, concrete labor cannot *already* be abstract labor; it must have a relative freedom. It cannot, like production work, *be designed from the beginning* to conform to the calculation of abstract labor power. For it must act as a motor force of change, continually producing "the new." Thus the relationship between concrete and abstract labor, in education and in ideological work generally, will always be an uneasy one, because that relation must somehow accommodate the incompatible demands on culture to function as both normalizing and productive.

Inglis knew perfectly well, however, that "culture" could not be recontained within the schools, despite the growing social importance of education. Indeed, his antagonism to mass market advertising results from seeing it as a competing cultural locale, unconstrained by any allegiances to the "higher" social values embodied in literature "at its best." The antagonism persists throughout the subsequent development of work skills and knowledges in English. But where Inglis feared advertising as a disruptive source of *changing* cultural norms and values, it soon came to seem instead, as my preliminary sketch of the development of work practices in English suggests, an apparatus of "manipulation," conforming potentially infinite differences to a set of static norms. Work in English could "battle" the effects of advertising insofar as it offered to a student clientele the skills enabling them to avoid being manipulated. Advertising thus *had* to seem everywhere manipulative, not necessarily because it is, *but because concrete labor in English was assumed to release "free," individual productive powers.* That is, once reduced to a utopian promise, this conception of social function becomes a way of purifying work skills in English and demonizing their "opposite."

Such purification, however, can only be prolonged interminably, haunted all the while by a sense of defeat and practical disengagement. For on the one hand, as a system of values the often complicated and shifting versions of tradition and the new, in whatever form, reward the internalization of work, disconnecting it from circulation to focus attention instead on the processes of concrete labor itself. Thus changes in concrete labor practices always seem possible. Work skills and knowledges can always be made more "concrete," more "material," more critically exacting, *more something*. But on the other hand, change seems doomed to defeat in advance, condemned to struggle heroically if futilely against appropriation, by an implacable and alien system of abstract labor in the schools, or by an equally insidious marketplace manipulation whose emblem is advertising. Because the source of an internal power of direction is also an internalizing power, it expels "to the outside" of work the means by which such work circulates in the culture, the ways in which it is put to use. Thus once it is begun, work of any kind can only be dissipated, compromised, appropriated *somewhere else*.

It is in these terms that it is possible to recognize the continually attractive force of arguments that the "value" of "literature" is finally how it has neither value nor use, escaping by that measure the relentless colonizing of behavior that characterizes the expansion of industrial and then postindustrial capitalism. But while there may well be ways to escape use altogether, I have yet to see any that don't either reinvent some form of aristocratic privilege for the lucky few, or romanticize a living condition in a way possible only to those who don't live there. In any case, it's an assumption you can't afford if you work in a university. Because if you do work in a university, whatever you do or refuse to do or drain away from "doing" into some as yet uncolonized territory *will be put to use*. The point where it would be possible to distinguish, once and for all, concrete labor practices from consequences, from what happens to those practices as they circulate, recedes further and further into the distance with each new approach to it.

Inglis's *Principles* is a good reference point, a convenient reminder of the historical connections between literature as studied and taught in a rapidly expanding educational system, and advertising as likewise an always-expansive influence on the same population moving through that educational system. Yet in another sense, as the subsequent development of literary study in the schools would attest, his arguments were perhaps already anachronistic, addressed to social conditions where the solutions he proposed with respect to literary study in the university especially seemed to answer to no recognizable problem. Where to some extent, for reasons I've sketched briefly, the imperatives affirmed in those solutions came to seem themselves a formidable range of problems. I'm beginning a chapter devoted largely to the relations between the concrete labor of literary study and the consumption of goods and services with this brief account of Inglis, not only because he is a convenient reminder of a great many things, but also because his arguments foreground issues of social value as a form of cultural politics. That is, and while I have no intention of trying to retrieve from Inglis's model some lost potential for concrete labor in English, I do intend to drive my own analysis of concrete labor toward a discussion in the concluding sections of this chapter of a cultural politics that has as one goal the circulation of specific sociocultural values. For *Principles* does at least supply the historical recognition necessary to realize that goal: work in English occurs in a specific, public, political location. To read the history of work practices at that location as a series of ultimately futile attempts to escape its gravitational pull is to succumb to the promise that yet one more attempt might somehow succeed. I want to read that history instead as a means of discovering what opportunities exist for a praxis of cultural politics at the location of work, and how to take advantage of them to wage a war of position.

I

The realization of surplus value generated in production depends on the consumption of goods and services. And consumption depends, Thorstein Veblen had argued in the 1920's, on "the fabrication of customers."[9] Part of that fabrication involved the massive transformation of formerly "unproductive" workers into "productive" workers who then had to exchange their wages for goods they had produced themselves in the past. The emblem for this new situation might well be the standard Depression joke about the farm family humping a wagonload of cabbage into town to sell, in order to have enough money to purchase cabbage at the store for slaw at dinner. (The story had its basis in fact, of course; in 1929 cabbage purchased from the farm at $6 a ton sold for over $200 a ton retail.) [10] By "the fabrication of customers," however, Veblen meant not only the transformation of unproductive to productive labor, but also a restructuring and expansion of the needs of that new labor force to conform to the means of producing commodities to "satisfy" those needs. Like other analysts, including Veblen himself, Braverman in *Labor and Monopoly Capital* understands the task of "restructuring" needs as accomplished by the marketing operations of large corporations: "But if the engineering organization was the first requirement" of a massive growth in productivity, he argues, "it was soon outstripped in functional importance by the marketing apparatus." Because production was increasingly redesigned and controlled by management working through engineers and technical experts, "markets must remain the prime area of uncertainty," with the result that "the effort of the corporation is therefore to reduce the *autonomous character* of the demand for its products and to increase its *induced* character." [11]

The Depression gave impetus to a whole folklore—as well as academic studies—that described the artful procedures of "inducing" consumption. It also led to legal restriction of advertising claims in the Federal Food, Drug, and Cosmetics Act passed in 1938, and to the Wheeler-Lea amendments—passed that same year—which expanded the authority of the Federal Trade Commission to prosecute "false" advertising. The issue of advertising power to induce consumption remained, however, and after World War II it became a highly visible focus of academic and legal attention once more. Yet there is something odd about the assumption that the marketing of goods and services involves reducing the "autonomy" of consumption and increasing its "induced character." For in these terms what is at stake is control over consumer desires: are one's desires one's own, to act on "autonomously," or are they in fact "induced" in us by the clever tactics of advertisers?

The question has obvious relevance *to consumers*, at least if one wants to believe that buying decisions are made freely and deliberately, choosing to exchange a portion of wages for the possession of a particular product. But for the work of advertising, it can be at best a second-order question. "Literary men, and reporters out of a job," the *Blue Book* reminds us, think of advertising as "so many written words" (*BB*, 18), the vehicle deployed to "induce" people to buy. The successful advertising agent must know better. At this level at least, it does not matter whether the words are used elegantly or ineptly, whether the customer "sees through" the words or not, whether the customer "freely chooses" to buy or is cleverly induced to buy. That is, the immediate issue is not a matter of reducing the "autonomous character" of demand, but of *reducing the uncertainty of selling*, which unlike the former is not necessarily predicated on a power to control or manufacture consumer desires. If uncertainty could be reduced by inducing people to buy, then it would be worth pursuing ways to induce people to buy. And advertisers, including the *Blue Book* of course, have done so. Nevertheless, these ways remain instrumental—the words "which compose the body of an advertisement are important," the *Blue Book* argues, "but only incidental" (*BB*, 19)—a *means* to an end that might well be realized by other and possibly more effective means.

Thus the analyst who assumes that advertising work is *primarily* a power of controlling/manufacturing consumer desires occupies a curious position indeed. On the one hand, it is a position where it becomes possible to expose the techniques of selling as manipulative, as a forced reduction of consumer autonomy. The analyst is then on the side of the consumer, contributing to consumer battles for autonomy against the power of advertising. But on the other hand, insofar as those techniques seem to work—insofar as sales accumulate—the process of exposure then becomes as well a mark of distinction *for the analyst*, a cognitive superiority to other people. To put it crudely, other people must be stupider than the analyst, for "they" must remain largely in the dark about their own "fabrication." But who are these "other people"? Where exactly does one find them?

I have often set a group of first-year university students the task of analyzing commercials, and I have been struck over and over with how much they already know about the process. At the very beginning of the exercise, they can tell me a great deal not only about how a Levis commercial, for example, distinguishes its product from other jeans, but also about how the commercial links the product to desires having little obvious relevance to jeans at all. At least minimally, they don't "identify" with jet-propelled people with jean legs; the women are insulted by "housewives" who collapse in hysteria at the first sign of bathtub ring; the men are insulted by New York models peeling off their overalls because now they can change the car's oil with products in plastic containers rather than messy cans; and *they can explain to each other* why they are insulted. We flatter ourselves indeed to think only "well-educated" college students evidence such prescience. "They" simply aren't duped into thinking the behavior represented in commercials is "natural." At the same time, of course (like me, and I imagine many other analysts of the process), they wear Levis to class to turn in the assignment. That is, there may well be a "mystery" here, but it doesn't involve demonstrating how "other" people's desires—or one's own, in a crisis of humility—are merely the fabrication of advertisers.

Recent educational texts on advertising tend to look back to the enormous expansion of advertising in the 1920's as the crucial period in the formation of modern advertising work, but also as a period that relied on a simplistic behavioral psychology of manipulation in the construction of ads. Testifying before the FTC hearings in October 1971, Donald Kendall of Pepsico was thus in effect passing judgment on this history of advertising no less than on current belief that advertising manipulates consumers: "To anyone who truly believes he can manipulate consumers, I would offer this humble advice: Try it. And after you've had some failures, let's get together and discuss 'manipulation' again." [12] Of new products and prospective changes in old products developed within his own company, he adds, only one of ten ever reach the point of test marketing, and nationally roughly half of all products test marketed are withdrawn. Only half of those finally put on the market remain there for over a year. That is, the *failure* rate even of those products that make it through the elaborate procedures of development and test marketing remains considerable.

Kendall's comments help focus two crucial directions of change taken by advertising in the decades since its expansion in the 1920's, and the social and legal reactions to that growth in the 1930's. First, the actual work of the advertising agency increasingly involves activities that do not contact consumers directly at all. Like the 1974 *Advertising Age* definition and most recent textbooks, Kendall continues to pay lip service to the *Blue Book* dictum that advertising is merely a substitute for the practices of direct, personal selling, as *Advertising Age* puts it, "a mechanized substitute for the personal salesman" (WA, 8). But Kendall's own data suggest that the notion of "substitution" has become more confusing than helpful. The "line" is no longer quite as "straight" as the *Blue Book* imagined. Even once a product is ready to be marketed, the account finalized and the necessary budget, market research information, and media analysis available, the creative services director of a large agency will then typically have to be responsible for coordinating the work of a large number of writers with the work of those involved in the art layout of the ads (often contracted outside the agency), all of which must then be put together with the departments actually in charge of print or television production, working to the schedules set by the "traffic" department, and so forth. You can understand about as much of this total process of work by inference from the practices of the "personal salesman" as you can about the production of the *Dynasty* funeral episode by watching my kid sit down to write an epitaph for his dead cat.

Second, and behind the *Blue Book* assumption about "salesmanship," is a claim that "an understanding of human nature" is a necessary "basis for all advertising" (*BB*, 19). In the *Blue Book* argument, the reason for such knowledge is immediately apparent; like the "personal salesman," advertising contacts a potential consumer, and in order to sell the product, the advertiser must know about not only the product itself, but the consumer as well. The work process of modern advertising, however, with its elaborate test procedures and high failure rate to which Kendall refers, suggests that *if* this direct reasoning still holds, then the general knowledge and intelligence of advertising agents has declined precipitously since 1909. The *Blue Book* had of course recognized that in managing an advertising campaign, an agency must be responsible for determining a great many variables. The nine points listed for a "successful" campaign include everything from the nature of the product itself to what in a later terminology would be refined into a complicated process of "product positioning." Thus major agencies like Thompson very soon begin to develop far more sophisticated models for measuring advertising effectiveness. For while sales obviously were the bottom line of "success," sales were just as obviously subject to variables that the agency had to be in a position to anticipate and control *if sales were to continue successfully.* "Sales," that is, had to result from more than just a local piece of luck and good timing. The importance of a knowledge of "human nature" in the *Blue Book* account, although not merely another variable like the others, was nevertheless understood as a variable *in the same way* as others. It was considerably more important, but not different in kind.

Its importance, following the direction of the 1895 *Printer's Ink* editorial, was registered throughout the first decades of the century in the attention given to psychological research as an invaluable source of knowledge about "human nature." In the 1920's, one of the fastest-growing segments of book publication dealt in one way or another with "advertising psychology," from technical models like the AIDA (Awareness, Interest, Desire, Action) to all manner of advice and testimonials about "salesmanship." Significantly, however, it was not until relatively recently that psychology became a component in assessing the *effectiveness* of advertising. For as a variable, the knowledge of "human nature" was located, as in the *Blue Book* account, at the point of contact between advertiser and consumer. That is, the efficacy of the knowledge, the contribution it made to advertising, occurred when contact was actually made. Thus the generally unspoken corollary of this working premise was that "human nature," however complex, was in some fundamental sense the same, a given of the situation. What was "variable" was how much one could learn about it and how well one could predict and control how it might manifest itself differently on different occasions and in different places. There would be little sense in deploying psychological research as a component of a model to assess advertising effectiveness, because such research provided knowledge of what lay on the other side, as it were, of the advertisement—the consumer. Psychology was a technique to control the "variable" of contact and what devolved from it; models of assessment organized the specialized techniques attached to each variable to determine the effectiveness of each technique.

In contrast, in the procedures preliminary to test marketing, for example, psychological research is not directed at understanding consumer desires, but at constructing the coherence of product and advertisement. It rehearses in conceptual and statistical form the *effectiveness* of past advertisements in order to generate an assessment model that can predict the form this coherence should take in the current ad under consideration. Thus the construction of an advertisement has as the immediate material of work a series of *effects*, a potentially infinite field of differences in which the work of construction intervenes to shape out of that material, as it might be available in any given data base, a local structure of coherence. As a result, the "human nature" of consumers is no longer the most important variable of the situation; it is no longer a variable at all. It is an "outside," something that goes on elsewhere and whose effects, again, are the material of work. Where the skills of the "personal salesman" were understood to be directly involved in the territory of "human nature," advertising work in this new sense has redefined its territory. It is not simply that the organization of advertising work has changed and become more complicated. The assumptions that direct it have changed as well.

In an argument about the "believability" of advertisements in 1963, John Maloney evidenced some of the new directions involved in using psychological research as a component of assessment models. "Few advertisers, advertising researchers, or psychologists," he admits, "would disagree with the statement that an advertisement is 'believed' when it leaves the consumer with that attitude, belief, or intention toward the product which the advertiser intended he or she should have after exposure to the advertisement." [13] But that does not alter the central thesis of his argument: "*no advertisement is likely to be completely 'believable' when its purpose is to change people's minds. Moreover, an advertisement need not be believed completely to be effective*" (AB, 1; Maloney's emphasis). It is worth following out some of Maloney's arguments to see how he makes his case. For his thesis suggests that the power to "manipulate" consumers—make consumers believe what the advertiser wants them to believe in this case—has become a secondary issue in assessing effectiveness. Successful advertising may, or *it may not*, "change people's minds," more or less completely. Whether it does or not, however, its effectiveness must be assessed in some other way. Manipulative power may well be a by-product of successful advertising, and to the extent it is, it will then continue to occupy the attention of those concerned with the influence of advertising. But for Maloney, manipulative power is not really what advertising work can aim to achieve.

Perhaps the easiest example in his argument to recognize the dif-

ference in aim involves, again, the question of "contact," in its most
elementary form a matter of gaining consumer attention. Everything
from the *Blue Book* to the most recent McGraw-Hill school text
assumes getting attention as crucial. Quoting from Alfred Politz's
"The Dilemma of Creative Advertising," however, Maloney's point
is that getting attention in and of itself affords no real *measure* of
effectiveness:

Imagine a room with a large window that looks out on a beautiful country-
side. On the wall opposite the window are three mirrors. The first mirror
is uneven, spotted, and dirty looking. The second mirror is clean and neat,
and in addition is framed by a beautiful ornamental engraving. The third
mirror has no frames or ornament, and is nothing but a plain, but perfectly
flawless mirror. Now, an observer (critic or client) is taken into the room
and his guide points to the first mirror and says, "What do you see?" The
observer says, "I see a bad mirror." His guide points to the second mirror
and asks again, "What do you see?" The observer says, "I see a beautiful
mirror." Finally, his guide points to the third mirror and says, "What do you
see?" The observer says, "I see a beautiful scene out of an open window."
(AB, 3)

Like good advertising, all three "mirrors" focus attention; the third
is of course constructed in such a way that it is most likely to sell
the "scene"-product.

The crucial recognition is that the process Maloney is illustrating
by means of Politz's story is not just a refinement of "creative selling," skillfully manipulating behavior to induce people to buy. The
differences among the three "mirrors" are understood as a matter of
having eliminated in their construction one form of what Maloney
calls "misindexing," connecting the codes by which the message is
transmitted to something other than the intended message. To the
extent the construction of an ad permits misindexing, it also allows
the entry of what from the advertiser's point of view—the "guide's"
finger—are *random* variables. Thus the criterion of effectiveness is
not the hypothesis that the "observer" will say "I see a beautiful
scene out of an open window." Rather, it is the degree to which the
coherence of message and code has reduced misindexing, thereby
reducing the randomness of the variables *as they appear in the construction of the ad*. The question of whether or not the ad might
manipulate consumers into identifying a single image of "beauty"
has been suspended as unanswerable in that form. Perhaps it will;

perhaps any given "observer" will "believe" that what she or he sees is in fact a *beautiful* scene, although as Maloney has pointed out earlier, "an advertisement completely believable to one person may not be at all believable to another" (AB, 1).

The question that *can* be answered, and that must then direct in this respect at least the work of constructing the ad, is how well the ad has reduced the chances of misindexing. For that at least can be controlled. Nobody can know *for sure* what in any given circumstances "human nature" might find "beautiful," and no matter how potentially powerful the means of persuasion, they can't be depended on completely. But you can know and control the construction of an ad such that *if* people think X is "beautiful," then this ad constructed in this way will increase the probability of a consumer seeing in the ad what she or he thinks is "beautiful." Insofar as the goal of marketing is to reduce the uncertainty of selling, Maloney's argument redirects attention to where, exactly, uncertainty can be reduced.

Psychology, especially the psychology of communication, obviously plays an important role in Maloney's arguments. His models, like Politz's in the article he quotes, are drawn from a familiar body of research. However, the use of these models is not itself positioned at the point of contact between consumer and advertisement, to play on the consumer's desires, manipulate them in the direction the advertiser wishes. They are used instead to control the construction of the ad, to reduce randomness and increase the predictability of connections within the ad. The 1950's and 1960's saw the development of whole new specialized research fields that transformed the "advertising psychology" of the 1920's into techniques for the construction of advertising based on similar assessment paradigms. And needless to say, this research was often in conflict with the "creatives" inside the same agency. Douglas Tigert, who had been involved in many of the early studies in "lifestyle analysis" on which one such specialized field—psychographics—was based, reports the confrontation as it took place at the Leo Burnett agency in 1967:

After the first round of research, in 1967, the research department at Burnett would schedule a presentation to the creative people for a particular product class, at which they reported the results and implications from the profile they had found. After the presentation, one of two things usually happened. Either the creative people would say "that's very interesting," and would then walk away, or they would argue with the data or their implications. It became clear that the creative people were *uninvolved* in the data that were being poured over them. Clearly the traditional schism between creatives and the research group was not closing.

Over the past three years, a workable and useful approach has evolved at the Leo Burnett company. Now, the *raw data* are brought to the meeting and the creatives participate in their analysis. They usually discuss their ideas about the product class, the kinds of people who are heavy users, and they play these notions against the new data to arrive at a new and fuller picture of the consumer.[14]

Tigert doesn't elaborate the reasons why "the creatives" were "uninvolved," but they should be clear enough. Psychographics is a refinement of market segmentation that develops a statistical profile of a potential marketing target group on the basis of a long list of psychological "predispositions" as research demonstrates them to have existed in past buying behavior. Applied to Politz's story, for example, it might construct patterns of predictable connection among known variables in a target group so that any given "observer" who had displayed in her or his past marketplace behavior such patterns would also be likely to perceive X "scene" as "beautiful" if the construction of the ad clearly linked product and patterns. The way the research had been presented in the meetings thus infringed on the territory of "the creatives" insofar as it was being used to direct the actual *construction* of an ad rather than simply as background information turned over to "the creatives." Changing the routine of the meeting to supply "raw data" then allowed "the creatives" to participate in the development of an assessment model by which the features of the linkage could progressively be determined in the construction. The result is a cooperative effort to arrive at a "fuller picture of the consumer," not as a representative of "human nature," but as a data base projection of a range of visible marketplace *effects*, a profile of effects.

If rather melodramatically, Theodore Chin demonstrated in his address to the *Advertising Age* Creative Workshop in 1973 the importance not only of the internal coherence of an ad, but also the "frame" that identifies the boundaries of that coherence: "Consumers are really smart. After all, it's their hard-earned money that they're spending. And they're only going to spend it for a product that gives them a benefit. A benefit means a solution to a real problem. After all is said and done, consumers are only interested in one thing, 'What's in it for me?' "[15] Good advertising for Chin must set itself the task of answering that question in such a way that the hypothetical frame of the situation is clearly operating. For the frame locates where the patterns of predictability and coherence will take place, as it were: in the formula "if this problem, then this solution" in Chin's argument, or alternatively, the specifically elaborated context of "believability" in an argument like Maloney's. Of course, as Maloney points out, the frame cannot *distract* attention to itself. But even more important, a good frame must signal that "consumer intelligence" has been respected. The frame makes clear that "random" or "free" forms of response to the ad on the part of consumers are always possible; it demarcates zones such that the advertiser is not put in a position of *competing* with consumer desires. Thus in Chin's terms, the operation of a "problem-solution" frame marks out a way of isolating the particular coherence of an ad from the full range of diverse interests, values, desires, and so forth in a consumer's life. The advertiser is not interested in the consumer's "human nature," nor necessarily in controlling its "autonomy." If *one effect* of that "human nature" can be made visible as X problem, then the coherence of the ad will supply the product as a solution. A consumer can then respond to a Levis commercial, for example, with a sense that the behavior represented in the ad, so far from "natural," is obnoxious or insulting, and yet still buy Levis "without contradiction." For the latter occurs within the frame, the former outside. If the frame is not clearly demarcating these zones, however, consumers instead will make *competing* connections across the board, with the result that if the ad is "insulting," no one is likely to buy.

What Chin then goes on to discuss as advertising an "attribute" rather than a "benefit" of the product can be understood in these terms as a failure to make the frame work. His example is the introduction of Mennen E deodorant:

Company ad executives budgeted $12,000,000 for Year 1 advertising. They were quoted as saying that Mennen E would be a leading deodorant in the $475,000,000 deodorant category. They called its discovery the first breakthrough in the deodorant category since germicides were introduced 25 years ago. They explained that the use of Vitamin E enabled the elimination of harsh germicides in the deodorant.

Results? On paper, Mennen E looked like a real winner. But it turned into a bomb during the national introduction.

A failure. Because Mennen E stressed an attribute, not a benefit that solves a real problem. The consumer is only interested in trying a new product if it solves one of his problems. Mennen E solved no perceivable problem. (NP, 108–9)

In the advertising for Mennen E there was no "if . . . then" frame —indeed, no operative, coherent frame at all. The "attribute" was connected to the product, but the potential coherence of a structure of variables in *response* to the product was left competitively open. That is, rather than respecting a consumer's "intelligence" and "autonomy" to move in and out of a frame at will, the absence of a frame *imposed a requirement on consumers* to "restructure" their needs in accordance with the attribute of the deodorant, which of course they refused to do. The advertising was a "disaster."

In sketching quickly here the kind of changes in advertising work brought about by the development of new models of assessing advertising effectiveness, I've emphasized "frames," "coherence," and "predictability" because the goal of these models is after all to ensure a greater control over the uncertainty of marketing. Braverman's corollary, however, that marketing therefore sets out "to reduce the *autonomous character*" of consumption, does not necessarily follow. The goal is to increase control, *by reducing uncertainty*. Now if consumption could be successfully manipulated, uncertainty would indeed be reduced. I have argued indirectly that such a premise informs the descriptions of advertising work, like the *Blue Book*'s, which center on the skills of the "personal salesman." It also informs arguments like Braverman's, concerned with the influence of advertising on the population, and where "autonomous consumption" then stands as the opposite to "manipulated consumption." But the changes in advertising work I have outlined here recognize that a "manipulation model"—if I can call it that for shorthand purposes—is not only just a means of reducing uncertainty. It is perhaps not the best means. For as it functioned in the practices of "personal selling," a manipulation model assumes (1) a relative homogeneity among potential consumers, if not quite in a metaphysical sense of some general "human nature," at least the homelier terms of an ultimately knowable, if elastic, range of needs and desires; (2) a force of persuasion sufficient to act in some way on that range of needs and desires, either by concretizing them in particular directions or reassembling the current balance of their existence so that different ones became prominent that had been "latent" before; (3) being at the right place at the right time to realize the benefit of that persuasion as a "fabricated" desire for the manufacturer's product. However, from the perspective of more recent advertising models, (1) and (2) especially, so far from contributing to a reduction of uncertainty, would generate reason for even more uncertainty.

If (1) is assumed, then the corollary is that advertisers must know a great deal more about "human nature" than consumers. Both the *Printer's Ink* editorial and the *Blue Book* in fact stressed that those who work in advertising must be specialists in the psychology of behavior. For in the practices of the "personal salesman," local success seemed to depend on such knowledge. That is, in one-on-one confrontations with consumers, a sales representative might indeed possess sufficient advantages in knowledge to proceed to (2), to the use of persuasive techniques. But advertising on a mass scale does not confront consumers in the same way, and in our culture advertising cannot really control either the production of or the means of access to knowledges of human behavior. Thus to the extent manipulation is made to depend on a monopoly of knowledge, it becomes fraught with uncertainty. Advertising would not only find itself locked in conflict with institutional structures specifically designed to produce always newer and more inclusive knowledges. It would also compete with consumers for access to that knowledge produced elsewhere. Reducing the uncertainty of selling would become secondary to reducing uncertainty about who possessed what knowledge. Advertising work of course remains intensely interested in the knowledges of human behavior; Maloney's article, for example, reflects a close attention to university research in the psychology of communication. But Maloney is under no illusion that as a result he knows much more about human behavior than any potential consumer. Nor does he much care. Unlike the "personal salesman," his work does not depend on such a monopoly.

The corollary of (2), concerning the techniques of persuasion, is that consumers must be kept in the dark about such techniques. That is, once again advertisers would find themselves in competition with consumers. For to the extent a belief in "autonomous" consumption generates as its opposite a belief that advertising manipulates consumption, the reverse is also true. Thus if advertisers work on the premise that their task is to manipulate consumers by techniques of persuasion, then they must also believe that left to their own devices, consumers choose "autonomously." As a result, should consumers become aware that they are being subtly persuaded, that their choices are *not* autonomous, they will promptly refuse to buy any products whose advertising employs visibly manipulative techniques. Reducing the uncertainty of selling would once more become secondary to something else, to maximizing internal security, in effect. Advertisers do attend closely to security, just as they attend closely to the production of knowledges elsewhere. Competing advertisers are always a problem, and authors like Vance Packard and magazines like *Consumer Reports* are a potential irritant. But they are not really the primary worry. One can imagine a "personal salesman" hiring a detective to halt the activities of someone who went around the village demonstrating that the "salesman" was perpetrating a fraud on consumers. But when General Motors hired a detective to follow Ralph Nader, the result was a now-legendary folly.

The directions of change in advertising work I have sketched, however, proceed on very different assumptions. Instead of (1), there is the assumption of potentially infinite different effects that emerge from consumer desires and needs as they become visible in the marketplace, and the research knowledge necessary to collect data on those effects. Instead of (2), there is the assumption of the power of a conceptual apparatus to isolate a set of variables that can be linked to each other in a predictable pattern or structure. Instead of (3), the measure of effectiveness is assumed to lie in the capacity to link *whatever* pattern to *whatever* product. The latter doesn't mean that advertising can sell anything to anybody. Rather, the notion of being in the right place at the right time is redistributed as a power to move with increasing rapidity from any one point in a coherent pattern to any other point in the linkage of product to pattern.

The advantages over a "manipulation model" should be obvious. At (1), it is no longer necessary to know more about "human nature" than consumers. It's not really necessary to *know* anything about "human nature" at all. What must be known are *the visible effects*— of whatever "human nature"—in the marketplace. The research task then becomes a relatively straightforward collection of differences, as it were, and the conceptual task a probable projection from this available data. Thus advertising would not have to open itself to the uncertainty of competition with the production of knowledges elsewhere. It simply puts knowledge to use for its own ends, wherever it comes from. Uncertainty in general is by no means eliminated. As Kendall reminds us, only one in ten new products are even test marketed. But that indicates how precisely the *scope* of uncertainty has been reduced, and more important, localized within a territory where advertising *can* exert real control. Research and conceptualization improve, refine, and detail work practices on the basis of past failures, *no matter what* is going on "out there." To a public, the result may look like advertising has become more efficient at manipulating consumers, but to advertisers it looks like the uncertainty of selling has been circumscribed. That is, the knowledges advertising has appropriated for use may or may not have the effect of manipulating consumer desires, but the issue is secondary in the practices of advertising work. For the reduction of uncertainty does not have to depend on successful manipulation.

At (2), likewise, the advertiser doesn't necessarily have to fear consumer awareness of how persuasive techniques work. For once again, the scope of uncertainty has been reduced, recontained within a local territory advertising can control. Consumers may find out something about advertising techniques of persuasion; they may not. What matters is that if the *effects* of consumer awareness become visible in the marketplace, the mechanism of the "frame" can accommodate those effects, translating them into a series of procedures for constructing internally coherent patterns. If "outside" the frame consumers find Levis commercials insulting, it won't necessarily determine whether or not they will buy Levis. The fact that Levis consumers are more often than not quite aware of some aspect of the techniques used to sell the product remains a mystery only if one assumes that advertising dupes and manipulates an unsuspecting consumer into losing her or his "autonomy." Consumers might know everything there is to know about the techniques of selling jeans, and still purchase Levis.

These new assumptions I have described, however, do not come without "cost." If in comparison to a manipulation model they permit a reduction in the scope of uncertainty, they also generate "failures" on a scale that would be disastrous for the "personal salesman." No work organized around the practices of "personal selling" could tolerate the stream of failures Kendall describes in his FTC testimony, let alone what Chin indicates in his example of Mennen E. Manipulation offers the promise of *reducing failures*; these assumptions in contrast seem almost to focus on them. Kendall adds immediately, however, that "failure" is only relative: "But if you step back a bit and look at the whole picture, something different emerges: a story of *success*, the successful functioning of an open, competitive, and *free* economy where consumers relentlessly weed out the products they don't want, and accept only those which serve some useful purpose to them" (FTC, 395). Apparently Kendall has forgotten his own preceding paragraph, which indicates that by far the greatest percentage of "weeding out" occurs before products are ever seen by consumers. But he is right that "failure" is relative. It is relative to the assumptions of a manipulation model, and to a conception of advertising work centered in the "personal salesman." Once that conception changes, "failure" becomes something different.

In a model of manipulation, the motor force as it were must necessarily come from a small and select group, reflecting the innovative power of "salesmanship" to devise always newer ways to fabricate new, or focus "latent," consumer desires in the direction of the manufacturer's goods. People can be persuaded to do what they don't usually "want" to do or didn't know they "wanted" to do. But the notion that the vast marketing apparatus of corporations could *depend* on advertising not only to continue, but to continually expand sales by means of such "persuasion" seems to me the result of refusing to think very seriously about what goes on "over there," about the actual work processes of advertising. Chin's "consumers are really smart" is not cynicism. It's just a recognition of the obvious to someone engaged in advertising work, that constructing ads on the premise that you are smarter than huge groups of the population and can "induce" them into acting in programmed ways *can't last very long.* Maybe the first time, maybe even the second or third, but not the fiftieth. At best it would be a process continually haunted by the fear of failure, of some smartass in the crowd who could muck up the whole thing. The image of the "huckster" and "con man" in American literature is popular with "literary people" because we like to think of ourselves as that smartass. It's not popular with advertisers, not because it "exposes" the "reality" of their work, but because it has almost no relevance to it. So far from control, manipulation in current circumstances would render marketing everywhere precarious, for it would be vulnerable everywhere to a potential for failure arriving from an autonomous "outside" that advertising is not in a position to do anything about.

In the assumptions I have been describing, however, failure no longer registers as the threat of an "outside" to disrupt the reduction of uncertainty in marketing. Instead, failure functions to redistribute the boundary between "inside" and "outside." For it shifts the dilemmas of reducing uncertainty from an issue of how work practices internal to advertising might exercise control over an external and unpredictable diversity of consumers, to an issue of how advertising uses the effects of that diversity as material to be transformed by work into multiple, and multiplying, local structures of coherence. Rather than a mistaken direction in the attempt to manipulate an autonomous consumption, failure becomes the sign of *a surplus of material*, the excess necessary to feed the development of still newer advertising constructions, newer products, more services, ultimately the expansion of goods and services in circulation. Failure itself thus contributes to the reduction of uncertainty by delivering the material of a continued expansion. Rather than indicating that an "outside" has frustrated the attempt to "induce" consumption, it marks the availability of *still more* "outside," as yet unused.

This doesn't mean that advertising never manipulates consumers, that it never employs techniques of persuasion that can "trick" people into buying, that it never applies whatever pressures possible to convince people that if they don't use deodorant, for example, they are social misfits. Advertising does all these things. But they have become local strategies, not the apparatus for the reduction of uncertainty in marketing. On the scale on which advertising now functions, to be forced to depend on such strategies would increase rather than decrease uncertainty. What can be depended on to reduce uncertainty is the expansion of consumption, which in turn depends on a continual surplus of material from the "outside." Thus Kendall's hymn to "an open, competitive, and *free* economy" of consumer choice is no ideological disguise for manipulative advertising practices, a deceptive appearance hiding a sinister truth only the expert analyst can ferret out. It is a powerful ideological instrument to expand the availability of material. So far from hiding anything, his argument reinforces the *necessity* for more choices, more effects of more differences, *more material*, by universalizing it as a moral imperative of freedom. The risk of course is the "failure" of any number of local strategies; the "whole picture," however, is "a story of *success*."

I I

For the *Blue Book*, the expertise of the advertising agency is located unambiguously between production and consumption. Production, the *Blue Book* argues, had undergone a revolutionary transformation, to enable the manufacture of massive quantities of goods cheaply, and as a result the consumption of manufactured goods was now possible to a far larger population. The expertise of the advertising agency connects one to the other, effecting a second economic revolution as dramatic in some ways as the first, making selling as cheap and efficient as the machine manufacture of goods. Advertising expertise, that is, must solve the problems created by the transformation of production, complete the promise of the revolution begun in the sphere of production. The *Blue Book* proposed to meet the challenge through an expansion of the practices of the "personal salesman." Although never stated directly, the analogy seems clear enough: just as the production of more goods more cheaply was made possible by the use of machinery, the selling of more goods more cheaply could be accomplished by the organized use of the media of communication. To span the miles from Connecticut to Ohio, an advertising agency would have to find a way to transform what had been done by hand as it were, by the "personal salesman," into a machinery of selling.

Industrial production, however, involves far more than the substitution of machines for craft skills. Likewise, an advertising agency is no giant, mechanized "personal salesman"; the selling of goods and services through mass market advertising entirely restructures the organization of marketing. The changes in advertising work I have been describing can be marked initially as a reversal of direction in the *Blue Book* model. Where for the *Blue Book*, advertising connects A to B, production to consumption, advertising in its new forms connects B to A. The "problem," that is, begins not in the increased productivity of manufacturers, but rather in the uncertainty generated by a mass market of diverse consumers. Thus as I have argued, the itinerary of change, of the reorganization of advertising work, moves from the issue of how to "induce" consumption of a greatly increased volume of goods, to the issue of how to make goods and services available in a way that can be connected to the coherent structures advertising work has made from the vast "material" of consumer differences. The product must obligingly alter its form to enable the connection to those structures. Once advertising begins systematically to connect B to A, then changes in production will increasingly be determined by the requirements of marketing, rather than the other way around, as in the *Blue Book* model.

Production became at once more specialized, and at the same time more "generalized" in the sense of being able to shift to the manufacture of what could be marketed in some terms at least as a "different" product. For as the reduction of uncertainty in marketing came to depend on expanding consumption, then it had to be possible to manipulate products in production. One result was the now-familiar "conglomerate" and then "diversification" structure of large corporations. This allowed a way of covering the losses involved in everything from plant retooling to management transfer until new designs and new products could be implemented at any one point in the corporate organization. Thus the new corporate anatomy is neither "vertical" nor "horizontal," in the classic manner of a monopoly, but instead *radial*, so that pressure at any one point can be distributed uniformly throughout the structure.

In these circumstances, the very fracturing of the labor process into always smaller and more specialized unit tasks, which had seemed so necessary to cut production costs throughout the massive gearing up of manufacturing to produce many more of the same product, now suddenly loomed as a liability. For it depended on a capillary network of tasks and workers so intricate that the rapid change imposed by marketing demands seemed impossible. One of the "answers" to the dilemma was what became known as planned obsolescence, based on a premise that change could proceed incrementally, calculated such that one single development could be introduced in a way that preserved the rest of the process intact until the next change. That is, what was "planned" directly was less the obsolescence of the product than the flow of change in production to conform to a marketing requirement of "new" and "improved" products. Obsolescence was the afterimage as it were of flow change.

Where possible, however, the more attractive corporate alternative was to shift the dilemmas posed by rigid, linear production to somebody else altogether. At least some of the smokestack industries even could avail themselves of such divestiture, and the automobile industry virtually "saved itself" by these means. More and more specific parts production could be farmed out to other plants, in the United States to some extent, but even better in other countries where labor was not only cheaper, but contracts were easier to terminate in order to move to still another location. "Franchising" grew enormously, shifting the cost burden of change to independent owners. And franchising works best, of course, when what is to be sold primarily involves services rather than goods. With a recent boost from the Reaganomics ideology of individual entrepreneurship, the rise of a so-called service economy thus derives in large part from the corporate attractiveness of franchising in all its multiple forms, with the corresponding shift of cost burden and the reduction of a skilled work force. In the industrial sector, high labor costs then became a greater liability, leading to solutions such as Reagan's union busting and to the complexity of employee stock option plans and the like. The latter have the added bonus for management of facilitating the currently fashionable practice of the leveraged buyout, which often depends on ESOPs and the differential between the cost of shares to management and to workers.

The point, again, is that as the perceived source of the problems faced by marketing gradually shifted from production to consumption, the result was a whole series of changes in production to accommodate the specific ways advertising reduced the uncertainty of marketing. For advertising work, however, the reversal of direction in the *Blue Book* model was not neatly symmetrical. The line from B to A could not be as "straight" as the line from A to B. What had to intervene was an organized apparatus of cultural production. For advertising work must transform the "material" of consumer differences into a series of multiple structures of coherence. That is, it produces cultural representations of the material of difference in order to determine where to locate A, the products of manufacturers. Rather than a "straight line," the result is a connection of B to A mediated always by A′, as it were, by an apparatus of cultural production. The interposition of A' then alters both A, as I have been arguing, *and* B. For it means that what is consumed are not only manufactured goods, but also the constructions of advertising. And as Maloney recognized quite clearly, these do not necessarily have to be identical. Consumers may buy manufactured goods without at all "buying" in its entirety the advertising construction. The two may seem to coincide, and thus appear as "manipulated" consumption. But strictly, manipulation of consumers as a motor force of selling can exist only within the coordinates of a *Blue Book* model, of a straight line from A to B.

In practice, of course, the *Blue Book* anticipated in any number of ways how the problems facing advertisers would be occasioned by a huge new population of potential consumers. The points of congruence between the *Blue Book* argument and the argument of *Principles* arise in large part from the recognition they share that the size and diversity of that population will determine the development of new forms of work expertise. For Inglis, education must change, and change dramatically, because the consumers of education are no longer simply "boys and girls from relatively well-to-do American families":

(1) Until toward the close of the nineteenth century pupils enrolled in the secondary schools of the country constituted a roughly homogeneous group in the sense that they were boys and girls from relatively well-to-do American families, who for the most part looked forward to a cultural education in the high school which would prepare them for college and for the higher walks of life. The past quarter century, however, has marked a period in the development of secondary education characterized by the expansion of the secondary school so as to provide education for classes of pupils never before represented in large numbers in secondary school. The result has been a very greatly increased heterogeneity in the high-school population, and consequently a demand for increased attention to the varied capacities, interests, and probable future activities of secondary-school pupils, and to the differentiated needs of society. (2) Within the past decade educational psychology has found no more fruitful field than that of the psychology of individual differences, and in no other field have the results of psychological investigation contributed more to our educational theory and practice. It has, of course, always been recognized that individuals differ each from the other in physical and mental traits. Only recently, however, have we begun to realize the full meaning of that fact and the implications for secondary education. It is probably no exaggeration to say that the adaptation of secondary education on the one hand to meet the needs of different capacities, interests, and probable futures among pupils, and on the other hand to

meet the differentiated needs of society, is the most important problem of secondary education at the present time. (*PSE*, 74–75)

For some time, of course, a literary education had involved the skills of evaluative reading. The new situation of the secondary schools, however, made necessary the expansion of those skills in unprecedented ways. Faced with the sheer size and diversity of a student population in the secondary schools, what worked in the past, with "boys and girls from relatively well-to-do American families," became in the *Blue Book* phrase "as obsolete as the Edict of Nantes." Further, the cultural products that new population encountered were by no means restricted to a canon of "high literature." Evaluation was no longer a matter of the relative importance of Milton or Pope; "modern literature," by which Inglis also meant everything circulated in magazines and newspapers, posed a problem that could not be ignored. Cultural products have (or lack) positive sociocultural values intrinsically, but those values must be realized in the process of consumption. Thus while the immediate subject of evaluative skills remained the identification of which *values* are significant and enduring, battles would be fought over which *cultural products* were circulated and consumed.

"Intrinsic" is of course vexed, difficult to define, and perhaps in conceptual terms merely a metaphysical illusion. Nevertheless, whatever intrinsic means exactly, and whether an illusion or not, it is possible to recognize how its force in Inglis's argument functions to position the teaching of literature very differently from advertising work in the battles over circulation. For if specific literary texts are understood to embody, intrinsically, desirable sociocultural values, then unlike the verbal constructions of advertisers, that textual location must be a constant in circulation. The words of an advertisement, the *Blue Book* argues, "are important, but only incidental" (*BB*, 19). If they don't help generate sales, they can be changed. Literary texts in contrast cannot be changed, nor exchanged for each other. In relation to this constant of textual location, the work of teaching literature is then a fixed variable, as it were. It may be done well or badly, of course, but so long as it remains tied to the constant of a textual location of value, the judgment of well or badly is a judgment of means, not ends. Students on the other hand represent a random or absolute variable. They succeed or fail insofar as they do or do not learn to "utilize" and "appreciate" the sociocultural values intrinsic to a fixed textual location. In the classroom, to put it crudely, Shakespeare's texts—unlike advertisements for Mennen E in the marketplace—do not fail; they have intrinsic value. Nor within fixed limits does the work of teaching literature. *Students fail.* In the development of advertising work, as I argued, failure begins to re-distribute the boundary between "inside" and "outside." In Inglis's argument, in contrast, the force of intrinsic expels failure to the out-side of the work of teaching, settling it in the only place left to settle it, with students.

Thus if a student "likes" Shakespeare, there is the reward of the teacher's approbation and the more subtle sense of having measured up to the qualitative norms of the culture. But the penalty for not evidencing such admiration, together with the "reading skills" ade-quate to the "demands" of Shakespeare's texts, is of course a desig-nation of failure. As a student, one is then faced with the rather stark alternative of accepting the structure of rewards and penalties as an accurate measure of one's individual capacity, or of finding ways to contest the accuracy of that measure. If on the other hand one "likes" comic book X, one rewards its author(s), manufacturer, advertiser, and distributor by buying it. If one doesn't like it, one penalizes them by not buying it. Instead of being the recipient of evaluative rewards and penalties, one seems at least in a small way in a position to deal them out. To be sure, all kinds of pressures are exerted on that posi-tion, from the disapprobation of teachers and parents or the derision of certain groups of classmates to, conversely, the comic book ad-vertiser's tantalizing promises of wondrous pleasures missed if you don't buy. But it is then in the process of *marketplace* consump-tion where those pressures seem to funnel toward the consumer's evaluation as the field of contention, in contrast to the classroom en-counter with Shakespeare, where everything funnels instead toward someone else's evaluative power.

Inglis had imagined the literature classroom as a battleground of sociocultural values, where in the midst of a barrage of reading material, advertisements for countless goods and services—includ-ing, of course, for "reading material" itself—the teacher's exper-tise helped make students aware of what values contend and what "reading" embodies the most desirable values. The teacher, that is, contends with the force and influence of "pernicious" values with the stake ultimately an influence on the future direction of society, as it is present potentially in the student audience. Thus as Inglis had imagined the battles ideally, what is expelled to the outside, what "fails" in the battle, are "pernicious" values. The force of intrinsic, however, as it distributes the work of teaching from the constant of the textual location of value to the absolute variable of the student, fails students rather than values. Instead of a battleground of values in which one is being taught to intervene "intelligently," from the students' perspective it looks inevitably like a structure of rewards and penalties visited on one from the outside. Thus the heavier the insistence on specific texts, opposed to others, as embodying positive sociocultural values, the more resistance is likely to be generated to the *circulation* of those texts on which the realization of sociocultural values for Inglis depends. The marketplace becomes far more attractive than the classroom, as an arena of at least some "free choice." For teachers in Inglis's model, to win the battle is to lose the war.

Advertising serves a profit interest of its clientele. As I argued, in a situation where "inducing" the consumption of specific products becomes increasingly fraught with uncertainty, failure not only redistributes the boundary between inside and outside, but perhaps more importantly specifies the content, the *material*, from which profits can be realized as the potentially unlimited effects of consumer differences. Thus Kendall is quite content to encourage in consumers a sense of evaluative power, evaluative "freedom of choice," with comic books as much as soft drinks or deodorants and in the advertising space comic books, television programs, and the like afford. For from the corporate side, it appears less a freedom *of* choice than a freedom *to make more choices*, to exercise evaluative power and thereby generate still more differences to be evaluated in the future. The more choices made, the more corporate movement and expansion are possible; the more, in sum, the uncertainty of marketing can be reduced to maximize the realization of the surplus value of production.

This doesn't mean that freedom of choice, or even the "penalty" one assesses by a negative evaluation, is an illusion—a hoax perpetrated on unsuspecting consumers. It simply means that marketing has found a way to capitalize on the circulation of evaluative decisions, to some extent regardless of "which way" those decisions go

in any specific case. That is, marketing can be relatively indifferent
to the values "embodied" in any product or any advertising construction it sells, because profit is not product-constant. Advertising
does not have to promote comic books *against* Shakespeare, unlike
teaching literature in Inglis's model, which has to induce consumption of Shakespeare. Advertising will emphasize as much as possible
the "desirable features"—in the *Blue Book* phrase—of Mennen E so
long as consumers buy, but profit interests do not devolve directly
from the wonders of Mennen E or its advertising, even if the company has invested a great deal of time and money in both. The corporation can market another product soon enough if Mennen E "fails"
its introduction. Thus cultural production as it comes to function
in advertising does indeed circulate sociocultural values that can be
connected to specific products. But the guarantee of profit is realized
not from those sociocultural values, but from the cultural surplus
value of failure, which continually delivers more material to feed the
expansion of circulation.

In contrast, however one imagines teaching literature it cannot
be dissociated from sociocultural values in quite the same way, and
certainly not in Inglis's model. If in the process of training "intelligent consumers" those consumers fail to "utilize" and "appreciate"
Shakespeare, the teacher cannot simply move on to promote the
Katzenjammer Kids instead (or even Dickens for that matter) without simultaneously altering, deliberately or inadvertently, the very
nexus of sociocultural value. It is in this sense that the "battles"
Inglis imagined condemned teachers to a no-win contest. On the
other hand, however, teaching literature *could* be extricated from the
uncertainties of circulation in a way advertising could not. That is,
where advertisers had to realize profits from capitalizing on change
to win an expanded circulation, teaching literature found ways to relocate the realization of sociocultural values somewhere other than
in the process of circulation. What enabled this escape from circulation was a shift in the force of intrinsic as it operated in Inglis's
model.

In *Textual Power*, Scholes identifies as one of the crucial "binary oppositions" organizing what he calls the "apparatus" of English a division "between the production and consumption of texts"
(*TP*, 5), crudely, between writing and reading. Such a division is
clearly operative in Inglis's arguments, as it had been throughout the

latter half of the nineteenth century in the teaching of literature in
the university. Given the opposition, for Inglis it had seemed obvious
that literature teachers must concern themselves with the consumption of literature, with training "intelligent consumers," because only
there was it possible to realize a "general and universal" social function. In contrast, the "literary critic" no less than the "producer" of
literature exercises relatively specialized work skills that only few
students could master, or would have any reason to want to master.

However, as the force of intrinsic shifted, the terms of this opposition between production and consumption shifted as well. Rather
than naming the "embodiment" of sociocultural values in specific
texts, intrinsic began to involve instead particular qualities of work,
to designate an "active" labor process in opposition to the "pas-
sivity" of marketplace consumption. Thus the alternative Scholes
proposes to the binary of production/consumption in English, "to
perceive reading not simply as consumption but as a productive
activity, the making of meaning ... and second, to perceive writing as an activity that is also guided and sustained by prior texts"
(*TP*, 8), is hardly the recent and revolutionizing practice he claims.
In one form or another, it has provided the directive force of the
concrete labor of both literature and literary study since the 1920's
at least. For as intrinsic value came to be associated with work
rather than with a cultural product to be consumed, it also became
a way of distinguishing properly literary study—*both* the writing
and reading of literature—from the marketplace, a way to create
a new "ground" as it were to escape a no-win contest. To the extent the intrinsic involves qualities of work, it can be dissociated
from circulation. Values are both constructed by *and realized in*
work; the circulation of those values is of course desirable, but it
is then incidental to work itself. Unlike advertising, teaching literature could not be separated from sociocultural values. But unlike
advertising as well, it could be extricated from the uncertainties of
circulation.

Inglis's distinction between the "limited and restricted" work
skills of the literary critic and the "general and universal" training
of consumers in education had neatly resolved the issue of what
social function literature teachers perform. Through literature, they
circulate positive sociocultural values to consumers. However, once
disengaged from this "universal" marketplace of consumption, not

only was social function far from clear, but less abstractly, it became rather more difficult to rationalize the professional status of
the work either to educational management or to students. Thus
Inglis's distinction could hardly be left in that form. The shift in the
force of intrinsic to qualities of work made it necessary as well to
construct an explanation of how the peculiar, specific, intrinsically
realized values of "literary work," whether generally circulated or
not, nevertheless realized some general social function, and did so in
a way that justified "literary work" being carried on in the schools.
To accomplish this double objective, the weapons, so to speak, could
be assembled from a range of practices and historical sources that
had been given relatively little play in Inglis's arguments. Kant's aesthetic, for example, with its complex elaborations in Europe, offered
a powerful precedent for the association of intrinsic value and work,
but there were other and equally crucial points of departure.

Through the latter half of the nineteenth century and into the
twentieth, professional work of all kinds was increasingly perceived
as located in a specific place of work: doctors in hospitals and clin-
ics; lawyers in the organization of law offices, courts, and the penal
system; scientists in the laboratory, of a university and then quite
often of a research department of a corporation; a whole range of
new professions with the location where they began. But while such
professional work was then in the process of being firmly tied to
a specific location, the work of the "artist" or "creative writer" in
contrast was associated with *placelessness.* "Bohemianism," exile,
expatriation, peripatetic "artists' colonies," and the like furnished
out a popular mythology of the artistic life (and one that still sur-
vives in what is felt as the anomaly of "creative writing" programs
as part of an English department, and in the periodically expressed
fear that such programs have ruined the creation of new literature
by "academicizing" it—that is, tying it to a specific location). On
the one hand, in the new circumstances of public education, this
mythology of placelessness had to be demythologized, as it were,
shorn of its "romantic" trappings of giant (if penniless) personalities
striding the continents, fueled only by the intensity of their artistic
passion. But on the other, what usefully could be preserved was a
sense that the work of writing literature was relatively unrestricted
by the immediate circumstances and conditions of the writer's working life. Bank clerks could write hauntingly modern poetry, which

might have come out of the circumstances of the writer's life, but whose range of reference could not be understood by forcing it back into those circumstances. No less specialized and maybe even "professional" than other forms of work, writing literature nevertheless was unique because the very terms of work implied no restricted social organization, no uniformly designated *place*, within which it had to occur.

Matthew Arnold's arguments for the social function of "criticism" offered a kind of complement to this placelessness of the "creative" writer. For the essential quality of critical intelligence for Arnold, and the basis of its indispensable contribution to society, was a "freeplay" of the mind. Like every other responsible member of society, critics too had their commitments, their interests, and their values. Their specifically critical function, however, begins at the point where those commitments, interests, and values are not abandoned so much as made available, with others, for interrogation. (For Arnold, at least, "disinterested" never meant that the critic had no interests.) Criticism at its best thus evidenced a freeplay of the mind across multiple possibilities and directions, a *dislocation* of the critic's own interests from their "natural" home where they could then be subjected to intellectual scrutiny. Here, too, a certain demythologizing was necessary before Arnold's concept of freeplay could be put to use in the circumstances of public education. His embarrassingly vague and nebulous "touchstones" of access to the conditions of freeplay, for example, had rigorously to be read and understood, translated from a realm of taste to a demonstrable set of reading practices, to *work*. His tentative historicizing of "epochs of concentration" and "epochs of expansion" as a vehicle for criticizing Romantic poetry in "The Function of Criticism" had to be rewritten into a consistently new version of literary history and a literary canon. Once accomplished, however, then Arnold's freeplay could become available as an effective complement to the placelessness of creative work.

Given this reserve of weapons, one immediate result was to focus new ways of distinguishing "genuine" literature from the "popular culture" circulating in the marketplace. Women writers, for example, had already been a target of attack in the latter half of the nineteenth century, not only because they were often popular, but because their work seemed neither placeless nor professionally demanding. By cultural definition, women wrote as an avocation rather than a vocation, and their writing seemed merely to reflect an extension of domesticity, of the "place," the "household" and all it entailed, where they spent their time. One can imagine perhaps that in another set of circumstances and another cultural definition, an increasingly hostile attack, via literary work, on the processes of consumption might instead have recovered in these women writers an ideal vehicle, their very "domesticity" *distinguishing* their work from the marketplace. But once placelessness had been mobilized as a weapon, a strategic resolution to the dilemma of connecting a special form of work to a "general and universal" social function for that work, a vast range of "women's writing" had no chance at all to enter a newly emergent canon of "genuine" literature.

In the more immediately pressing terms of justifying professional work in the university and in secondary schools, the combination of placeless "creative" work and a freeplay of the mind in "critical" work could generate a pedagogy directed at both educational management and students. Unlike other professionals whose place of work as well as field of expertise targeted a specific range of potential clients' needs and interests, literature could be understood to address if not a general public—the evidence seemed too overwhelming to support such a claim even as fantasy—something more important, namely, what a general public might eventually become. That is, insofar as Inglis's argument that education is a "process of producing, directing and preventing changes in human beings" (*PSE*, 3) remained a force in the organization of education, then the unique nature of the work of writing literature as placeless and the work of reading critically as a freeplay of the mind could be argued to educational management as justifying the indispensable importance of the study of literature in the curriculum. For unlike the limited territories of other professional fields of teaching, they permitted the educative pressure of "producing, directing and preventing changes" to be exerted *generally*. To take the most familiar kind of claim, education in the sciences was said to train people to be scientists, whereas education in literature trained people to realize and understand the full complexity of their nature and potential as human beings. And one of the explosive ambiguities of this premise, which accounts in part at least for the screeching back and forth movements of literary study, is that it can lend itself either to "progressive" or "conservative" ideologies, depending on whether that "full complexity" is understood as something to be realized in a different future, or something to be maintained and preserved from the past against a hostile present.

In relation to students, the complement of placelessness/freeplay could justify *the work process itself* as affording something unavailable to consumers in the marketplace. Inglis himself had emphasized that most of the "reading material" in the marketplace—to say nothing of advertisements—was calculated to "appeal" only to one aspect of a consumer's interests. In buying a comic book, one didn't have to put one's whole character and value system on the line. "At its best," however, literature requires just that for Inglis. And in subsequent arguments for the value of literary study to students (in Brooks and Warren's *Understanding Poetry*, for example, twenty years later), Inglis's hints in this direction were expanded to suggest that unlike marketplace reading, literature discovers new powers for the individual. Challenged with the intensity and complexity of a *King Lear*, one discovers new and heretofore unexpected capacities in one's own imaginative grasp of experience. The "reading" of *King Lear* is thus work rather than consumption, often requiring very specialized skills and knowledges exercised with patience over a long period of time. But just because it *is* work in this sense of imaginative expansion, it also commands into being the kind of engagement with a fullness of experience impossible from the commodified products consumed in the marketplace. Rather than more "intelligent" consumption, the access to the tale of the tribe Inglis had found "embodied" in literature, the work of reading could instead release and extend an individual power of imaginative growth better and more completely than the relatively trivial powers of evaluative choice exercised among consumer goods.

To a remarkable extent, these justifications of work and work skills were accomplished through a series of textual distinctions, whose function then involved a way of transforming the location of and audience for work into a new *material of* work. That is, in order to realize the complement of placelessness/freeplay in a situation where work so obviously occurred in an educational institution in front of a specific audience, there had to be some means of converting both location and audience into a textual form, into a material thereby available to be worked on by literary texts and the study of literary texts. Thus location, the place of work in the university, was textualized in a familiar New Critical terminology as instead a "referential" or "scientific" *discourse.* "Place" becomes professional discourses of knowledge. In such discourse, the connections among the elements are deliberately specified as clearly and coherently as possible in order to facilitate the transmission of a message. For its purpose was conceived as emerging from its power of "abstraction," its power to restrict and identify a field of expertise. Literary texts in contrast complicate and proliferate the complexities of communication, "working *on*" referential discourse to the point where the continually expansive play of signifying possibilities in the literary text begins to resemble something like the density of experience "unabstracted," a "simulacrum of reality," as Brooks would put it in *The Well-Wrought Urn.*[16] Thus literature would not itself be a professional discourse of knowledge in any sense, for all that both writing and reading it involved a range of skills and knowledges as specialized as those of any other discourse. For not only "at its best," as Inglis claims, but by *the very nature of its discourse*, it cohabited with the very stuff of knowledge, the irreducible multiplicity of experience.

Audience, conversely, appeared in a double form, a "latent" or as yet unrealized potential on the one hand, and a textually programmed apparatus almost on the other. That is, audience in the good sense was a coming-to-be as yet masked by the manipulative textual forces of still a third form of discourse. Such discourse might often masquerade as either "scientific" or "literary" (although it operated just as often in perfectly "ordinary" contexts of everyday speech) because it was in essence a masquerade, a facade. Its efficacy lay in how the labor of its construction had been effaced: the cliché of "ordinary" language; the "pseudoscientific" appearance of a truth claim; the sentimental or popular or debased literary form; and preeminently of course the advertising text whose success depended more than any of the others on deception and disguise, effacing not only the labor of construction, but the manipulative intent of that labor on an audience. Literature in contrast only begins to unfold as the work of its making is revealed. For it labors on "ordinary" language and its masquerades until by a kind of sea change they reemerge newly alive with the luminous power of literary work. Literary meaning thus continually expands the more one knows about and brings together in the encounter with it the labor of work in words, of *making* meaning. Reading such a text helps construct the "latent" sense of audience, for it offers the possibility of participating in an "authentic" experience rather than just a glittering mirage masking a manipulative end. It deprograms an audience textualized by the manipulative forces of their social world.

The changes I've described briefly in literary work were directed at the points where a model like Inglis's could not be accommodated to the actual conditions shaping the development of education and the society within which it functioned, conditions that in effect condemned Inglis's model to a losing battle. In the most general terms, the result of these changes was a shift in the focus of expertise in the school from the teacher of literature to the "literary critic." The latter of course was also a teacher, and in large part the success of New Criticism in the university was due less to its conceptual power, as opposed to the other and competing directions that it battled in the 1930's, than to its relentless pedagogical reforms. However, the expense of this shift—from "teacher" to "critic" as the dominant figure, and from teaching consumer skills of evaluation to the critical skills of work—was a disengagement from the functional ends of literary education, which had organized Inglis's arguments. For the focus on work skills involved an idealization of the intrinsic to the point where the ends of concrete labor were effectively recontained in the performance of the work itself. That is, unlike Inglis's sociocultural values, which were "embodied" in literature, but which were then transferred somewhere else in the process of consumption as literature circulated, once intrinsic became associated with work skills, it was consummated, as it were, in the process of work itself, which became its own end.

I I I

Although it is difficult to specify conceptually a definition of intrinsic in this new sense, its *force*, again, can be registered in how it redistributed the practices of work in the classroom and in "research." On a visit home in 1967, when I was a junior in college, my mother brought me a first paper written by a friend of hers who had just returned to the university in town for enough hours to meet the requirements of the next pay step for secondary school teachers before retiring. The woman had graduated with a minor in English in 1928, and throughout her years in college had never received less than an A— on a paper. On her return, she had anticipated some trouble with "modern" literature, which had been one reason for choosing instead a course in Romantic poetry. But this paper, on Wordsworth's "Westminster Bridge," got a D. In the paper, she had discussed something of Wordsworth's biography, his love of nature and delight in observing natural processes (all of which had been simply X'd by her professor as "irrelevant" to the topic at hand); described Wordsworth's ideas regarding plain, direct language with a heightened imaginative intensity ("are you ever going to get to the point?"); written one paragraph about the sonnet form as Wordsworth adopted it ("OK, but see much earlier examples"); and concluded with three paragraphs detailing the "picture" of London as it must have appeared to Wordsworth that morning. The summary comment was "yes, but what does this have to do with the *poem*?" My mother had explained that what her friend wanted to know from me was what *did* have to do with the poem if not the things she had written. When I finally spoke with her about her paper, and reconstructing as best I could my own course in the Romantics a semester earlier, I began by outlining the possible plays of meaning between "show" and "fair" in the first line. It became clear very quickly that there'd been a lot of that in her class also. It hadn't made much sense, she said, because though it was interesting, she had no idea what to connect it to. She eventually got a B in the class.

In fact even a late and baroque New Criticism connected such verbal analysis to all kinds of things, and the New Criticism of the 1930's is a revelation to those who come to it for the first time now expecting "close readings" of poems. However, behind the woman's comment about connections was another question, namely, how was one supposed to know which connections to make and which ones not to make? To her, it had seemed obvious that part of her task must involve pointing out how the poet's love of nature found expression in this particular way of seeing early-morning London. Thus the rejoinder, that she was to attend instead to what was "intrinsically" available through the poem, so far from offering a criterion for making connections, seemed merely redundant. She'd known that all along.

The "break" that marks the idealization of intrinsic in work is

then less a matter of strict conceptual definition ("New Critics" dif-
fered strikingly among themselves, and in their reconstructions of
arguments in Kant, Coleridge, and so forth) than of a kind of tacit
assumption of equivalencies. However defined exactly, intrinsic
named a uniquely poetic work and a textual location of that work
where both the revelation of what was *worked on*, and the constructions of value that *resulted from* work, could be read off from the
verbal movements of the "poem itself." A poem, that is, comes to
us (to borrow what in the context is a rather unfamiliar term) as
so much "congealed labor," which reexpands to its potential fullness of being by means of the critic's ceaseless dialectical shifting
back and forth from "precondition" or "material" worked on to "result," as such shifting recovers the contortions exerted through the
working of the poem, which then in turn validates the authenticity
of the critic's own hesitant movements. That this circuit remains in
some simple and direct sense "tautological" is no discovery of recent
theory, but something understood as constitutively necessary to the
very assumption of intrinsic. That the assumption led unavoidably
to conceptual paradoxes was one sign of its power. The other and
more visible sign was how it projected a whole new range of work
skills that were virtually unrecognizable as such to a student like the
woman whose literary education had occurred in the 1920's. In this
sense, at least, the objection that a Brooks or a Blackmur or whoever
habitually brought information from "outside" the poem to bear on
its context simply misses the point. One of course brought such information; it would be impossible not to. Whatever the source of
the information, however, its authority was derivative. It might cor-
roborate or even clue one into what to attend to about the poem
in the first place. But it didn't command the field. In her paper,
the woman's information about Wordsworth's love of nature was
perceived as "irrelevant," not because it came from "outside," but
because it was as yet so much inert matter, unfurrowed by the labor
of the poem.

The effect of new critical skills of work on the production of
scholarship soon enough became obvious in the growth of the various "author industries" by which publication increasingly was organized. For rather than marking a point of recurrence, a return over
and over to the "same" values "embodied" or "contained" within
a text, this assumption of the intrinsic as a set of equivalencies

directed attention instead to the potentially almost infinite multi-plicity of relevant "material" available to the making of a literary text. The debates between New Criticism and historical scholarship thus confused the way in which, in its own terms at least, New Criticism was also a program of historical scholarship. The point of the latter, however, was not to "place" literary texts in an exact historical context. It was, crudely, to unplace them. That is, just as criticism transformed its location of work in a university into a discourse that supplied the material of work, in this larger sense literature transformed "historical context" into so many available and often competing discourses that the literary text then compre-hended. So far from being ahistorical, New Criticism offered the unique qualities of literary texts as in effect a kind of master code of *interpreting* history, a way of reading the human significance of historical material.

By the logic of intrinsic equivalencies, the presence of such his-torical material, once revealed by scholarship, then meant—if ever so minutely perhaps—both a necessary refocusing of how the work of the text itself could be understood, and a clarifying of the values constructed through that work. The pervasive "imagery" of light-dark in the scholarship visualized the connecting features of work as a process whereby critical analysis "sheds light" on heretofore mysterious aspects of the text (how the text verbally "moves" in ways never seen before), which is itself engaged in "bringing to light" previously unrecognized qualities and complexities of human experience in the labor of its construction. Thus by means of the logic of the intrinsic, criticism in the university could possess a kind of "equivalent" to what was perceived as a progressive structure of knowledge in other disciplines, a production of scholarship that continually expanded and refined the meaningfulness of literature. The idealization of the intrinsic, that is, not only redefined the skills of work, but afforded a justification for them to educational man-agement.

In retrospect, living now in the midst of such "light" that MLA must tax us to support the computers to handle the "information flow," it's easy enough to satirize the whole process as an illusion. David Shumway and James Sosnoski, writing for the GRIP report on the dysfunction of institutionalized scholarship, make the point succinctly: "There are far more interpretations of major texts than can be of use or interest to even the most specialized readers." [17] Unquestionably they are right. In itself, a "major new" interpretation of any given poet is about as exciting as the addition of lemon scent to Cascade. What they ignore, however, is a sense in which there does exist an audience for scholarship. Not the "public" certainly, nor even "specialized" readers, but precisely educational management as a potential client hiring our services. The client doesn't have to *read* the scholarship, any more than the latest research in molecular biology. What counts is the appearance of a progressive structure of knowledge, "illusion" or not. That is, it was not entirely some perverse "protocol of disagreement," as Shumway and Sosnoski theorize, which "allows an infinite number of positions, an infinite amount of articles, and an infinite amount of 'work' for literary scholars to do" (CP, 4). It was a justification of work to educational management. No justification no work, no matter what the "protocol."

The effects were equally visible in the curriculum of English departments in the university. Despite the changes in a canon of literature since *Principles* in 1918—something itself likely to be taken for granted now—it remained of course impossible for the literature teacher to move anywhere as it were. Powerful as it was, the process of canon reformation certainly did not permit teaching "just anything." However, by means of the logic of the intrinsic, it was possible to conceive of every *encounter* with the "same" text as yielding new discoveries. Thus English majors could find themselves facing a particular author, and often a particular text, first in an intro to lit course, again in a survey course of English or American literature, still again in a "period" course, and finally one more time in a senior seminar or "special topics" course. And even in this "last" encounter, they would be excused from class on the final day with apologies that there hadn't been "enough time" to really study the subject, for which see graduate school. Thus if with respect to educational management as a client, the logic of the intrinsic provided an equivalent to the progressive structure of knowledge in other disciplines in the university, with respect to a student clientele it provided an equivalent to the ceaseless marketplace motion from one product or service to another. Knowledge was always "new and improved." Further, it also ameliorated at least the assignment of "failure." For once the intrinsic was relocated in qualities of work, failure named only a *relative* incapacity to perform that work, a failure to perform it yet rather than a failure to live up to the norms of the culture.

Anatomy of Criticism, which arrived in the midst of the growth of "author industries" and curricular layering in 1957, begins with an attack on evaluation, on "value judgments," to which I want to return in the concluding sections to this chapter. But in another sense it was Frye who remembered as it were that "intrinsic" ought really to be part of a connected phrase, that it designated not just an "internalization" of work, but "intrinsic *value*," work with a purpose and an end. Thus one of the signal perceptions in the "Polemical Introduction," anticipating Shumway and Sosnoski by nearly 30 years, was that the data base of critical work had gotten out of hand. It was in danger of jeopardizing the rationale of work to both educational management and students. If the university is institutionally responsible for preserving the progress of knowledge across the generational discontinuities of professional experts in a democracy, then each discipline in the university must assume its responsibility for constructing a *theoretical* matrix to act as the organizing form of that knowledge toward some collective, social end. Simply the continued production of scholarship could not suffice. Likewise, each discipline must be able to demonstrate to students more than endless variations of work skills. There had to be explicit principles that explained *why* one did this kind of work in this order. Perhaps the most miraculous achievement of *Anatomy* was to have made these two directions, toward educational management and toward students, appear not only compatible, but identical.

Yet *Anatomy* is hardly unique in the double attention to practical pedagogy and to educational principles. It is worth pursuing Frye's arguments specifically, here and later, because of how *Anatomy* as a "polemically" introduced theory of the importance of theory was positioned in what has now become a familiar apparatus of circulation for theoretical texts: as the subject of journal issues and conference sessions (including an unprecedented English Institute that at least one participant, William Wimsatt, compared to a canonization), and thus as an authorization for the production and circulation of often quite different theoretical directions, and as a matrix for the reorganization of new textbooks for use in university literature classrooms. In many respects similar to the *Blue Book's* advertising of advertising, *Anatomy* theorizes theory in ways that permitted precisely the terms of circulation necessary to extend the explicit roles of theory in the discipline. That is, in large part the influence of Frye's ideas lay in how they were materially embedded in and through new forms of circulation.

For Frye, the conversion point between work and value yields the possibility of an elaborate, progressive, specialized structure of knowledge, while at the same time it makes available to any potential reader of literature a "power" to be possessed, an imaginative liberation. In one stroke, Frye thus unites the explosive ambiguity of "work" into a single force directed simultaneously at educational management and at students. As object, as text, the "work of literature" can be seen as participating in an always vaster intellectual construction, an intricate system of expandable "units" of meaning whose itineraries it is the task of criticism to trace at every level of connection. It is in this regard that Frye can claim he is not asking critics to do anything differently, but merely to recognize how the ends inherent in what they *are* doing already conform to the pattern visible in every other field of knowledge in the university. Once that pattern is clear in its specific critical form, it is no mystery how pedagogy is organized, for the principles that operate at the most refined level of research operate no less compellingly in an intro course.

But the text, the "work of literature," is also and at the same time *literary work* for Frye, a liberating activity, the culmination of an "imaginative revolution" whose goal is nothing less than the transformation of an alien environment into a fully human home. Ordinarily, of course, such transformation is understood in rather more mundane terms, something to be accomplished by doing things other than reading books. Cities to be sure "emerge" from fields and stones and trees in part at least by conceptual direction as well as physical labor, but such existent cities are not quite what Frye means by a human home. Existent cities in fact are more likely to be a place of human misery. Their story, the history of *this* labor of transformation, occupies the "tragic" narrative of *Anatomy*, the "Theory of Modes."

For the plot of "Theory of Modes" is the most familiar of tragic patterns Frye himself identifies, in its simplest form a fall from prosperity to adversity. Through the sequence of modes, the "hero's" power of action devolves from godlike superiority over natural forces to subhuman brutalizing by those forces, from "myth" to "irony." (Frye's assertions to the contrary, "heroine" cannot be conveniently substituted for "hero" in this formulation without changing the context. For in the texts he cites, insofar as women have a "power of action," it is not a power *over* natural forces, but power *as* a natural force.) The mechanism of this fall from prosperity—which Frye calls displacement—is mimetic plausibility, the imitation of external things, or more exactly of things as external. The work, the "power of action," which goes on here is then what in another terminology would be called "alienated labor," and what it produces are commodities: external things, objects that can be exchanged insofar as the labor of their making is gradually effaced and they seem to stand on their own as external, as objects. The result of this effacement is of course a perceived diminishment in the power of action of the hero, to the point in irony where the hero has almost no power of action at all and must conform his life, such as it is, to the objects that surround him, so many elements of a prison house. The last motion of the narrative, the way irony bottoms out and returns to myth, thus comes as a fantasy ending, at once a dim memory of something different and a desire for escape as the last gasp of power of action, of "work" in these terms.

The proper narrative of this desire is not the tragic movement of "Theory of Modes," but the comic movement of "Theory of Symbols," where for power of action, which can only diminish, one now substitutes imaginative labor. This labor moves from the isolated word, the opaque and vaguely sinister sign ambiguously pointing outward to objects and inward to other words; to the "work of literature" proper as a text, an individual, integrated system of words; to the totality of the literary as one single Work; to the level of anagogy, the literary *as work*, the continuous imaginative revolution where nothing is external any longer, where intrinsic finally comes into its own as an immense human body potentially available through every individual "work" to every individual reader as home. The movement would thus recuperate everything lost as power of action to everything possible as a single, connected *making of meaning*, an apocalyptic labor.[18]

It is at this point as well that literature and literary study as work reveal as finally identical the apparently incompatible directions toward educational management as a client and toward students as a client. For to the former, literature can claim a justification for *all* education as "compensatory," as the imaginative realization of an ideal classless and inclusive community, a genuine "home," over against the fallen world of social powers of action organized in competing privileges and exclusive hierarchies. To the latter, to students, it can claim to offer a power of possession, an imaginative life where one has complete autonomy and control of ethical choices in a way never fully possible in the shimmering but illusory marketplace of consumer goods. *Anatomy* is thus a kind of ultimate idealization of the multiple development of a whole range of concrete labor skills of literary work, and one of the most comprehensive statements— perhaps the last—of the liberal educational ideals that helped shape a twentieth-century conception of public education in the United States.

IV

However, for all that *Anatomy* represents a *summa certa* of decades of change and development, its rapid itinerary in recent critical history (from the early controversies and its immense visibility, to its current status as a kind of mnemonic rune that had prepared those over 40 for What Was To Come) suggests at the same time how those developments had deferred rather than resolved the problems occasioned by the location of literary study in a system of education. Frye's argument would make professional expertise in the study of literature an indispensable structuring principle of a liberal education generally; as I argued in the previous chapter, however, English actually became indispensable not as such a structuring principle, but as a sorting mechanism to demarcate the achievement levels of that vast new student population Inglis had witnessed entering the schools. Thus the specific skills of literary work increasingly appeared a marginal benefit for the English professor, wrested from educational management, precarious, continually in danger of being eroded by pressures to do something else. Likewise, the principles of intrinsic value that Frye had generalized then promised to students a democratization of reading. Freed from the culturally imposed norms of taste and sensibility, from the centralized archives available only to the trained philologist or historical scholar, from the mystically silent worship of "genius," reading was no more and no less than a productive effort of imaginative work, potentially possible to anyone to be carried on anywhere. Instead, what happened is that such work seemed to appear a remote professional hierarchy, organized around craft guild territories whose names—"Donne," "Shakespeare," "Milton," "Eliot," "Yeats," "Conrad," "Joyce," and so on—were bafflingly similar to the putative authors of term paper material.

What intervened after Frye in the circumstances of these disjunctions has often been characterized rather hastily as the arrival of "theory" in a discipline for obvious reasons hostile to it. But theory of course is a term that can lend itself to almost any strategy of revision, insofar as that strategy attempts simultaneously to foreground the internal dissonances in what had seemed a compact ensemble of practices, and in the process to name its own intervention as a conceptual reorganization. And that had been going on for a long time. Literary study, that is, did not suddenly become "theoretical" after decades of practical torpor. Where Frye had attempted a theoretical justification of English as a profession, carrying through to a certain logical conclusion the assumptions of an intrinsic relation between work and value, the eclipse of *Anatomy* signaled on the one hand the surfacing of a whole complex of *antiprofessional* tendencies. Evident in some form or another throughout the growth of English departments in the twentieth century, the exacerbation of tensions between how work was conceived internally in English and its location in an educational system permitted these tendencies to assume the critical force of new and alien perspectives focusing a series of challenges to the very professional aims of work in the discipline itself, questioning everything from its organizational structure to its ideological role in education.

On the other hand, the eclipse of *Anatomy* also signaled the shock of a rapidly proliferating armature of new concepts and methodologies appropriated largely from other disciplines (and other countries). They made it possible to isolate in view, as if for the first time, those obligingly amphibious formulations of the *material* of literary work, as they wriggled back and forth across the boundaries of "experience" and "text." Poems, Cleanth Brooks had explained in *The Well-Wrought Urn*, "return us to the unity of the experience itself as man knows it in his own experience. The poem, if it be a true poem is a simulacrum [because itself *textual*] of reality—in this sense, at least, it is an 'imitation'—by *being* an experience [and hence *not* textual] rather than any mere statement about experience or any mere abstraction from experience" (*WWU*, 212–13). Frye had carried this paradoxical logic to a kind of ultimate resolution in the form of anagogy. The arrival of new concepts "from the outside" made it instead available for study like some curious biological freak.

Thus what arrived in English was not theory, which had been there for some time, but rather multiple and often contradictory interventions *directed at changing the very terms of concrete labor*. That is, and unlike Frye, whose intent in *Anatomy* had been to explain and organize theoretically what critics were already doing haphazardly in practice, these interventions transformed the term "theory" itself to name a necessity for a different concrete labor. Although constructed to a larger purpose, Raymond Williams's argument in *Marxism and Literature* is useful to distinguish, at least provisionally, "residual," "dominant," and "emergent" forms of work that followed on the eclipse of *Anatomy*'s influence.[19] "Residual" in Williams's argument describes the survival of earlier cultural practices in a situation where the social formation that had sustained their deployment is disappearing, to the extent that such practices continue to function but in a different way, the original function almost soundless as it were, with fewer and fewer corroborating echoes from its surroundings. I will use his argument in this context to designate instead a more conscious and deliberate direction toward the past, a claim for the power of earlier cultural practices of work to afford opportunities increasingly foreclosed by the specialization of literary criticism as a discipline in the university.

Almost unavoidably, then, the central figure of the "residual" becomes some version or another of the "public critic," the critic whose work practices have as their material *general* cultural values, and whose allegiances are thus to the general culture rather than to a specific location as a working professional. "Public" creates confusion, however, insofar as it also suggests some primary and direct contact between critic and audience against which the institutionalization of literature and criticism in the university might then be measured historically as a restriction, the interposition of an elaborate institutional structure between critic and audience. And in fact, of course, that structure permitted an audience for criticism larger and more diverse than any addressed by Matthew Arnold or his predecessors. Inglis had rightly anticipated that teaching literature in the schools *made literary experts public* in a way they had never been before.

However, the issue focused by the figure of the "public critic" is not historical in the sense of actual contact or the numbers of an audience for criticism. It is theoretical, involving a conceptual connection between work and cultural authority. For as an intervention, the challenge of the "residual" is directed immediately at the "technologizing" of work in literary study, and ultimately at the dissolution of cultural cohesion that makes of the university with its array of specialized disciplines little more than a servant to whatever local and specific interests command the services of those disciplines. Thus what in historical terms appears a mythologizing of the "public critic" nevertheless supplies the conceptual articulation between these two levels of critique: in current circumstances, "public critic" names a no longer available potential of work *to produce general, cultural values*. Whether or not, historically, literary work ever engaged in such production with authority is less important than the fact that now it is conceptually incapacitated from doing so. For rather than step into the cultural "vacuum" left by the fragmentation of knowledges across the educational structure of the university, criticism instead condemned itself to a voluntary suicide by collapsing attention to larger social and cultural ends back into a relentless proliferation of specialized techniques and methodologies of work. The result was supposed to look like other disciplines; instead, and quite rightly from its perspective, educational management treats literary study like a pseudodiscipline, and students treat it as an easy grade on their way to more consequential things.

Though this "residual" theorizing of work undoubtedly exists, the "dominant" forms of intervention have in contrast found ways to accommodate its virulent antiprofessionalism to an educational structure. Locally, they take up an already evident strategy of "modernism"—the foregrounding of the act of making itself, the play that is at least in part "about" the making of itself as a play, the novel "about" the making of a novel, and so forth—in order to narrate a kind of cultural double plot, an "undoing" conducted in the very interstices of the endless "doing," the business of culture in the university. From within the university itself, work manages nevertheless to tell the story of its own location, shattering the illusion that professional practices of all kinds, beginning at home with one's own, are simply "natural" conditions. Work thereby restores a sense of specificity of function within a newly enlarged awareness of how these practices are being constructed in the first place and for what end. That is, the question is not "what is the nature of these practices," but rather *how do they work*, how do they function. Thus at a macro level the object of inquiry becomes the range of connections in what structuralism valorized as "the human sciences," and at the micro level the structures of textual exchange as they can be charted across the appearance of discourse at the motor point of every production of knowledge.

At best, criticism in these terms might seem to have reinvented a rigorously second-order and methodological equivalent to the "placelessness" of the creative writer and the "freeplay" of the Arnoldian critic. For shorn of their idealizing transcendence of local circumstances, their power of work reemerges in the terms of an *immanent* critical interrogation, again, an "undoing" that exposes how the business of culture attempts to seal itself off from inspection. At worst, however, and as such dominant forms of intervention came under attack from a residual theorizing of the loss of cultural authority, the result appears more of the same under a new guise, merely an extension of the endless "light" shed on literary texts in the heyday of an institutionalized New Criticism. The boundaries of the "literary text" become more fluid, the depths murkier, the process of exploring them more convoluted, and the equipment and training more expensive and specialized, but with pretty much the same outcome. Literary study simply arrives at a degree of insular professionalism so blind that it mistakes its technical expertise for "radical," antiprofessional critique.

Although they have taken a number of different directions, the conflicts between what I have characterized as "residual" and "dominant" theorizing are of course familiar features now of critical debate. And as Edward Said has argued persuasively, any recognizably distinct and elaborated theoretical position is likely to occupy different and even contradictory points in the ensemble of relations that marks out the terms of conflict.[20] In turning to consider the appearance of genuinely "emergent" new directions, however, Williams warns that "it is exceptionally difficult to distinguish between those which are really elements of some new phase of the dominant culture (and in this sense 'species-specific') and those which are substantially alternative or oppositional to it: emergent in the strict sense, rather than merely novel" (*ML*, 123). In my far more limited context here of literary study in the university, such distinctions are if anything more difficult, for even Williams's own language sounds suspiciously like a version of Eliot's attempt in "Tradition and the Individual Talent" to isolate "the really new" work of literature from mere alternations in fashion and taste. Yet to the extent theory as I've been describing it involves changes in concrete labor, in the very terms of work, it is possible to shift a focus on emergent directions from the "arrival" of new methodologies, concepts, and directions of analysis—with all the critical debate they have generated—to the issues raised by the composition of the work force. For changes in concrete labor are also related everywhere to changes in *who* works, to the arrival in the work force of new and different populations. That is, and unlike "residual" and "dominant," a discussion of "emergent" theoretical directions might well have to "arrive at theory" by means of something like a sociology of work in the discipline of English.

New Criticism then affords an instructive historical precedent. For whatever else was involved, the rise to prominence of New Critical practices followed very closely on the enormous expansion of public education and the growing intraeducational importance of English, and they supplied in these circumstances the necessary rationale to recruit into the profession of teaching English students who a mere generation earlier would have gone into other professions, or who might not even have been in the university at all. That is, to be "successful" in the university, a critical theory must also be a recruitment rationale. In his presidential address to MLA members in 1982, Wayne Booth gave the following account of his decision to become an English major, reached in the spring of 1940:

"All right, then," I intone, pounding my points out on the roof of an old Ford, "I'll *be* an English major, even though it does mean that I'll always be poor. Let's go over it again: I want to work at something that I enjoy doing, something that will contribute to my continuing to grow (Oh, yes, we talked like that, back then). So that means I should be a teacher.... If I teach English I can do what Prof. Young was doing last year in Litcomp, and Prof. Christensen has been doing this year in Advanced Comp; I can learn to read and write and think."[21]

Booth's testimony is a good example, since neither by choice nor training was he associated with New Criticism as a "theory" or "practice" of literary study. Nevertheless, his statement echoes everywhere the terms of New Criticism as a recruitment rationale in effect. For it is the idealization of intrinsic work values that provides the justification for such a narrative of a "career" decision. It makes the very specific skills and knowledges of literary work appear simply what it means to "enjoy" work, to "grow," "to read and write and think," and it makes the *terms* of choice appear a moral decision between a potentially very lucrative career in another profession opposed to the possibilities of individual, imaginative freedom and growth in a career in English, "even though it does mean that I'll always be poor." English, that is, had to recruit against other professions on grounds other than pay, or highly visible social prestige, or public authority. Likewise, the students who could be recruited were those like Booth to whom the intrinsic work values of English offered a moral way to resolve the dilemmas of work and careers in a rapidly changing social environment.

Booth, however, surrounds his account with an elaborate rhetoric of apology, which reflects an almost inescapable awareness that both the work force and the rationale for recruitment have been altered fundamentally. With characteristic prescience, earned by attending to a larger context than the immediate situation in the United States, Blackmur had warned of the impending problems in the very midst of the euphoria of growth in English departments during the 1950's: "Call it what you like, the double apparition of mass society and universal education is producing a larger and larger class of intellectually trained men and women the world over who cannot make a living in terms of their training and who cannot, because of their training, make a living otherwise with any satisfaction." [22] That is, the economy of work in English, as in so many other expanding sectors of work, had also begun to generate a "reserve army" of labor, and as Blackmur notes, an army which in this case included a significant percentage of highly trained women. The ease and cost efficiency of expansion—the addition of Ph.D. programs and new areas of study, for example, sometimes of new departments altogether—depend on an available pool of labor. But it is a reserve that, because of the values associated with work itself, occasions a peculiarly

acute form of dissatisfaction having little to do with the morality of
Booth's vow of poverty.

The dilemmas of recruitment and training Blackmur had fore-
seen are of course familiar enough now; everyone who was around
sat through endless faculty meetings in the 1970's trying to balance
the "ethics" of a desire for large Ph.D. programs with the uncom-
fortable awareness that few if any new Ph.D.s would get jobs even
remotely comparable to those held by their exam and dissertation
committee members. What ought to be familiar as well, however, are
the changes in expectations occasioned by the expansion of literary
study into the new "areas"—in the still current euphemism—of
"minority" literatures, women's studies, popular culture, interdisci-
plinary studies, theory itself, and so forth. As "areas," these may well
reflect a theoretical crisis of direction, with its furious conflicts of
"residual" and "dominant," but as possibilities of work they both so-
licit and promise a different population in the work force of English.
And it is a population for whom the carefully negotiated boundaries
of "work" and work as it were, the balances and trade-offs by which
English could preserve a degree of internal autonomy in return for
accepting its intraeducational responsibilities, can make little or no
sense. That is, what is at stake in English changes depending on who
works in English. Such changes may not be as immediately visible
and dramatic as the conflicts over new methodologies, new concepts,
and so forth. But they are likely to be far more crucial as a source of
"emergent" directions of concrete labor.

v

I have suggested that it is curious to think of literary study as becoming "theoretical" in terms of the relatively recent, post-*Anatomy*
arrival of multiple conceptual models and methodologies of analysis.
For in this sense, there was never a time when the study of literature
was not theoretical to some degree. Nevertheless, it does seem that
Anatomy marks a kind of break, a moment that in retrospect at least
can be identified as the visible appearance of a fundamental shift in
the organization and direction of work in English. Rather than the
arrival of new conceptual models, however, or an analogy like Frye's
own to the development of other disciplines in the university, it is
perhaps more useful to focus the terms of this shift through a com-

parison to the advertising work discussed earlier. For while I have already argued the intricacy of connection between advertising early in the century and the teaching of literature in the schools, I think the subsequent development of agencies like Thompson continues to offer an instructive paradigm.

The *Blue Book* argument insisted that advertising on a new scale demanded a new work expertise, but as yet the location of that expertise in an agency was still understood as an extension of the "personal salesman," the latter writ large. Theories of selling were legion in the nineteenth century, and doubtless before that as well. However, it is possible to identify what might then be called, in contrast, *advertising theory* emerging not at the point when conceptual models began to organize and direct sales practices (certainly that is evident enough in the *Blue Book* and its predecessors), but rather when the discourse advertising holds about itself foregrounds a recognition of the centrality of location. It is when the advertising *agency*—not the "personal salesman"—as the workplace of marketing becomes a primary focus in theorizing work. For that is the recognition that in effect assigns *everything* prior—no matter how conceptually sophisticated or innovative or historically important, like the *Blue Book* itself—to the status of a "pretheoretical" activity. *Printer's Ink*, for example, had frequently enough urged the necessity for advertisers to become conceptually aware of how to use psychological models. The difference between such arguments and those of Maloney, detailing the use of models from the psychology of communication, is not one of degree of sophistication or paradigm shifts or whatever. It is a difference between a "pretheoretical" assumption of how psychology might extend the "craft skills" of personal selling, and a theoretical recognition of mass marketing as predicated on a means of cultural production organized around the specific work practices of the advertising agency.

What I have distinguished crudely and schematically as "residual," "dominant," and "emergent" directions of theorizing concrete labor in English likewise mark the "arrival of theory" in literary study as a recognition, in however different forms, of a transformation of cultural production organized around the location of work in a university discipline. For even more obviously than theories of selling, theories of literature, of "beauty," of the "aesthetic," and so forth, had been around for centuries. The *making* of literature had been theorized as a craft skill of work, in far more intricate detail than the skills of personal selling. The difference, again, involves not paradigm shifts, but the recognition of how a specific, organized location of work employing a large and diverse work force intervenes to transform the networks of cultural production and consumption. Advertising is an instructive comparison, because in a relatively much shorter period of time it is possible to isolate the itinerary of change from the craft skills of the "personal salesman" to the mass marketing practices of advertising agencies. In "literary work" in contrast, the idealization of intrinsic work values deferred for decades the effects of change, by appropriating and reshaping the craft skills of the past to the economy of cultural production in a system of education. That is, as its force shifted, the intrinsic functioned to preserve a value-charged space of freedom for concrete labor to be distinguished—by some version or another of "tradition" and "the new"—from the *circulation* of ideologies in the marketplace, which had become the business of education every bit as much as of advertising.

Anatomy in this context is a monument to "literary work" as an intellectual craft skill. Unlike his immediate predecessors, however, Frye rarely forgets the informing significance of where that work is carried out. Thus even in the midst, now, of relentless "arrivals" of new directions, *Anatomy* affords an opportunity for a kind of reconnaissance of ideological circulation in the workplaces of English. It is not the argument to invoke in order to find out *what* ideologies circulate, nor to learn the practices of analysis which expose their consequences. For the most part, ideologies—like commodities—are too full of "metaphysical subtleties and theological niceties" to be detected by the relatively crude instruments available in *Anatomy*. But like Marx in *Capital*, Frye realized that the initially mysterious power of ideologies, no less than of commodities, lies not in themselves so much as in the process of circulation. Thus though in comparison to more recent conceptual models, *Anatomy* lacks a sustained means of ideological analysis, it provides nevertheless perhaps a more comprehensive reconnaissance of circulation. For Frye's critical target throughout *Anatomy* is *evaluation*, the form taken by whatever ideologies are current in English *as they circulate*.

As always in *Anatomy*, Frye's attention to evaluation was directed at the practices of literary criticism familiar to him. And given that focus, evaluation then appeared directly in two forms. On the one hand, it represented as a governing ideal of critical work the discrimination of relative significance in "reading material," the attempt to press into rational, ordered logic an explanation of why certain texts were better than others, and to communicate that explanation to students. On the other hand, however, evaluation also named the detail of what in larger terms is the formation of a literary canon. It fills out the terms of consensus about the identity and values that constitute a canon. In making his argument for Blake's long poems in *Fearful Symmetry*, Frye had understood perfectly well that it is impossible to intervene decisively in this process of canon formation without taking as your subject over and above the poems at issue the very ground rules of consensus. Thus a great deal of *Fearful Symmetry* is less about Blake directly, than about what a poetics would have to look like that excluded *Milton, Jerusalem*, and so forth, and what alternatively it would have to look like to include those poems. That is, evaluation at this level is the activity that constitutes in detail a community of interest and value; it limns the boundaries of what is included and excluded.

These two forms or levels of evaluation help explain at least one otherwise confusing ambivalence in Frye's attack. At times in *Anatomy*, evaluation is dismissed as irrelevant, merely a loose, general index of the assumptions of an age rather than a genuine contribution to critical knowledge. At other times, however, Frye seems to suggest instead that it is redundant; "everyone knows" already that in some ultimate sense reading Milton is a more rewarding and comprehensive experience than reading Blackmore, and nothing much can follow from insisting on the recognition. It may be true enough, but even if it is it has no consequences for critical work. The distinction, then, between "irrelevant" and "redundant" corresponds to the two levels of evaluation identified. As a refining power of discrimination, evaluation can be dismissed as irrelevant, a mechanical process of lining up a range of literary texts with the appropriately given category of cultural value. As canon formation, however, evaluation cannot be dismissed in quite the same way, for it participates in the very construction of the categories of value in the first place. It is neither similarly "generalizing" nor similarly "mechanical." Thus to label it "redundant" marks still a second kind of ambivalence.

For while constitutive, the evaluative judgments involved in canon formation are nevertheless represented in Frye's argument as strangely incommunicable. The experience they comprehend is said to be at once "central" to the very project of literary criticism, but at the same time "forever excluded" from the structure of critical work.[23] When pressed into actual practice, the result appears merely a redundant value judgment. In contrast, the locus of communicability that authorizes critical work is intended as a counterpremise to evaluation in *any* form, "the total acceptance of the data of literature" (*AC*, 25). Unless that premise is itself accepted, Frye argues, critical work communicates no knowledge whatsoever. What is curious is how in any ordinary sense of the term, "communicability" has been radically reassigned. For insofar as canon formation lies at the boundaries of community, in the detail of evaluation indicating inclusion and exclusion, it must be communicable in one form or another. That form may offer a mystified or ideological projection of boundaries (it may not *really* be knowledge); it may be tacit rather than explicitly detailed. But it is hardly an evaluative activity at all if it provides no way of communicating among the members of the community what the work of the community involves, if it is "forever excluded" from the structure of work. Frye's counterpremise in contrast ("the total acceptance of the data of literature") is empty, a kind of "non"-communication, like being told to "go thou and do likewise" without knowing what was done in the first place. As ostensibly a principle of communicability that, unlike canon formation, *can* further critical work, it fails even a minimal requirement, of suggesting how one might know what *are* "data," let alone how one might "accept" them.

Frye's attempt to connect his counterpremise to the organization of knowledge in "science" confuses the issue even more, for its source is obviously not in any structure of science. It is instead in the development of intrinsic meaning that finds expression in "Theory of Symbols" as the vision of an apocalyptic labor *of value* that excludes nothing as external. For Frye, it is only when measured against *this* ultimate communicability, where everyone is transparent to everyone else, that the irrelevance and redundancy, respectively, of the two levels of evaluation he has described can be resolved into a single process. In whatever form, evaluation must continually project an "outside," an unknown or alien or—at the level of "irrelevance" most obviously—inferior term by which the privilege of value bestowed on the primary term appears in contrast. The process is then not so much "wrong" as, even in its more powerful version as canon formation, *cyclically endless*. It is "redundant," a process by which judgments continually circulate, for each new formation carries within itself—as its "outside"—the seeds of its dissolution and reformation into a new set of terms. The process itself can then be understood as the "natural" and recurrent cycle of a kind of intellectual capitalism. The results of each effort of concrete labor in building a human world of mutual transparency are *exchanged* against another set of results, with a privileged class of intellectual entrepreneurs able at each turn of the cycle to grow fat on the work of others.

Such an argument can reveal relatively little about the ideological function of any given set of terms, of how Eliot's criterion of "impersonality" for example rationalized the judgments of "marginal" poets like Hart Crane and H.D. as having nothing to do with Crane's homosexuality or H.D.'s strikingly different use of myth than her male contemporaries. That is, it does not explain any specific ideological function of "impersonal." However, as a reconnaissance of how ideologies circulate in English, it charts in considerable detail the way a process of circulation can be controlled even when the terms of value change. For intellectual *profit* does not emerge directly from this or that privileged term like "impersonality," but rather by investing in the exchange of one term against another. Control is then exercised by means of a structure of exchange that plots the *movement* of circulation. It does not have to depend on an authority to impose fixed requirements on what circulates. Indeed, such authority must at some point itself be contingent, for profit accrues from exchange. Thus as Frye recognizes, profit *requires at least* two levels of evaluative activity. To the extent exchange is necessary, evaluation will be productive; it must always "produce" new terms of value and new "revaluations" of canon if exchange is to continue. To the extent control is necessary, however, a *structure* of exchange will normalize the direction, the movement of circulation. What Frye "anatomizes" is how a process of circulation in English mediates the double obligation of culture to function as both productive and normalizing.

The crucial operator in the apparatus of control, in determining the direction of movement, is then the link between the two

—or however many—levels of evaluation. It is what ensures that circulation will expand, becoming always more general. The structure of exchange normalizes the articulation of links between levels of evaluation such that whatever exchanges take place will result ultimately in a more general economy of circulation. In the evaluative activities Frye discusses, the direction of circulation moves *from* the relatively more detailed work of canon formation *to* the more general and mechanical linkages of abstract categories of value to particular texts, which can then circulate more widely.

Frye's examples are all drawn from specific criticism, but it might be easier to understand the operators in this generalizing movement by shifting his focus instead to what is after all by far the most common evaluative activity in English, grading students. Within the classroom, evaluation typically results in the form of instructor comments, in more or less detail, on papers or tests assigned to students. Like canon formation, this is at least a relatively restricted circulation, because though the commentary anticipates and is guided by other things, the detail of the commentary is also local, reflecting both the specific terms of the assignment and the instructor's perception of what kinds of comments are more likely to connect to the individual students whose work is being graded. Of course, it is not absolutely restricted by any means; there is "carryover" of all kinds. But in any case, at the end of the term the instructor's complex of judgments, comments, and grades on a succession of assignments, together with the more nebulous and often tacit assessment of a student and whatever other factors have entered, must *in some way* be reported on a grade sheet as a final grade for the course. This final grade then imposes on the instructor the invention—more or less consciously, more or less consistently—of a code of "translation," an operative link between the level of a relatively local formation of that complex of judgments and a relatively more general level articulated through a system of numbers or letters used to report a final grade.

The translation is sometimes characterized as a change from "qualitative" to "quantitative" judgment, but though the difference is real enough, the final grade is no less "qualitative" for being a number. It is a different order of judgment because its communicative power ranges so far beyond the locale of the specific formation of commentary on papers, tacit judgments, and so forth.

That is, its communicative power now extends to contexts beyond the classroom. Administrators, counselors, prospective employers, school admissions committees, parents, friends, can all "read" number grades, *and exchange them against each other*, in a way they might not necessarily be able to "read" three paragraphs of detailed commentary on a student's reconstruction of sexual imagery in "Leda and the Swan." Further, as number grades, these evaluations are then available to function within still more general contexts, to be linked by some other operator to an expanded circulation.

Given such a movement of circulation, it is not hard to see why Frye would describe *all* evaluative activity as an ultimately empty cycle—either irrelevant or redundant—and the expansion of what I have called "communicative power" an illusion. Because from his perspective of concrete labor, at each movement of the process, each shift in levels, the "gain" in communicative power would be a loss with respect to the work of both students and instructor, a canceling or emptying. For they can no longer control the work or the result; the "gain" accrues only to those in a position to *use* the operative links of translation from one level to another. (Hence among other things, the necessary student move when a "low" grade reaches an audience outside the classroom becomes the gesture of "let me explain," let me recover what I think was lost in the transaction.) For Frye, that is, intellectual profit is a *surplus value*, a gain that represents the power of appropriating concrete labor from those who perform it.

It might then be possible to coordinate in the following way Frye's attack on "evaluative" criticism with the other focus of attack in *Anatomy*, the burgeoning of scholarship as simply more and more "commentary" on literary texts, with no direction or end in view. For insofar as it lacks direction, the result of such scholarship can only reinforce that most familiar "binary opposition" in the "apparatus" of English, which Scholes's list in *Textual Power* ignores: between "research" and "teaching," or more exactly, between writing for publication and teaching. At the university level, of course, whatever pieties to the contrary, publication is always the privileged term, because it names the power of producing "the new." Teaching in contrast merely circulates in the classroom what has already been made available in one form or another in publication. That is, the link articulating the translation from one economy to the other is *repetition*. Teaching repeats to a larger audience—doubtless in "simplified," more "normalized" form—what has already been done. The relation between writing for publication and teaching itself then duplicates the relation between in-class evaluation of students and assigning a final grade to students for the course. Thus whether or not published writing is intended as directly evaluative in Frye's terms, if it lacks direction in itself, it can only cross from one economy of circulation to the other and more general economy of the classroom as a "loss," which in that expanded circulation then contributes to a "gain" in surplus value, to the practices of classroom evaluation of students. The privilege accorded writing for publication at the same time makes it a *restricted economy* of circulation, available to be appropriated elsewhere as circulation expands.

However, Frye's idealization of concrete labor as the source of intrinsic value and direction makes it very difficult to pursue the issue further, to ask what exactly "restricts" the economy of writing for publication in English. In one sense, to be sure, writing for publication can be more closely monitored internally than other practices of concrete labor in English. What one says in the university classroom, for example, is likely to be heard by no one else "in" the profession. Students may, deliberately or inadvertently, report it. But except in extreme cases, the authority of such reports is always suspect. In contrast, writing for publication will be seen minimally by one person and probably more, and in "ideal" terms it is available to be read and understood by anyone "in" the profession. That is, unlike teaching in the university at least, the organization of publication can lend itself to a kind of tacit censorship that actually *curtails* the appearance in print of new directions for change. Further, while there are many diverse journals available to publish in, obviously all publications are not equal. In hiring, promotion, and raise decisions, some publications count more than others simply by virtue of *where* they appear. It is an organization that can and has made it possible to block, harry, and penalize individuals whose writing for whatever reasons appears suspect.

Yet in another sense, this is itself an effect of the privilege accorded writing for publication. It is in large part *because* writing is assumed as the point of departure for an itinerary of change—for Frye no less than for the scholarship he attacks—that its organization permits careful monitoring. And what must be specified beyond this effect is how writing for publication becomes a point of departure in the first place. What makes it not only a restricted economy, but one where the "restrictions" *at the same time* position it as the most "natural" point of departure for changes in concrete labor? Very simply, I think the latter answers the former. That is, writing for publication is a restricted economy because it *is* assumed as the point of departure for change. This answer then reflects still another shift in the force of the intrinsic, in how it distributes the practices of work in English such that significant change itself becomes identified with the production of something distinctive, new, and different rather than with a collective power of action to effect consequences in how sociocultural values circulate and are acted on. Change is *intrinsic to* specific work practices, to writing, as distinct from how writing circulates in the classroom or elsewhere. In one way or another, circulation can only repeat change as already having happened, as a fait accompli. Thus circulation is perceived as what begins to "normalize" writing, which at its best at least opens up the possibilities of "the new."

To take an obvious example, whose point is precisely its obviousness, one cannot really publish that *The Sound and the Fury* is about an aristocratic Southern family and *As I Lay Dying* about farmers. There is nothing at all "scandalous" in writing that; what "restricts" the economy of circulation at this point is not the possibility that someone might censor such a statement as dangerous. But nevertheless, in print what is likely to emerge instead will be something on the order of how Faulkner's investment in the tragic narrativizing of the aristocratic Compsons results in an almost neurasthenic suspension over physical detail that is conspicuously relaxed when he turns to the farmers of *As I Lay Dying*. The difference I am concerned with between these two statements is not a matter of "simplicity" versus "complexity," or "direct" statement versus "jargon." There is no particular reason students couldn't come to understand either statement, and of course versions of either *could* be said in class. The difference is that the former *cannot* be said for print *without the invention of some new context in which it can occur*, such as supplied by the second formulation. For the organization of writing for publication not only makes it possible that certain statements may be denied publication, or denied publication in the "right places," and so forth. Perhaps more important, it restricts the economy of circulation by determining that writing for publication is cumulative for those "in" the profession. Somebody at some time has written that *The Sound and the Fury* is about an aristocratic Southern family and *As I Lay Dying* is about farmers—or at least it seems as though someone must have written that. Therefore, it "bears repeating" only as a tacit accompaniment to something else, to where the "real work" of writing is being done. It can of course be circulated in class, because *students are new* to the "material." But when it is circulated, directly in class or tacitly in writing, *it makes no difference.* "Everyone" in the profession knows it already. Change is intrinsic to "real work," to writing that "breaks" with available knowledges.

Frye's own analysis, however, suggests as the devastating corollary to the intrinsic in this sense that when circulated elsewhere, "real work" *can only* be appropriated. Writing will appear as simply more "commentary" on more texts, to be appropriated and used somewhere else. Hence the effort of *Anatomy* is to locate an "end" for such endless textual commentary somewhere other than in the appropriating mechanisms of circulation. It is to *rewrite* the whole massive apparatus of circulation into the symbolic order of anagogy. Repetition then becomes *identity*, where it is no longer necessary to cross from one economy of circulation to another because the evaluative levels dividing them have been dissolved, and change has become a permanent, "apocalyptic" labor of the intrinsic. Given his analysis of circulation, writing for publication must have as its goal an imaginative transcendence of circulation itself. Criticism must be restored to its status as an immense "craft skill" of imaginative work, against the appropriating mechanisms of an intellectual capitalism feeding on the structures of exchange in a process of circulation.

V I

When Marx arrived at the point in *Capital* where it became necessary to explain a specifically *capitalist* genesis of surplus value, it was not enough to have identified money as the agent of circulation, the bearer of exchange value. Capitalism becomes capitalism to the extent that capital itself enters into the sphere of material production, reorganizing production such that *abstract labor* actually generates surplus value. For the effects of capital as a force in production were evident everywhere to Marx: the appearance of factories concentrating large masses of workers; the rapid growth of cities around these new workplaces; the astonishing proliferation of machine technology; and perhaps most importantly the disappearance of craft skills of work, to be replaced by the very different effort involved in the repetition of single, detailed unit tasks.

To some extent, however, similar effects are also visible as a result of the transformations of ideological work. The growth not only of universities, but also of hospitals, government offices, and so forth as distinct institutions, each with its own organization and hierarchies of work, its own division of labor, its own specific research facilities and archives, likewise concentrated large groups of people in single locations doing work in completely different terms. Although not as dramatically perhaps, the presence of such institutions likewise altered the settling of populations in cities. The "industrial revolution" in both the United States and England marked the midland farm regions as also centers of heavy industry in cities. But it was no less significant how the chartering of land grant universities in the United States, for example, helped create the phenomenon of the "university town" as a cultural center in Midwestern states; how the choice of often small, rural villages for the establishment of state government created the situation of the capitol city mediating the political tensions between farm and city populations in a state.

In another sense, however, the effects of this transformation of ideological work are not always so easy to see as the effects Marx discusses. In literary study, the ideological equivalent to the craft skills of material production certainly changed form considerably. But such craft skills did not altogether disappear in the new workplaces, as craft skills disappeared in the factory. Samuel Johnson's pen and ink largely gave way to typewriters, and then to computers; his personal library to the archives of research libraries; his laborious efforts to resuscitate a classical terminology as a means of describing a different literature, to a vast range of textual knowledges; his "literary circle" to a university department. What still persists at the center of the work of criticism, however, is an image of the often lonely, always isolated, but intellectually productive encounter between individual reader and text embodying the basic *skills* of work. It is the focal point through which whatever labor of "research" in whatever communal and institutional settings must first pass in order to emerge on the other side to be circulated in print, in the classroom, in other communal and institutional settings.

It should hardly be surprising that Frye's critical attention thus focuses on the expansive movement of circulation. For the persistence of this stubborn, "irreducible" crafting of work against the molar changes in the organization and economy of circulation makes it seem obvious to Frye that however mistaken locally, however influenced by their surroundings, such craft skills nevertheless contain their own potential for self-correction, as it were. Given this persistence and this intrinsic potential, the apparatus of control for him will be located "outside," in the movement of circulation, and the immediate critical task will be to expose that apparatus as parasitic. As Frye could explain it then, abstract labor—the "work" of evaluation that circulates in an intellectual marketplace—is always in itself absolutely empty. It is not "real," productive work at all. Surplus value appears merely as the *appropriation* of concrete labor, the way in which at every shift in level in the process of expanding circulation, concrete labor is appropriated as intellectual profit for the entrepreneur who parasitically feeds off the exchange of value terms.

I think it is true that the transformation of ideological work has not evidenced the same massive destruction of craft skills as the transformation of labor in capitalist material production. But it does not follow necessarily, as Frye argues, that circulation in itself is then an ultimately empty process, the appropriation of "intrinsic" values of concrete labor to "extrinsic" sequences of evaluation. Though Marx identified the destruction of craft skills as one result of how capital enters into production, the persistence of craft skills in ideological work might simply be an indication that *cultural* capital enters into ideological production in a different way.[24] Unlike Frye's analysis, intended to expose the emptiness of circulation, the problem would then become one of explaining how it is that abstract labor generates ideological surplus value every bit as surely as abstract labor generates surplus value in capitalist material production, but without at the same time completely redesigning concrete labor to conform to the requirements of abstract labor, as in material production.

I want to argue that the answer has to do with the redistribution of gain and loss in ideological work. In Frye's terms, the gain in communicability that results from an expanded circulation, a shift from one level of evaluation to another, is always an illusion. For he assumes that "real" gain, real communicability, can only be measured intrinsically, in the terms of concrete labor that are lost in the process of circulation. Anagogy recovers what has been lost, restoring the centrality of an "eternal, apocalyptic" work as the measure of all communicability. Cultural capital, however, enters into production not by interfering directly with this or any other "intrinsic" measure of value, but rather by determining what it is that concrete labor *works on*, what counts as the "material" of work. That is, rather than redesigning concrete labor completely as in the material production Marx analyzed, cultural capital grounds that labor in a specific point of departure. For the ground, or point of departure, can then determine the measure of gain and loss. Gain accrues from a movement that begins in labor on a diffuse, chaotic, alien material, and goes toward a clearly demarcated and communicable system of distinct elements. (It should be obvious just how thoroughly New Critical discussions of literature "internalized" a version of this determination of ground, as the work of the poem is understood to have transformed a chaotic "experience" into the luminous communicability of poetic form.) Loss is simply the *reversal of direction*, back toward the point of departure.

Once understood in this way, as direction with respect to the material of work, gain and loss mark the access of cultural capital into the organization of ideological work. For it is of course abstract labor that holds in place the system of distinctions, realizes their communicability. However concrete labor is conceived "intrinsically," whatever internal explanations it constructs for the material of work and the rationale for the necessity of work in the first place are *formally* subordinate to the determination of gain and loss by the requirements of abstract labor. They are not completely subordinate, for again, the process of work, the actual skills of concrete labor, are by no means completely redesigned. Nevertheless, the communicable form in which they circulate is congruent with the redistributed terms of gain and loss. Thus abstract labor no longer has to appropriate the results of concrete labor. Nor does it have to fear concrete labor that claims to multiply indeterminacy or chaos or whatever. For this, too, obeys the determination of ground, in a sense validates the authority of the ground. The redistribution of gain and loss can systematically *convert* concrete labor, whatever forms it takes internally, into the abstract labor that generates ideological surplus value.

It is here that the remarkable agreement between such otherwise diverse representations of new work expertise as Inglis's *Principles* and the *Blue Book* becomes most revealing. For both Inglis and the Thompson agency agree that the "raw material"—as Inglis puts it— of work, for the expertise of the literature teacher and the advertising agency respectively, is *consumer differences*. The recognition of "individual differences among secondary school pupils" (*PSE*, 74), Inglis explains, is the fundamental fact from which all educative work must begin. No increase in the level of education in the general population is possible that ignores this point of departure. The *Blue Book* is if anything even more emphatic in insisting on the range of such differences as basic to advertising work. Only the agency that recognizes the sheer size and diversity of potential markets can compete successfully. As I argued, the development of advertising work extends the *Blue Book* premise even further. "Markets" become the visible effects of an *incommunicable* field, a mute assemblage of differences in which the work of advertising intervenes to shape local structures of coherence connected to a particular product or service.

The reduction of uncertainty as the goal of advertising work must then involve a correlative increase *in communicability*. For uncertainty is reduced insofar as consumer evaluative decisions in the marketplace can be registered as communicable effects. That initial field of potentially infinite differences is thereby transformed into a data base for the conditions of a coherent structure. "Profit," gain, becomes something considerably more than the happy result of consumers choosing to buy product A rather than product B. Whichever way the choice goes in any particular case, the result can still be used. The choice itself has reduced uncertainty by adding an increment of communicable coherence. Again, advertising work has no interest in eliminating "choices." For the "failure" of a particular sale nevertheless generates a surplus, an access of communicability out of incommunicable differences. It is a gain for the total process of circulation, for the "whole picture" Kendall praises. Loss is a reversal of the direction of movement, a lapse back toward the incommunicability of the material, the point of departure, rather than a local "failure" to make a sale.

Advertising can thus depend increasingly on the cultural surplus value generated in education because education helps in the task of reducing uncertainty. Abstract labor, circulating in the schools as a system of evaluative distinctions, generates an increase in communicative power. Students in the schools need not at all be educated *what* to buy in a way that conforms to what advertisers want them to buy. Contrary to Frye's model, the concrete labor of education is not appropriated for use somewhere else. As it becomes abstract labor, it circulates evaluative distinctions and multiplies the opportunities for evaluations. The result is a cultural surplus value whether or not people are educated to buy particular products, and *to some extent* no matter what cultural codes and values reinforce their decisions. Once the terms of gain and loss have been redistributed in accordance with a determination of the material of concrete labor, there is no longer a necessity for appropriation. The conversion of concrete to abstract labor will assure the power of abstract labor to generate surplus value.

If as Frye argues, evaluation is nothing more than the appropriation of the values that emerge intrinsically in concrete labor, then, as "Theory of Symbols" is intended to demonstrate, the circulation of evaluative distinctions not only can but must be circumvented entirely. There is no reason to intervene directly in circulation, because there is nothing at stake. It is an empty process. Instead, the whole apparatus must be rewritten to reveal its emptiness, arriving ultimately at the point of anagogy where circulation appears from beyond its circumference as a recurrent, "natural" cycle of bondage. But if, through the organization of the workplace, circulation systematically converts concrete to abstract labor by determining the ground or material of concrete labor, *then no such rewriting is materially possible*. It remains *only* symbolic, a form of compensation available to an individual imaginative power as a "craft skill," a release from the relentlessly programmed social world whose archetypically tragic story Frye tells in "Theory of Modes." And as compensatory, almost despite itself, "Theory of Symbols" reinforces the *use* of education to maintain what Frye himself will indict as a degradation of value to a system of invidious sociocultural distinctions. Frye's idealization blocks such recognition by conceiving of abstract labor as an empty category, nothing more than the appropriation of value as evaluation. That is, it remains an idealization to the extent that it does not account for the emergence in distinctively modern, capitalist societies of a reorganization of ideological work permitting abstract labor a direct, productive role. It remains a description of a "premodern" formation.

Gramsci's discussion of "traditional intellectuals" indicates how historically, even under the rule of an aristocratic class, the concrete labor of ideological work enjoyed a relative freedom. Because aristocratic patrons, in court or church, had uses for that work, it was appropriated, often ruthlessly, and continual pressures were brought to bear on its exercise. But its availability for use at all was contingent on at least the appearance of freedom, and often considerably more than an appearance. Under capitalism, this freedom has taken different and more "progressive" forms to be sure, the outcome of long and bitter struggles. Nevertheless, and however altered in form, it is always the nexus of freedom/appropriation that defines a central problematic of the traditional intellectual. Frye's idealization simply extends that problematic into the present, where it then becomes singularly powerless against the modern reorganization of ideological work. It is no longer possible, as Frye would have it, to avoid ideological circulation altogether, to "intervene" like a traditional intellectual from "above," by rewriting the whole process to conform symbolically to a desire for an absolute freedom of concrete labor. The reorganization of ideological work condemns a praxis of intervention to specific locations.

The direction of Frye's argument has remained immensely attractive, however, because it reserves to the immediate practices of concrete labor the possibilities of real change. Thus while the local terms of the argument (the swirling system of archetypes, the levels of meaning in "Theory of Symbols," and so forth) became suspect quickly enough as the explosion of new concepts and methodologies in the "arrival of theory" exposed the range of hypothetical assumptions involved, the promise of concrete labor practices persisted. If those practices could just be made concrete, "material" enough, then consequences would take care of themselves. What is too often characterized as a kind of theoretical fashion parade, the dizzying whirl of new models that make even last month's sensation obsolete, might then be better understood as an index of frustration imposed by the peculiarly modern organization of ideological work. For it is an organization that continually permits changes in the practices of concrete labor. Such practices can be made more "concrete," "material," or whatever, but the consequences of change will not only seem incommensurate with this new level of concreteness, but actually to reinforce business as usual.

One result is that new practices—"deconstruction" is perhaps the most convenient and visible example—then appear to lead curious double lives. On the one hand, they travel increasingly rapid itineraries from an early moment of radical promise (confirmed more often than not by the almost obligatory attacks suggesting such practices destroy "the very fabric" of something or other); through a kind of middle period of growing familiarity, where they become topics for conferences and special issues of journals; to a point where the focus of attack is no longer their "destructive" potential, but rather their "failure" to go "far enough" presaging the next highly visible itinerary. *On the other hand*, however, they circulate through the profession. In contrast to the first, this second "life" is shadowy, nebulous, and if remarked at all usually with critical disdain. For it is made to seem merely a phase of the former, when appropriation has become more or less complete, when "deconstruction" simply takes its place as evaluative categories to continue the business of sorting out "work in the field."

It shouldn't take much thought, however, to recognize that such disdain perpetuates a finely Arnoldian vision of cultural change. Change moves from the top down, accommodating new ideas to the diminished capacities and responsibilities of those on the lower levels of cultural hierarchies as new ideas eventually circulate to them. And since we all know revolutions are not supposed to move from the top down, the process becomes disgusting to see. Somewhere, somehow, the mysterious forces of reaction have worked their magic, so that what left France as "radical" and passed through Hopkins and Yale as a new arrival in the United States, reaches graduate students in Idaho as "always already" appropriated and declawed, suitable only for leavening the multitude in just the way Arnold thought Bishop Colenso's book should have if Colenso had done his cultural homework before writing it.

However, if one does not assume, like Frye, that concrete labor can internally construct its own concreteness, then the image of this double life is altered considerably. Rather than the long, smooth slide from the Ecole Normale Supérieure to the terminal moraine of Idaho, and the dramatic contrast between the purity of radical practices and the compromised exchanges of circulation, one finds instead a complicated ensemble of relations *in circulation*. A growing series of contested positions appears within which loosely affiliated "deconstructive" practices exert a variable force marked on the one hand by the relative degree of freedom of concrete labor in these positions, and on the other by the process that converts concrete to abstract labor. Unquestionably deconstructive practices can and do circulate as abstract labor. They function categorically in the evaluation of new books and articles (X "extends" the implications of Jacques Derrida; "misreads" and neutralizes Derrida; reinforces reactionary tendencies in Derrida; demonstrates the inapplicability of deconstruction to pre-1600 literary texts; accelerates the recondite technologism of literary study; provides a satisfyingly incomprehensible answer to unclear questions; discovers Derrida is actually compatible with Gilles Deleuze—or Wayne Booth—after all, etc., etc.); of dissertations; of candidates for hiring, tenure, and promotion decisions; of proposals for grants, for curricular reform —the list is a long one indeed. Yet as they circulate, deconstructive practices can also exploit the relative freedom of concrete labor as an opportunity to proliferate positions where it is possible to intervene in the process of circulation by disrupting the determination of a point of departure for concrete labor. For the sliding cluster of terms like *différance* can function to contest the epistemological grounding of that point of departure *in a "material" of differences*.

Thus as deconstruction circulates, as specific positions proliferate in circulation, what Derrida will designate as a philosophical discourse of "presence" can begin to be understood in a vast range of everyday educational procedures as instead the circuits of communicability emerging through the hierarchies of evaluative distinctions. For such distinctions seal and confirm the internal homogeneity of any given unit insofar as the boundaries of that unit are etched in the contiguity of each unit with any other unit. In the practices of IQ testing, for example, the index of evaluation rigorously abuts each closed, sealed unit against the next in order to read off the *presence* of intellectual capacity in every different, "individual" subject tested. IQ testing thereby confirms as the material of educative work an incommunicable field of heterogeneity, of mute differences, and at the same time, by means of the communicative apparatus of the test, transforms that material, "without loss," into a precise index of differentiation contingent on the communicable presence of every individual unit of difference. Deconstruction in contrast generates multiple practices where such a "gain" in communicability is revealed as a surplus itself contingent on the complicity of *différance*. That is, the opposition to be bridged by the test, between the point of departure (the field of mute differences) and the point of arrival (the systematic *elucidation* of difference as distinction), is recognized instead as from the beginning a mutually reinforcing *systematicity* of the system.

The result is perhaps "only" an epistemological disruption. But to the extent it is not confined to those apparently interminable *Critical Inquiry* debates about whether literary texts do or do not have determinate meanings, deconstructive practices can also exploit the specificity of location, take advantage of how thoroughly epistemology saturates the abstract labor of educational institutions. For rather than an attack on IQ tests as concealing the cultural bias of those who construct them, such practices would question as precisely an epistemological ground the determination of cognitive gain and loss which the tests affirm. That is, there would be no denial that IQ tests are culturally biased. What deconstruction can demonstrate, however, is how the determination of gain and loss permits *changes* in that cultural bias, in the cultural values encoded into the tests, without at the same time any loss of normative authority. For unlike Frye's analysis, which dissolves this normalizing power into the emptiness of circulation, is the recognition of the abstract labor of evaluation as something other than merely appropriation, as instead the generation of a *surplus* that helps constitute normative authority even when, as is certainly the case historically, the cultural biases of IQ tests have changed.

More directly than most forms of evaluation in the schools, IQ tests conceal the historical genesis of specific sociocultural values. In the elaboration of the test, it's as if questions do no more than inventory as "always already" in place values whose dominance, historically, was contested—and are perhaps still contested—along a whole range of circumstances. However, the process of testing not only minds the force of that dominance. In itself, it also generates a *differential* force, a cognitive sorting of students tested whose yield is a communicable index of differences. It is assumed students who take the tests all differ in their cognitive capacities, but the test then generates as a surplus, over and above the reinforcement of dominant sociocultural values, the communication of those differences to others as the measure of evaluative distinctions. Thus as the results of the test circulate, sociocultural value and surplus value appear identical, but they must be *realized* separately. For though the test conceals the historical contingency of sociocultural value, the gain in surplus value constitutes still another form of contingency. Stripped of historical genesis, sociocultural values become contingent instead on the necessity for the process of testing to generate surplus value. Whatever sociocultural values are coded into the test cannot not function to yield a gain in communicability as an index of evaluative distinctions. The "material," the students tested, cannot be left as mute differences if gain is to be realized. But conversely, if this surplus value is not jeopardized, the sociocultural values in the test need not remain the same. Should their historical contingency be exposed elsewhere as evidence of cultural bias, other values potentially can be substituted so long as testing continues to yield a system of evaluative distinctions. Sociocultural values and surplus value appear identical in the cognitive norms of the test, but they are realized nevertheless in separate terms.

Sociocultural values will be held tenaciously, and coded into evaluative practices like IQ testing, so long as it seems that abandoning them will jeopardize the realization of cultural surplus value. If, however, the power of a dominant cultural formation can produce alternative sociocultural values to enable the realization of surplus value, then more or less gradually, more or less completely, the original values can change. Gramsci quite accurately registers over and over in the *Notebooks* how the strength of modern democratic societies inheres less in their capacity to maintain certain "central" sociocultural values against all pressures for change, than in the *variety* of culture. He didn't mean that such societies don't evidence lines of distinction, hierarchies, class structure, gender and racial discrimination. But they also evidence a continual capacity to produce multiple ways of realizing the surplus value of such distinctions, preserving a dominant formation by expansion, as it were. For this capacity makes it unnecessary to "dig in" and "hold the line" to preserve specific sociocultural values *on every occasion* they are challenged. Because culture functions as both normalizing and productive, the expense of coercive force can be conserved for "special" occasions. The price for that simultaneous normalization and production is that concrete labor must then be left relatively free if it is to generate alternative sociocultural values that can potentially be used to substitute in the accumulation of surplus value as cultural capital.

Deconstructive practices can take advantage of this relative freedom, however, to disrupt the epistemological ground that permits substitution. For what is challenged directly are not specific sociocultural values or the use of those values in circulation, but rather the *material* of cognitive difference that distributes the direction of gain and loss in accordance with the requirements of cultural capital. Thus certain feminist theories, for example, have employed deconstruction so widely, and multiplied its possibility of disruption, in part at least because feminists have had to be acutely aware of how changing cultural codes of behavior for and about women have in circulation more often than not accomplished an even more efficient means of normalizing women's roles. This is not a "degradation" of deconstruction, so many banal activities on the plains of Idaho that have reduced the grand task of deconstructing All Of Western Philosophy to fidgeting with the mechanisms of IQ tests or the allocation of women students into particular educational "tracks." If indeed philosophy were a master discourse, then such activities would simply be following in the footsteps of the Master who has demonstrated how to deconstruct it. But IQ tests and the like are not Husserl writ small. Philosophy is only *a* location of discourse. In moving from that location to others, deconstructive practices risk of course a conversion to abstract labor. Unless they circulate, however, nothing much changes at any other location. Contrary to Arnold, and his heirs, cultural change does not move from the top down. Arguably deconstructive practices will only *begin* to be disruptive when they have been "forgotten," when they are no longer recognizable to a "top" that has unveiled a new sensation.

The relative freedom of concrete labor marks a divergence of the organization of ideological work from the organization of capitalist production Marx studied. In ideological work at least, concrete labor must be *converted* to abstract labor, and the conversion involves a certain *durée*. For value is not immediately realized as double; sociocultural value and surplus value appear identical, but are realized separately in the process of circulation. Despite how conversion then seems instantaneous, nerve-layered into the very structure of the workplace, it can never eliminate *durée* entirely. The accumulation of cultural capital requires both a continual production of value in concrete labor and a continual conversion of concrete to abstract labor producing surplus value. The two are continuous but not coincident. Thus in contrast to material production again, ideological work in English evidences not only a relative freedom of concrete labor, but also a necessary *durée*, an interval that intercedes between value and surplus value, and that affords a second point of intervention in the movement of circulation. The relative freedom of concrete labor permits counterpractices such as deconstruction that challenge the epistemological grounds of redistributing gain and loss; the *durée* of conversion likewise should permit counterpractices that function to *dislocate* sociocultural value and surplus value, which keep the interval from closing. The result is then a *misrealization* of surplus value, which forces a kind of disaccumulation of cultural capital.

The immediate difficulty is that unlike deconstruction, praxis at this point of intervention cannot be an option as it were, to be engaged now and then, in individual and isolated circumstances even, like a craft skill. For rather than a way to take advantage of a freedom of concrete labor to reveal epistemological incongruities, it is instead a way to *use* all such incongruities to effect a dislocation in the very process of cultural capital as it enters into ideological production. And unless used, *no matter how "radical" the counterpractices initiated*, the *durée* of conversion will lapse. In the circumstances of work in an English department, in a distinctively modern organization of ideological work, there is no break, no rupture, no emergence, no reversal, no counterpractice, no "destruction" of value so unbelievably *radical* that it can't be plotted in some way in a general economy of circulation. For unlike in the "premodern" formations Frye and other theorists continue to describe, the results of concrete labor are not appropriated in circulation, such that if that labor could just be made concrete enough to resist appropriation, the battles would be won. Concrete labor practices may well resist appropriation, but *anything at all* can be converted to abstract labor, even practices like deconstruction, unless they involve a deliberate, sustained, and collective pressure at the very nexus of conversion.

The difficulty, again, is not the radical daring of emergence, but the patience necessary to keep up pressure, to build up as much as possible at as many different points as possible, to undertake as Gramsci argues a "siege" war of *position*, directed at the process of conversion. For whatever emerges can be converted, and must be fought for in necessarily variable and location-specific terms at every point in the movement of circulation. To imagine the target instead as a "master discourse" from which all others follow is to struggle with premodern strategies against a bafflingly "invisible" enemy.

The second and correlative difficulty is that *durée* cuts two ways. If it affords an interval of conversion where pressures can be exerted, it also marks an interval before the consequences of such pressures become visible. As I argued, *to some extent* at least any given term of sociocultural value can be substituted for another without immediately jeopardizing a gain in surplus value. In the practices of IQ testing, for example, it is possible to work toward eliminating cards that score six-year-olds a "correct" answer for identifying a picture of a Caucasian woman as "prettier." The function of IQ testing, however, is twofold. It may mind the social force of specific cultural images of "beauty," but it also sorts students, yielding as a surplus value a communicable index of differential student "capacities" that helps track students into their "appropriate" places in social hierarchies. The two are connected of course, but not inseparable. For there are multiple ways the second function can be accomplished; it does not necessarily depend on preserving in the apparatus of the test any given cultural image of beauty. Thus the pressure to eliminate such cards does not immediately destroy the gain in surplus value from the test.

If in perhaps more refined and complicated ways, the whole complex of practices in English classrooms—from teaching "grammar" to the subdivisions of a literary canon into "historical" periods—likewise both minds the force of sociocultural values and sorts students. The *durée* of conversion—the interval that holds apart concrete labor and abstract labor—makes it possible to contest the former at specific workplaces of English. Rather than grammatical rules of "good English," students may be taught to recognize grammar as a variable system of ethnic and class norms of speech. Rather than an ambiguously signifying endorsement and criticism of "the American dream," students may be educated to read *The*

Great Gatsby as perpetuating the myth of an unpopulated wilderness available to the white man to mold as an image of *his* desires. Regardless, students will emerge from those classrooms more specifically differentiated than when they entered. There will be another increment of sorting to be read and exchanged against already existing increments. Even if one should refuse to assign grades to students altogether, the result is easily plotted. It simply marks that *no work has been done*, because no surplus value was realized. As in the practices of IQ testing, challenges to specific sociocultural values do not immediately disrupt the presence of cultural capital in the locations of ideological work. The *durée* of conversion permits opposition to sociocultural values, but it also functions to redistribute the consequences.

For it is only later, and in another situation, that the consequences can become visible as a kind of bend in the direction of circulation. That is, at some point later in the movement of circulation, it will become necessary to *do again* an earlier stage in the process if the force of specific sociocultural values is also to be realized, if value and surplus value are to be held together. Students must be retrained to write grammatically "correct" sentences, retrained to read *Gatsby*, and so forth, or something else must be substituted. Substitutions are possible—as Gramsci argues, the strength of a dominant cultural formation lies in the variety of culture—but there is a risk in that strength. Multiplying the necessity for substitution reduces the efficiency of the system and increases risk. There can be no guarantee that what is substituted will compensate *exactly* for what is replaced. In any case, redoing—whatever form it takes—cannot be neatly plotted as conforming to the directions of gain and loss. It generates waste that delays, perhaps interminably, the realization of surplus value. Or to put it rather differently, the realization of oppositional sociocultural values can at last appear in the *misrealization* of surplus value.

The crucial point is that such misrealization never occurs immediately. In time it might appear, but not as a direct consequence of classroom practices in a particular course, a letter of recommendation, a decision about a job candidate, a reading of a literary text, an explosively "radical" theoretical essay, or indeed any concrete labor practice in and of itself. Oppositional practices in all these situations must begin, of course, but given the relative freedom of concrete labor in English, it is often possible they *can* begin. What counts is what happens next, how their initial pressure can be extended, continued, forced at every available point. For substitution and re-doing are simple enough if confined to isolated, individual "bends" in the direction of circulation. It is only when practiced across mul-tiple points, at multiple locations, that counterpractices generate the "work" of misrealization.

A modern organization of ideological work cannot eliminate a relative freedom of concrete labor and hence cannot eliminate the possibility of counterpractices. Nor can it eliminate a *durée* of con-version, even if it risks the accumulation of waste. That is part of the price for the peculiar efficiency and expansiveness of dominant culture. But while *durée* cannot be eliminated, there are insurances against the risks it entails. In this context what I described earlier as a restricted economy of writing for publication in English can be understood as, precisely, an insurance. So long as it can be made to seem that "real work" enacting the possibility of change occurs in writing, and is then only repeated and degraded as it circulates, it does not much matter what is written or how it is written. It will be made to *function* as merely the psychodrama of the writer, as a kind of massive therapy program for disaffiliated intellectuals.

By far the most effective insurance policy, however, has been the idealization of "the new." It is easy enough to recognize why the new exerts such fascination, in "conservative" no less than in "radical" practices. Poets like Williams and others saw in Eliot's "Tradition and the Individual Talent" a means of recontaining the explosive energies of an emergent new literature, but it is perhaps more exactly understood as a complication and refinement of them. For the bur-den of "tradition" in the essay is to isolate from the mechanisms of fashion, mass appeal, personality, the multiple and wavering anten-nae of the times, what could be registered as "the introduction of the new (the really new) work of art." That is, tradition is a second-order and ideal projection within which "the really new" can be identified as such, and which then provides a permanent home for the possibility of the new against the inevitability of appropriation. *For it is the new that is the emblem of the relative freedom of our concrete labor*, the visible proof of work that, for however fleeting a moment, realizes an escape from its circumstances.

It becomes an idealization of the new not only when, as in Eliot, it is folded back on itself to be reconvened as an ideal order of signification, as "tradition," but also when it is condemned to repeat itself endlessly as a hope, against appropriation, that the freedom of concrete labor, while relative, is as Frye argues infinitely *renewable*. The result, in the circumstances of a modern organization of ideological work that no longer functions by appropriation, is to prevent a continuing war of position at the *durée* of conversion. No counterpractice, no matter how new or radical, can generate immediately congruent consequences; position depends, again, on *what happens next*, on an interdependent collectivity of concrete labor. This by no means implies that all collective work is inherently a force of social change; it can just as easily be a conservative force. It does mean, however, that a war of position cannot not be collective, for the interval of conversion will always distribute consequences into different locations. Likewise, an idealization of the new is not inherently an individualizing of counterpractices, an intellectual craft skill. But insofar as it eliminates the "next" of a war of position by repeating the emergence of the new, it shatters the interdependency of work necessary to a war of position.

Thus so far from the threat to dominant culture it is often perceived to be, the hope of the new can and does function instead as an insurance policy for a dominant formation in the organization of work. Neither the relative freedom of concrete labor nor the *durée* of conversion to abstract labor can be eliminated, despite the risks of disaccumulation they entail. But they can be insured against risk by perpetuating idealizations of the new. There is no surer indication of the effectiveness of this insurance policy than the circulation of "newness" as a criterion of evaluative judgments. Decisions about literary texts, about journal and book publication, fellowships, hiring and tenure decisions, all turn at some point on the presence or absence of the new in some form. Not *every* successfully distinguished work of course is "the really new." But for those times, like the images of inexhaustibly renewable virgins paraded through television dramas, there is always Eliot's tradition.

VII

I began this chapter by emphasizing the similarities between the formation of English departments and the formation of advertising

agencies in the early twentieth century in the United States, as new
sites organized in the midst of what was perceived as the entry of a
vast new population into the cultural economy. The comparison is
instructive for a number of reasons, not the least of which involves
the effects on concrete labor in English of how advertising agencies
and other sites of cultural production function in the circulation
of sociocultural values. My brief "reconnaissance" of a history of
concrete labor in English is then intended to show how an English
department is a location of work where specific opportunities for
a praxis of intervention in that process of circulation do exist and
can be exploited. For the organization of the workplace is neither
a seamless whole nor a massively smooth functioning machinery. It
is a complex, shifting, at times even tenuous formation. All English
departments of course are not the same, and praxis as location specific must learn in far more detail than any survey like this one can
provide to take advantage of what local possibilities are available.

A comparison to advertising is generally instructive, however, for
I think it helps explain how and where such possibilities might exist.
But no comparison will show that English occupies a structurally
comparable position to advertising agencies in the *circulation* of
what cultural production produces, because it doesn't. There are a
lot of ways to grasp this perhaps obvious point, but it's unnecessary
to go very far afield to make it convincingly. Work in advertising
is organized to circulate what the advertising agency produces as
the means of selling its clients' products. Work in English, in contrast, is by no means organized to circulate what a permanent faculty produces, nor even what they teach. Indeed, the percentage of
total labor time in English generated by a permanent faculty is relatively very small. For administrative and clerical personnel, graduate
assistants in many English departments at least, "temporary" and
nontenured faculty all work in English as well. And most obviously,
in very large numbers, so do students. That is, as I argued in my
first chapter, total labor time in English is a matter primarily of a
mobile labor force *circulated to English*. As a location of cultural
production, English is organized around this circulation of a mobile
labor force to the location, rather than to facilitate the circulation of
what is produced by the concrete labor of permanent faculty. Thus
for all the similarities, and despite how the concrete labor of literary
study as carried out by permanent faculty has been shaped in re-

sponse to advertising and the like, English occupies a fundamentally different *kind* of position in cultural production than an advertising agency. As a result, however necessary in immediate terms, an emphasis on concrete labor practices in English, like mine in this chapter, is particularly dangerous if isolated for attention.

First of all, there is no way to read off, as it were, just what kind of position English *does* occupy from the concrete labor practices of a permanent faculty. As I argued in Chapter 3 as well, those practices are likely to tell you very strange stories indeed—ranging from the social importance of humanistic values, to the centrality of English as a propaganda office by which a dominant power structure indoctrinates the young. But, crudely, if either were the case (or anything in between), work in English would be organized more like work in an advertising agency, to facilitate the circulation of what concrete labor produces. We may occasionally think our work is organized in this way, albeit in a "higher form," of course: "selling" values to groups of 20–200 students at a time for 10–15 week intervals. In which case the reasons why thousands and thousands of such "personal salesmen" would be employed to do a job of work that advertising with its massive resources of communication technology has demonstrated how to do far more comprehensively and efficiently remain mysterious, to say the least. The less fanciful explanation would begin by recognizing that English as a site of cultural production does something else.

Second, while I have extended Marx's terminology of abstract labor and concrete labor as usefully explaining aspects of work in English, given the particular valorization of "concrete" in literary study, they are also potentially misleading terms. That is, concrete/abstract functions in English as a value-charged distinction. Rather than a way to focus an understanding of the work process, alternatively, on the intellectual and physical effort of work, and on the organization of social relations at the workplace, concrete/abstract names *qualities* of work, qualities of what in my context are then concrete labor tasks. Thus while the privilege so often accorded "concrete" in the opposition concrete/abstract can indeed function as a critical tool to restore the specificity and detail of situation against the manipulation of abstractions and so forth, the study of concrete labor practices in either sense remains only one part of understanding work. When you shift to consider abstract labor, it is not a move from "the concrete" to "the abstract," but from concrete labor tasks to the organization of social relations in work.

I've spent so much time in this chapter with sketching a history of concrete labor in order to suggest, again, what opportunities for a praxis of intervention in the circulation of sociocultural values exist in English, how it is possible to work against the organization of work. But recognizing what might be at stake in such intervention I think necessarily involves returning to the subject of my third chapter, to abstract labor, to the social relations of work. For what remains mysterious about the functions of cultural production in English begins to make a great deal more sense once that production is understood as connected to a specific process of circulation. English is not organized to circulate sociocultural values directly; as I argued in Chapter 3, work in English as abstract labor sorts and evaluates—primarily students—in the process of education. That's why work in English, unlike in an advertising agency, centers on the circulation of a mobile labor force to the locations of English. That labor force generates most of the total labor time in English, because its work must be sorted and evaluated. Thus what is at stake in a praxis of intervention involves how concrete labor practices can be put to the tasks of exerting positional pressures on the way in which English functions to *distribute* social relationships in and through the production of evaluations.

For a working class and for "minorities" (and for others as well, even if less willing to admit them as such), class distinctions are of course visible everywhere in the social structure of the United States. Class *boundaries*, however—the contact points where the authority of class is actually exercised—are not necessarily congruent at all with these visible class distinctions. As working class, for example, what you encounter as boundaries in this sense typically do not involve people distinguished as "owners," "capitalists," "rich people," "rulers" in any way, but rather intellectual functionaries. To take a simple and obvious example, when you go to apply for a warehouse job, the power of class, marked as a boundary, is not encountered in terms of a "worker" who must seek employment from a "capitalist owner." It is instead a worker who must first of all perform the task of a job application that will be judged as satisfactory or unsatisfactory by the person(s) who does, precisely, the intellectual work of evaluating applications. And among other things, the "information" to be supplied as part of the application procedure will doubtless reflect the evaluations of other intellectual workers—in the schools, in employment offices, in the personnel division where you were employed in the past, in medical offices, and so forth.

Now "everyone knows" that somewhere behind that intellectual worker is the "real" authority, the person(s) distinguished by class who owns the warehouse. However, the authority over who works in the warehouse is not usually determined directly by this owner, nor in most cases is the authority to determine the actual processes of work in the warehouse. Further, it is by no means clear how a job applicant might even arrive at a direct encounter with the owner. It may be possible under the right circumstances, but it is equally likely that it would take the expertise of another intellectual worker, a lawyer say, just to exfoliate the layers of corporate anatomy that enfold "ownership." What is immediately clear and visible as an exercise of authority, marking a class boundary, are the intellectual workers in the personnel office who manage the apparatus of hiring.

To think of an English department as also a contact point in a network of class boundaries is to emphasize its affiliations with a rather different range of work locations than advertising agencies and the like. For while you "contact" an advertising agency through a circulated cultural product, an advertisement making a claim on your attention, English is encountered in ways not altogether different from how you encounter voter registration offices, driver's license and employment and welfare offices, debt counseling, insurance and tax forms, traffic tickets and other legal citations, arithmetic, medical advice, credit ratings, draft status, and countless other examples. For unlike seeing an advertisement, each of these encounters, including English, involves: (1) a specific location to which, in person or by mail, you are circulated, (2) the performance of a certain intellectual task of work required by the location, (3) a group of intellectual workers who evaluate your performance of that task, and (4) the payoff, of whatever kind, on the basis of the evaluation. Obviously the intellectual work required of you is very different in each location, as is the payoff. Writing a paper on determinism in Theodore Dreiser is not quite the same as filling out an application for a warehouse job or taking a test on highway driving signs. Where and how you get to "circulate" if you complete each task "successfully" is not the same, either. The common point is that nobody comes to any of these encounters neutrally. Working class *consciousness* is largely forged in the humiliations at the boundaries, in feeling that you never have enough of the right resources in *any* of these specific locations to assume that the outcome of the encounter will be "natural" or inevitable.

Class boundaries in this sense then form part of a larger process of the distribution of what is often called "human capital," those resources of skills and knowledges, as socially recognized and certified in one way or another, which among other things enable smooth passage through the innumerable contact points in the social circulation of people managed by intellectual workers. Nor is class by any means the only determinant of human capital resources, and hence of movement. Far more visibly and directly in the United States at least, race and the structures of racial domination exercise their force at these contact points. Gender constructions, too, not only function in the distribution of human capital, but like race and class are an element in the determination of what counts as a "resource" in the first place. The range of skills and knowledges necessary to "housework," for example, for all that it *does* involve specific skills and knowledges of work, is not socially recognized and certified as such. Thus as Heidi Hartmann points out, television commercials that sell the means and materials of housework typically represent the women who do the work as incompetent idiots.[25]

Specifically class boundaries are worth emphasizing in this process of certifying and distributing human capital not because class is more or less important than race or gender, but because it has been made to seem more purely the result of a failure of "achievement" in the certification mechanisms of the educational system especially. That is, to the extent "class" is recognized at all as a factor in educational certification, it is explained as if the "individual capacity" of certain people just naturally predisposed them to sink toward the bottom of a system of social stratification. There are now in place, the argument goes, significant programs available for "disadvantaged" children to catch up educationally. Those with the "capacity" to do so will; others probably do belong where they find themselves, drifting toward the bottom.

It is this naturalization of class that is then exploited in the recent proliferation of conservative attacks on affirmative action policies and the like, where race and gender are in effect assimilated to a concept of "natural" class as an underlying cause. Thus the fact that an enormously disproportionate number of women and "minorities" occupy low-paying and less prestigious jobs (if they occupy any at all), live below the "poverty line," lack the possession of socially recognizable human capital resources, and so forth is attributed to a natural process of social stratification rather than to gender and racial inequalities. And once assimilated to these class terms, it is then an easy step for such arguments to imply at least that such people are probably where they ought to be anyway in the social hierarchy. They should be content to wait until the benefits of the system as a whole "trickle down" to improve their lots as well. Human capital, that is, like economic capital, is mysteriously assumed to move just like water, obeying the laws of the natural world rather than the constructed environment of a social formation. It is very different kinds of intellectual work, including of course work in English, that carries much of the burden of constructing the details of that environment as it controls the social circulation of people.

For literary critics, however, much of the interest in Gramsci's focus on "intellectuals" in the *Notebooks* has involved his discussions of traditional intellectuals, since historically that was the group who made the study of literature a culturally important project. His remarks about organic intellectuals, in contrast, are used to contribute to a discussion of counterpractices, to questions about the relations of a working class political praxis with a new stratum of organic intellectuals from the working class. This twin focus of attention then leaves out not only Gramsci's analysis of organic intellectuals as they emerge as functionaries of a *dominant* class, but also most of the actual history of the formation of English departments in the United States in this century. For the rise of English does not mark the "institutionalization" of a traditional intellectual cultural authority. It was instead part of a process by which "in the modern world," as Gramsci argues, "the category of intellectuals ... has undergone an unprecedented expansion. The democratic-bureaucratic system has given rise to a great mass of functions which are not at all justified by the social necessities of production, though they are justified by the political necessities of the dominant fundamental group."[26] Intellectual workers in English were not traditional intellectuals, and were even less likely to be the organic intellectuals of the working class. Intellectual workers in English belonged to this immense range of organic intellectuals who had emerged in all kinds of fields and locations, as the "functionaries" of the dominant class, and who in English at least initially encountered as a *threatening* presence "categories of intellectuals already in existence" (*SPN*, 7), that is, encountered traditional intellectuals.

Thus "organic intellectual" is not immediately a descriptive category itself, but for Gramsci a way of outlining a problem of class analysis: "The relationship between the intellectuals and the world of production is not as direct as it is with the fundamental social groups but is, in varying degrees, 'mediated' by the whole fabric of society and by the complex of superstructures, of which the intellectuals are, precisely, the 'functionaries.' It should be possible both to measure the 'organic quality' [*organicità*] of the various intellectual strata and their degree of connection with a fundamental social group, and to establish a gradation of their functions and of the superstructures from the bottom to the top" (*SPN*, 12). That is, the problem posed by the term "organic intellectual" is not a matter of asking to which class intellectuals belong, but rather of asking how the various strata of intellectuals function to push the divisions and boundaries of class further and further into the details of social organization. For the dirty work, as it were, of maintaining, extending, and reshaping where necessary the boundaries of class is not accomplished largely by a socially dominant group, but by intellectual functionaries. These functionaries are then positioned for the most part at what I have called the boundary "contact points," like English, in the social circulation of people.

I would add to Gramsci's account, however, that these contact points involve a series of locations where the concrete labor carried out at the location generates in more or less detail, more or less complex formations, constructed rationales for work that are internal to the workplace and not necessarily congruent at all with their functions in elaborating class boundaries. As I have tried to show in this chapter, English as one such location evidences particularly complex sequences of such internal rationales. Thus "the degree of connection with a fundamental social group" is neither determined in advance, nor determined entirely by "the political necessities of the dominant fundamental group." It is a zone where these "political necessities" are at once contested and modified by the internally constructed rationales for work. However, they are not contested necessarily on behalf of *all* subordinate groups, but specifically on behalf of the intellectual workers at the location, by means of their internally constituted rationales for work.

Clearly the allocation of personnel, the process of selecting and certifying the intellectual workers who will manage the different locations, is a crucial task that is continually fraught with tensions. I think just as clearly it will vary depending on the internal history of formation of the workplace. Teachers in English are not trained and recruited in quite the same way as high school counselors or civil service employees, and so forth. Nor are secondary school English teachers even trained and recruited in the same way as university English teachers. In every case, however, the allocation of personnel is legitimized in some way, and in the United States to a greater extent than perhaps in any other country the means of legitimation involve demonstrable "merit" as measured by the schools. The development of education, as Gramsci remarks, is then "an index of the importance assumed in the modern world by intellectual functions and categories" (*SPN*, 10).

For the same reasons, however, schools will often emerge as a particular focus of working class hostility. Education not only functions itself in a series of boundary contact points; it also distinguishes and to some extent trains the intellectual workers who manage other locations. Schools appear *the* motor force where a system of class boundaries reproduces itself. It is then only an apparent paradox that working class hostility and "anti-intellectualism" will so often in the United States find an ally, not among intellectuals—and certainly not "left" intellectuals, to whom it is a continual embarrassment—but in a *socially dominant class contempt* for intellectuals and intellectual work.

For some time, women have held a relatively high percentage of positions in the less "technical," less "professionalized," and less "politicized" lower echelons of the locations of intellectual work. To a certain extent, in the schools themselves, this trend has accelerated rather than diminished. In 1928 some 55 percent of elementary school principals were women. Currently, and although nearly 90 percent of elementary school teachers are women, the number of women principals has declined to around 20 percent.[27] Thus in terms of actual contact, of who it is one encounters *first* and most visibly at the lower levels of the locations of intellectual work as part of a system of class boundaries, the answer is women. It should then come as no surprise either that working class "anti-intellectualism" is often also antifeminist, on the part of both women and men.

In this context, however, the presence of women in such positions of intellectual work should be understood as an expression of dominant class contempt not only for women, but for the jobs of intellectual work themselves. For given the legitimation of suitability for intellectual work on the basis of merit in the schools, the perceivable reasons why otherwise meritorious individuals would consent to working under the conditions of salary, organization, and routine the positions require do not involve the internal and often idealizing rationales for the work constructed by intellectual workers at the location. Instead, they involve a perception of some deficiency of "character," a failure of nerve, a reluctance in the face of the risks and the exercise of power required by the real world of high-level business, politics, and at least certain professional ranks. Or of course being a woman, where such character deficiencies come "naturally." Working class hostility on the one hand, and dominant class contempt on the other, thus continually pressure and exaggerate the importance of generating internally constructed rationales of intellectual work, particularly for men who after all largely occupy the higher positions at any given workplace. Together, these pressures make it all the more likely that the defenses of intellectual work and the ways of contesting the directions of its social function will be articulated not on behalf of all subordinate groups of the population, but, again, on behalf of quite possibly only a leading fraction of the intellectual workers at the location.

"Class" may be difficult to define exactly; class consciousness—as it finds expression in humiliation, hostility, contempt, defensiveness, and so on—even more conceptually nebulous; race and gender convenient to keep as separate items altogether on the agenda. Nevertheless, the transformations of intellectual labor have positioned the work carried on in English departments in the midst of their entangled formation. And that is where a "reconnaissance" of concrete labor at *any* location of intellectual work, pursued far enough, will I think inevitably lead. It is where a praxis of change, in contrast, must begin. For in English, "literature" and "literary study" as forms of cultural production do not directly circulate as competing discourses with advertising and the like, or as ideology or the distantiation of ideology or the negation of ideology or whatever. They don't have to be textually deciphered, submitted to a "radical" concrete labor of criticism to yield a content of social antagonisms and struggles. They are already, in English, an immediate occasion for a range of *work practices* imposed on a mobile labor force circulated to English, at the boundaries in the process of being shaped and distributed by intellectual workers. Thus in my concluding chapter, it seems to me necessary to turn first to the labor process itself in English, to the determinations of work and of what counts as work, as those determinations function in the construction of class, race, and gender boundaries in the social circulation of people.

Cultural Work as Political Resistance

According to this conception, the "new working class" embraces those occupations which serve as the repositories for specialized knowledge in production and administration: engineers, technicians, scientists, lower managerial and administrative aides and experts, teachers, etc. . . . it has escaped their notice, for example, that the occupations of engineer on the one side and janitor-porter on the other have followed similar growth curves since the start of the century, each beginning at a level between 50,000 and 100,000 (in the United States in 1900), and expanding to about 1.25 million by 1970. . . . Why is one to be considered "new working class" and the other not?[1]

That a university English department is a site of cultural production seems so obvious as to require little comment. It is, after all, a place where any number of texts are produced, reproduced, read, studied, and passed around all the time. In any given course during any given school term, the total number of pages of writing produced—student notes and papers, instructor lecture notes, syllabi, instructions for papers and tests, responses to student work, and so on—is likely to be considerable, and when multiplied by the total number of courses and added together with the number of administrative memos, committee minutes, letters, and faculty research and creative writing of whatever kind, it is very considerable indeed. "The immediate process of production," however, as Marx remarks early in volume 3 of *Capital*, "and the circulation process, constantly run into one another and intertwine, and in this way their distinguishing features are continually blurred."[2] Had he been thinking specifically of cultural production, he might have been even more inclined to add that it "runs into" and "intertwines" with a specific form of "the circulation process." For despite the manifest evidence of cultural production in English, it is by no means a general circulation of cultural products with which that production is inextricably connected. Rather, cultural production in English is far more directly connected to "human capital," the resources of skills and knowledges concentrated to a great extent in certain fractions of the population and certified by educational attainment. That is, as I have suggested, cultural production in English "intertwines" primarily with the social circulation of people, as a crucial point in the distribution and certification of human capital. Thus the "distinguishing features" of production in English are "continually blurred" with the distinctive possession of human capital generated in and through the social circulation of people.

The differences between at least some aspects of cultural production in English and cultural production as carried out in an advertising agency for example have often proved difficult to generalize when the comparison is made in terms of "distinguishing features" of their respective cultural products. "Everyone knows" that a poem published by the director of a Creative Writing program or Professor X's latest essay demonstrating levels of structural recombination in Wordsworth's *Prelude* is neither one the same kind of thing as the construction of an animated video redoing "I Heard It Through the Grapevine" to sell raisins. Yet it's not so easy as it might seem to explain clearly what "everyone knows" by focusing on the results. Thus school texts like *Advertising*, on the one hand, and on the other the internal rationales for literary study in English typically begin to shift from "the thing itself" to the qualities of labor that went into its making, and the end it serves, to construct explanations. If instead, however, you keep in mind the "blurring" of production and circulation, the differences are obvious. They can be marked most succinctly by the relations between work and the material means of production.

For in English, work is for the most part carried to completion with material means that by comparison to advertising at least are astonishingly simple, cheap, and easy to obtain. Students writing papers and exams usually use pen and paper, or at best typewriters and personal computers if they own one. Student notes in class are a matter of pen and paper, perhaps a tape recorder if the instructor permits. Instructor comments on those papers and exams involve the same material means. Syllabi are either typed and run off on the department's ditto machine, or perhaps printed on the instructor's computer. Letters of recommendation, committee minutes, faculty news, memos, class lectures, and so forth, again involve a similar range of means, sometimes with the aid of copiers. The Texts (that does feel better in caps) assigned for reading, whether "literary" or "critical," are an exception, yet even here they are not often "mass produced" with quite the same means as raisin ads or the latest Louis L'Amour novel or color layout for Swiss Styling Mousse. In contrast to advertising, the work of cultural production in English is generally done with cheaply available material means, and there is often no very clearly marked division between who does the work and who actually owns those material means, as there certainly is in advertising.

As texts, or as cultural products of some kind or another, what is produced in English and what is produced in an advertising agency are often far more similar than most people who work in either would admit. But the "distinguishing features" of the production process in a site like an advertising agency (and by extension *any* site which, like advertising, depends on a concentration of complex material means not owned directly by those whose work is realized through the material means) are determined by the necessity of expansive and rapid *circulation* of the cultural products produced. The peculiarities of English as an organized site of cultural production might then be summarized in more general terms as involving a production process whose design does not have to facilitate rapid and expansive circulation, whose products in fact do not necessarily circulate very far. For unlike an advertising agency, what English must produce directly are not cultural products to be circulated. What English produces is, precisely, a *labor* process, which is then available to function in the social circulation of people as one basis for the distribution and certification of human capital through the terms of evaluation. English is not only a place of work; English makes work.

To think of an English department in these terms, as a site of cultural production producing a labor process, helps explain a great many otherwise curious features about work in English. First of all, it suggests why, unlike in an advertising agency, the material means of production in English remain on the whole cheaply available, and are more often than not owned directly by workers in English. If as Inglis had assumed in *Principles of Secondary Education*, English was crucial to the general circulation of sociocultural values, surely this would not be the case. Students might still have to make do with cheap means, but faculty and perhaps advanced students would have available the technological developments that have been so much a part of the transformation of cultural production elsewhere. Those technological developments would have had far more and more far-reaching effects in English as well. They have not, because insofar as what is produced in English is a labor process, the most important thing is that everybody who is circulated to English must have the means in hand to realize *on their own* a process of work. For material means in English, for a mobile or a permanent labor force, do not function to facilitate and expand the circulation of what is done, but rather to make it possible for everyone in English to do something, to be engaged completely in a labor process, at whatever "level." This doesn't imply material means used in English haven't changed since *Principles*—obviously they have—but simply that the changes must always be accommodated to the requirement that everyone have the means in hand to do something.

Second, the production and evaluation of a labor process in English gives considerable substance to Terry Eagleton's claim, in *Literary Theory: An Introduction*, that the study of literature in English is "a question of the signifier, not of the signified. Those employed to teach you this form of discourse will remember whether or not you were able to speak it proficiently long after they have forgotten what you said. Literary theorists, critics, and teachers, then, are not so much purveyors of doctrine as custodians of a discourse."[3] The linguistic analogy is useful to emphasize the importance of "proficiency," the evaluation of a labor process, over the circulation of "what you said," of what gets done. For it's not just that those who teach you will remember proficiency rather than what you said; on the whole, others won't have a clue to finding out what you said. Because what circulates directly is the mark of proficiency.

At the same time, however, the analogy is also misleading. To a certain extent after all, *any* cultural construction involves "a question of the signifier," advertising no less than the discourse of the English classroom. Further, "discourse" is neither singular in English nor—in English—particularly valuable such that society requires us to act as "custodians" for it. If it were, English would not include in fact a great many critics like Eagleton himself who are not exactly faithful custodians. Proficiency is important to emphasize because unlike in other sites of cultural production, it indicates the overriding importance of a certain kind of monitoring of a labor process. That is, Eagleton's point about "what you said" can apply almost as well to how you say it, to specific forms of discourse. English doesn't have to purvey *a* specific form of discourse any more than it has to purvey *a* specific doctrine. For as a site of cultural production, the organization of work in English is enormously inefficient to *purvey* anything at all. That task has moved elsewhere, where the material means exist and are concentrated toward the end of circulating efficiently whatever is up for purveyance. English in contrast must produce a labor process available to be monitored for proficiency.

"Doctrine" and "discourse" thus have a double form of appearance in English. On the one hand, what is often a remarkable range of both are constituent elements of a labor process and hence a part of how that labor process is evaluated for proficiency. English may not be organized to circulate either doctrines or forms of discourse very efficiently, but they influence nevertheless not only the evaluations of the labor process, but the very detail of determining work *as work*, what counts as work in the first place. On the other hand, however, the appearance in English of any given "doctrine" for example is hypothetical. For it's not only when doctrine (or a particular form of discourse) is recognized as such, and students are asked by the instructor to entertain it as an hypothesis, a proposition to be tested by critical inquiry, that it looms in quotation marks as it were. Even when unrecognized (when it seems neither doctrine nor discourse, but just "natural," "obvious"), it does not circulate directly from instructor to student. Rather, it functions as a constituent of a labor process; it is continually "quoted" within the terms of producing a labor process. Thus the test of its presence, and the way it is maintained and elaborated, occurs within the terms of the instructor's evaluation of a student labor process.

Finally, English as a production site of a labor process helps explain the *material* of work in English, what it is that is worked *on*. For not just any material will do. If on seeing an "Exit" sign students simply walked out the door, an "Exit" sign would not be suitable material for classroom work in English. It can become suitable material when a speech act theorist, say, asks her or his students to reflect on the characteristic language behavior exemplified in an "Exit" sign. That is, whatever appears as the material of work in English must be construed as the occasion for a prolonged, detailed, and multiple labor process. Until it is understood in this way, it is not material for work in English. "Literary texts," even in composition courses, are then often felt to be the "obvious" textual material for work in English, because literary texts for some time have been distinguished from other texts, like "Exit" signs, precisely by the quality and effort of work "necessary" to read them. The possession of formulas, empirical data, basic literacy, general cultural information, even personal attributes of sensitivity, and so forth is never quite sufficient. None of it can ever quite substitute for the detailed, exacting labor of working through *this* text at this time.

As a result, even very experienced literature teachers who don't, or who don't any longer, teach composition regularly often face a moment of panic at the prospect. What exactly can you have students work on? What possible material could they write *about*? Likewise, it's taken a great deal of often ingenious theorizing to permit the use of so-called "popular culture" forms, "propagandistic" texts, "Exit" signs, and the like in English classrooms. For it's not until these texts can be construed as the occasion for something comparable to the familiar, extended labor of reading "literary" texts that they are deployed as material of work in English. Such theorizing always insists that you can't read, for example, *Superman* comics "new critically." But this means first of all that new and equally complicated methodologies of reading have finally achieved currency. For if *Superman* comics couldn't *in some way* be understood as an occasion for a complicated labor process, they couldn't be "studied" in English.

The cheap availability—often the ownership—of material means, the double appearance of "doctrines" and forms of "discourse," and the characteristics of the material to be worked on: all these peculiar features of English as a site of cultural production begin to make a great deal more sense when it is understood that what English must produce is a labor process to be carried out by a large population circulated to English. Thus, in the simplest terms, the availability of material means implies that it is relatively more important in English that everybody work rather than that some specific work get done to be circulated elsewhere. Imagine for example the fate of a Ph.D. candidate explaining to her or his examining committee that while s/he had not actually read and written about Pound's *Cantos*, it was all right to count the work anyway because someone else had read and written about the *Cantos*, and the committee could refer to that if they wanted to know what the *Cantos* were all about. Likewise, it is relatively more important that doctrines and forms of discourse function as constituent elements of a labor process to be evaluated rather than as ideological constructions to be circulated generally. The familiar "tolerance" and "pluralism" encouraged in English are not only limited in specific ways, but also reflect the prior require-ment that whatever the doctrine or discourse, it must function first as a constituent of a labor process. And finally, it is relatively more important that the material worked on in English is construed so as to permit an extended labor process rather than belong to a fixed canon of literary texts or a rigidly structured program of read-ings of any kind that must circulate to everybody. Which is why for all the pressures regulating canonicity, in fact changes are con-tinual, and new courses addressing different texts continue to be developed.

The material means of cultural production in English, as I have suggested, differ significantly from the material means of other fa-miliar sites such as advertising, film making, television, radio, mass circulation magazines, books and newspapers, and so on. But they do not differ significantly from the material means of production available in what I called in my first chapter "popular cultures." For in the sense I have given the term, rather than what is circu-lated widely for consumption, "popular cultures" names the mul-tiple range of practices in which people engage daily, in all kinds of circumstances. That is, crudely, though "Miami Vice" is not popu-lar culture at all in this sense, it is very often the material popular cultures work on. What people do with "Miami Vice," how they use it, how they *work on* it is part of popular culture. And the material means available to most people most of the time for popular culture work remains roughly the same range available to most of the work done in English most of the time. The availability of material means, however, marks only one of the specific conditions of cultural pro-

duction in English. Although English shares that availability with
a whole diffused range of popular culture practices, in other respects the labor process in English is very different indeed. As itself
the *production* of a labor process "intertwined" everywhere, unlike
popular cultures, with the social circulation of people, English involves: (1) a specifically allocated labor time for cultural work; (2) a
certain structurally imposed remove from the immediate circulation
of doctrines and forms of discourse; and (3) a necessity to understand the material worked on as *undependable*, as the occasion for
an extended labor process.

As a result, and despite the similarity of material means, the
relations between work in English and popular culture practices do
not admit any symmetrically linked politics of resistance. It is not
possible simply to "take the side of" popular cultures as somehow
congruent directions of political resistance. Nor, conversely, is it
possible to imagine English as a training ground for the critical refinement of popular culture practices, a place where others are educated in our work skills and knowledges in order to exercise them
critically on their own, in whatever circumstances. Alliances must be
forged instead in terms that recognize where cultural work involves
continually contested zones existing along the boundary points of
contact, the movement of a population through the educational system. To the extent, again, that these zones share a roughly similar
availability of material means of cultural production, they all occur
within a similar "territory," which is not at all the same territory as
advertising or television production, for example. But depending on
where you are and what you do, what is at stake in this territory is
by no means the same.

I

Theories of a "new working class," as Braverman notes in the
passage I quoted at the beginning of this chapter, typically focus
on groups of the population who possess "specialized knowledge
in production and administration."[4] That is, such theories focus
on groups who possess certain resources of human capital even
though, in more strictly economic class terms, they may also be
wage laborers working alongside numerous other people at the same
place, doing the same kinds of work. Certainly these groups have

proliferated, to such an extent that a prescient commentator like
Blackmur as early as 1951 would register the curious optical illusion
of living in a whole world gone professional, with nobody left to
practice on. Everywhere you turn, you seem living in the midst of
what Blackmur was already led to call a new "intellectual proletariat."[5]

Perhaps accordingly, within Marxist class analysis, theorizing
about these new groups of the population has rapidly become more
diverse than Braverman implies. André Gorz in *Strategy for Labor*
and Serge Mallet in *Essays on the New Working Class* both acknowledge that the groups isolated for attention have a kind of "middle class" consciousness reinforced by their education and training.
But what these groups come to discover in the objective conditions
of their work as wage laborers is a structural position as working class. Nicos Poulantzas in contrast distinguishes what he calls
class "places" existing on three levels—the economic, the political,
and the ideological—and argues that people often occupy different class "positions," dominant or dominated, at different levels of
these class "places." Erik Olin Wright, refining Poulantzas's analysis still further, explains as "contradictory class locations" at least
some of the intersections among economic, political, and ideological
levels. As an alternative to this increasingly complicated anatomy
of a new working class, Barbara and John Ehrenreich propose instead to recognize the emergence of a distinct new class altogether in
late monopoly capitalism, what they call the "PMC," a professional-
managerial class.[6]

As Braverman points out, however, this emphasis on the growth
of certain "new" groups of the population comes at the expense
of failing to register *often comparable increases* in what must then
somehow be identified as "old" working class jobs. For the decline
in assembly-line work, heavy manufacturing, and so forth in the
United States has been more than offset by the numbers of people
employed in clerical work, product distribution (warehouse work
and the like), and most obviously of course "service" jobs. After all,
those formerly employed—or who would have been employed—in
heavy manufacturing, for example, do not for the most part move
into employment in "new" working class occupations. They move
into other and expanded versions of "old" working class occupations. Thus for a great many women at least, for men who grew

up in "old" working class families, and for "minorities," access to "new" working class occupations seems if anything as remote as access to managerial positions in heavy manufacturing had seemed in the past. The differences between the groups identified as PMC or "new" working class and the growing numbers of workers who focus Braverman's attention are not a matter of the gradual disappearance of a working class "in the old sense." Indeed, as Braverman suggests, the terminology of "old" and "new" is at best a confusing way to describe a shifting working class composition where expansion is as much a matter of "old" occupations as it is of "new" ones. There are differences to be sure among these groups, but they are a matter first of all of profound differentials in human capital resources. And the possession of human capital resources involves not only class, but race and gender constructions.

If, broadly, the workplaces of economic production concentrate the battle lines of class across the accumulation of capital, the structure and organization of an educational system likewise concentrates battle lines around the possession of human capital resources. That is, and increasingly, education becomes a battleground where an analysis that assumes Marx's inheritance as a basic, two-class model articulated through positions in economic production finds instead both new problems of analysis and new possibilities for political strategies of resistance and change. But what has to be thought as well is the differential angle of entry into education as this contested territory. For the (usually implicit) assumption of "new" working class theories involves the conditions of a *downward* social mobility, a large and heterogeneous "middle class" population forced to recognize, in the terms of job distribution and work organization, a structural "proletarianization" running everywhere counter to expectations generated in the course of often very specialized educational training and high levels of educationally certified skills. In the circumstances of this angle of entry, education as a battleground, a contested zone, will then mean first of all finding ways of using the educational system to *arrest* downward mobility, to transform education itself into a resource in conflicts fought out between classes and class fractions already heavily invested—albeit for very different reasons—in the organization of education.

To the extent education becomes a visible battleground in these terms, it then contributes to the growing invisibility of that growing number of people Braverman identifies as also "new" working class. *Their* conflicts do not seem "politically productive," since for these people after all, the angle of entry into education as a battleground is not a downward social mobility. Nor is being "proletarianized" despite educational qualifications a real problem. Nor are ways to transform education into a means of arresting downward social mobility a source of new and potentially more diverse forms of political resistance. Race is a problem. Gender is a problem. Class in the all-too-familiar terms known to a working class for a long time is a problem. And education, so far from being a battleground to organize specific resistances to a dominant social formation, remains pretty much what it has always been: a place where, with still very few exceptions, you learn your place.

English as a production site of a labor process is strategically located within the educational system. For that labor process is simultaneously a necessary and a peripheral aspect of the distribution of human capital resources. In simple terms, it is necessary to the extent that the labor process as evaluated in English at some level typically has been made to function as a prerequisite for admission to training in the more specialized skills and knowledges that constitute the multiple forms of human capital, and hence as a way of legitimizing the intricacies of selection. Work in English, that is, functions strictly as a labor process and not itself human capital. Those who manage the labor process in English—especially at the upper levels, in the university—must then *convert* that labor process into the terms of a specific fraction of human capital that might be understood, as I argued in Chapter 3, to more closely resemble what Pierre Bourdieu calls *cultural* capital, the powers of cultural distinction. As involving strictly cultural capital, however, the labor process in English becomes a peripheral concern to those who are in or would move into scientific, technical, and administrative positions. It is an adjunct rather than the whole focus of attention. Thus conflicts over "composition" and "literature," "basic literacy" and "textuality," "service" department and "professional" discipline, and so on articulate continually new series of intersections around defining how, in what way, for what end, and for whom work in English is carried out.

Now from a certain angle of entry, the presence of these conflicts marks English as a politically charged field, a contradiction-crossed territory whose very instability affords opportunities for political direction and use. Composition teaching, for example, long relegated by the upper reaches of literary theory to simply part of the routine performance of responsibilities for general education in the university—to be assigned whenever possible to graduate students, temporaries, and beginning staff—instead reemerges as singularly appropriate for the practical elaboration of theoretical directions initially worked out across the more familiar domain of a literary canon. For at the point when, as either promise or threat, the boundaries of the "literary text" begin to dissolve into the mobile apparatuses of "textual production," then composition courses, so far from rote exercises performed as a "service" or to distinguish students with sufficient talent and interest to proceed to literary study proper, become the laboratory zone to test the possibilities of a pedagogical expansion of territory. Likewise, a whole range of material that had seemed "extraliterary," useful at best for "background" and "contrast" to the establishment of central texts in a literary canon, assumes a new importance. Its very visibility in the culture generally marks out a territory where once again work practices and knowledges heretofore circumscribed within an increasingly marginal form of cultural production might test the possibilities of expansion.

Composition on the one hand, and mass circulated cultural products on the other, thus afford ways to generalize the terms of a labor process of literary study in English. For such expansion exploits the double system of affiliations within which literary study occurs in English: "internally" as it were, insofar as departments of English in the university typically have institutional responsibility for the teaching of composition as well as of literature; and "externally" insofar as strictly "literary" cultural production of course now jostles, however uneasily, with multiple forms of production such as advertising, television, film, and so forth as they permeate the social field. Yet in either case, whether as internal or external connections, the point of departure remains work practices specific to the labor process in English. That is, both directions of expansion assume that labor process as immediately a *resource* in whatever conflicts emerge. The result is that though everything from composition courses to television commercials suddenly seems fraught with possibilities for political redirection, who it is that can be recruited to do this work appears already plotted across a familiar and closed economy of social movement.

For it is precisely the labor process in English that *cannot* be assumed generally as a resource for the work of political resistances. Indeed, so far from a resource in the emergent conflicts of direction that mark out English as a politically charged territory, from the rather different angles of entry of "minorities" and an "old" working class, the effects of these conflicts make the labor process itself in English, increasingly at all levels, appear an always more baffling, contradictory, changing, and ultimately impervious cloak of fire warding off outsiders. That is, what looks from a certain angle as unsettledness and hence political opportunity, looks from another as the proliferation of local demands arbitrarily imposed at impossible to predict points whose sole purpose is to generate a shifting configuration of requirements that will preclude successful passage. For from these angles of entry, the immediate stakes don't involve what can be done with a labor process in English as a resource you control, but rather the complications of access to the very possibility of human capital resource in the first place. *You* may see the stake in deconstructing the paradigms of representation in *Gatsby*, but it's hard for at least some of your students to share that stake immediately at the point of discovering that the knowledges of *Gatsby* that got them through high school English must now be completely turned inside out in order to get through this class. The process simply begins to look arbitrary and interminable.

This does not mean that those victimized by an educational system have no cultural powers, can engage only in the "consumption" of mass circulated cultural products unless somehow, and against the organization of work itself in English, we find ways to "liberate" them. Rather, it imposes a recognition that cultural work that goes on elsewhere, that becomes visible if at all as "popular culture" practices, will likely occur in very different contexts of political struggle. For all that popular cultures share a certain range of material means with work practices in English, the resources available for work and the stakes at issue are not the same.

For unlike work in English, popular cultures involve no specifically allocated labor time for cultural work. The implications of this difference are easy to ignore, but in fact they are considerable. To the extent work time is taken for granted, as a "natural" resource in effect, it becomes a relatively insignificant factor in any calculation of *use*, of what cultural work is good *for*. Faculty in English think nothing of asking graduate students who might, for example, be interested in analyzing the ideological conjunction of forces by which the "Rambo" films achieved their popularity to read an astonishing range of critical material to prepare themselves for the task. That material might well include everything from Adorno on mass culture to transcripts of the Westmoreland suit against CBS, sociological studies of film audience distribution, and technical discussions of the semiotics of camera angles and shot composition. That the result of this work will likely circulate no further immediately than a graduate seminar, and perhaps a fifteen-minute aside in the midst of an English 101 composition course the graduate student is assigned as a TA, poses no particular problem of incommensurability. Even if the local yield is small, the long-term possibilities have a potential efficacy that cannot be ignored. And in any case, as a graduate student and TA in English, the worker possesses at least a modest amount of allocated labor time that would be filled in some —and probably less politically challenging—way regardless.

Clearly for popular cultures, however, such incommensurability would be disastrous. What time you can snatch to think about, talk about, work on, find a use for in some way of your viewing of "Rambo" is hardly going to be taken up with a similar task of research. The knowledges involved may be no less crucial and intricate, but what use you can make of the film will occur in contexts where what is at stake does not involve anything similar to the stakes in a graduate seminar, a comp class, a published essay, and so on. Further, the stakes are not likely to be visible as such to work practices engaged within the terms of ideological analysis as carried out in English. For they may well have to do with conditions whose relation to the film itself are a matter of local conjunctions. I'll have more to say in the next section about these kinds of local conjunction. The immediate point is that without the resource of allocated work time, the connection of work and use is profoundly altered.

Second, the double appearance of "doctrines" and forms of "discourse" as constituent elements of a labor process in English makes possible a certain isolation of attention to their constructed properties. To be sure, work in English by no means always takes advantage of that refocusing of attention; otherwise, there would be little need for the continual flow of publications that expose, precisely, the terms in which English "naturalizes" a wide range of both doctrine and discourse. Nevertheless, as the existence of these same publications attests, the possibility does exist. The price of what that structurally double appearance permits is a location in a rigorously epistemological field of struggle. That is, and almost inevitably, questions occur within a context of challenging the conditions of knowledge itself under which cultural constructions of both doctrines and forms of discourse are produced. It is then all too easy to imagine that similar epistemological challenges mark the first, necessary priority of *any* cultural work of political resistance, no matter where it occurs.

But for popular cultures, where neither doctrines nor forms of discourse appear as also constituents of a labor process in the same way, epistemological issues are at best secondary. That is, what is involved is rarely a question of how do you know what you know, but what do you *need* to know in order to focus your resistance to authority at the weakest link. If your boss tells you warehouse paper deliveries are expected to conform to management-generated standard times, the most immediately important direction of resistance is not your capacity to expose such standard times as a constructed discourse to rationalize company profits at the expense of workers, to produce an epistemological challenge to the conditions of management control. You don't need to know how you know you're getting fucked over by those standard times. The possibilities of resistance begin instead in the knowledge of what variables the discourse of standard times cannot necessarily predict with accuracy. Thus your cultural work in the circumstances is much more likely to take the form of inventing a wonderfully complicated story about the unexpected traffic jam at 15th and Central that delayed your return from the delivery for a full 30 minutes. Now in so doing, of course, you haven't immediately realized the proletarian revolution. But then neither does deconstructing for a graduate seminar the entire Taylorized epistemological logic of Western societies. The traffic jam story is just as surely a local form of political resistance; it just happens to be resistance that does not at all depend on first having exposed the conditions of the *epistémè*.

Finally, the material worked on, the material available for the work of popular cultures, is not likely to be construed as undependable in the same way as the material of work practices in English. If you work eight hours a day as a secretary, are on call every minute of every day to manage a household of husband and baby, you probably won't worry your time overmuch with a PBS nature show by asking if the filmed images of tree frogs mating are "really" how tree frogs mate, culturally produced "simulacra," a forest outpost in the relentlessly colonized "nature" as a determined quantum of "leisure time" for consumers, or whatever. For rather than an occasion for an extended labor process that slows down the details of the TV images, exposes their constructed properties as it isolates their gaps and contradictions, the material must be depended on in the terms in which it arrives to supply details *to be used differently* than in the TV construction itself. You may not care at all how tree frogs really mate or why anybody would produce a show about tree frogs mating, but the images of the TV show can be valuable as a way to extort at least one measure of local control against the demands you face in a thousand different circumstances throughout the day. They could be used, for example, as one former student explained to me, as a lever to pry your husband into changing the diapers for once, on the grounds that since you're taking an extension course in poetry writing and never have enough time to take a walk by yourself, you at least need to watch the show uninterrupted as material for your first assignment in writing a nature lyric. In sociological studies of TV viewing, you may well then turn up as merely an integer in some impressive statistical evidence for how a significant percentage of the audience for nature shows are bored housewives. Your cultural work then becomes invisible, and your "self" a construct of "ideology in general" or some such thing. This kind of explanation, however, thus functions as a convenient disguise for how it is that at least one reason why you might find yourself as a secretary/wife/mother whose political struggles occur in *this* specific ensemble of relations, rather than in the very different ensemble of explaining to graduate students a concept of "ideology in general," is the terms of evaluation that attached to your performance of a labor process in earlier English classes.

For the recognition that popular cultures use material differently, and are engaged in different fields of struggle, unavoidably raises the issue of how English nevertheless functions as a connecting link across these different fields. That is, though work practices in English may involve different stakes and different focuses of conflict than popular culture practices, English *as a location in the social circulation of people* cannot be defined solely in and through the conflicts surrounding the work of permanent faculty. Obviously permanent faculty are not the only ones whose lives are affected by the authority designated to English in the social circulation of people. And insofar as that authority affects other people, it affects the possibilities available to popular culture practices as well. Secretaries make poems out of PBS nature shows, not necessarily because they are "duped" by ideological powers and don't know enough to challenge instead the very terms of discourse of nature shows, but first of all because such poems are one way to marshal their resources to resist the dominant structures of their lives. And in some small part at least, those dominant structures are determined by the mechanisms of human capital distribution adjudicated in and through the social authority of English.

The conclusion I would argue is a twofold one. First, there seems to me little reason to change the multiple work practices in English that attempt to function as "cultural critique" by trying to bring them more into line with popular culture practices or, alternatively, indulging in the fantasy that others might be educated to perform work similar to what goes on in English. There *is*, for example, a singular appropriateness to the kind of extended ideological analysis work time in English permits; English is a location where the incommensurability of work and use does not enforce an immediate penalty, and I can't think it worthwhile to give up that advantage. Second, however, it seems to me also necessary to understand how there are other ways to take advantage of a position in English. For as a site of cultural production, English is "intertwined," as I argued, with a specific process of circulation, with the social circulation of people. That is, it's not a site from which you can expect your ideological analysis, in whatever form, to circulate generally, but rather where it can take its place in an educative process of exchange that uses the position of English in the social circulation of people to build a support structure for multiple forms of resistances diffused throughout multiple locations. "Exchange" in this sense recognizes no single standard of equivalence. For while English is a position designed to facilitate a normalizing of human capital distribution, the labor process that goes on in English can be used instead to take advantage of that position, to facilitate educative exchanges that benefit any number of different locations where a war of position is engaged. Which means, among other things, finding ways to use the terms of a labor process in English not only as a resource for work practices internal to English, but also as a resource to continue the efforts of popular culture resistances in the contexts in which they occur.

I I

I've often thought Gene Vincent singing "Be-Bop-a-Lula" near perfect male working-class rock, the sappiest and most conventional lyrics in the world, but sung like you're just waiting for some clean-looking asshole to make fun of how sappy and conventional they are so you can kick the shit out of him. As an image circulated for consumption, the song by now seems part of a much larger and stylized rationalization familiar everywhere, from refighting the Vietnam War on film to selling Beamers to Boomers, and above all of course to keeping women in their place. So that it's particularly worth recalling in this late context that "Be-Bop-a-Lula" could and did function in a rather different way, as a strategic weapon against a different enemy, a gaudy lure to shift territory. For nobody but a class enemy would be dumb enough to walk into the trap, to think you sang it to or about your girlfriend. You sang it, precisely, as a trap.

Popular cultures often inventory the means for such territory shifts as strategies of resistance in local circumstances, and widely circulated material such as rock songs can provide those means. Thus popular culture work also relies very often on the "realistically" conventional in circulation because the conventional can be relied on to supply the necessary details to work with. It has the virtue of being familiar and recognizable, and hence available for immediate use, saving you a lot of time. I remember reading somewhere, as a pejorative comment of course, that the lyrics of "Be-Bop-a-Lula" were a matter of about twenty minutes' effort. It's too good not to be true. In any case, even in junior high it didn't take us more than about twenty minutes to learn enough of them, to have them ready for use in the matter at hand.

"Realism" in all its multiple forms functions in circulation as

a powerful instrument of hegemony, naturalizing the details of an
ideologically constructed world. It can do so, however, because realism is an art of detail, because it helps generate the details of differentiation to be exchanged in the process of how ideas, values, and
norms of behavior circulate. Thus advertising research spends an
increasing amount of money, and has developed increasingly specialized technologies, to construct as exhaustively as possible a "realistic" picture of the routine of "realistic" daily activities. In setting
up a campaign to market a new men's shaving cream, for example,
it is important to determine a target group of potential consumers,
to isolate the factors that will be involved in product positioning,
to develop new ways to use in advertising constructions the normative values of hygiene, "comfort," sexual attractiveness, and so
forth. But it is important as well to have available in minutely accumulated details the motions of shaving. For somewhere in those
motions it will be possible to fix a recurrent pattern: a hitch at the
cleft of the chin, a necessary delicacy under the nose, finesse near the
ear—*some* identifiable pattern of motion. The pattern can then be
used, in Maloney's terms that I discussed in Chapter 4 as a context
of "believability," or in Chin's terms as a "problem" to which the
new shaving cream can be posed as a "solution." Such a pattern will
emerge only from a relentless scrutiny of motions, and hence from
the power, first, to represent research constructions as the material
detail of shaving, and second, to represent that representation in
such a way that it conforms to the narrative of "problem-solution"
or whatever.

If realism thus multiplies detail, however, it multiplies just as
surely the number of positions where "misuse" of that detail is possible. On a visit home not long back, I ran into a junior high friend
wearing a singularly greasy-looking mustache on his way from work
in the mixing room of a large bakery where, as I knew from my own
work experience there, company rules specify a short haircut and
no facial hair. He explained how he had argued, successfully, that
with a skin condition susceptible to prolonged irritation, he ought
to be excused from shaving at least the especially delicate area under
his nose. The idea, of course, had come to him from the detail of
television commercials about the wonders of a clean, smooth shave,
and the mustache collected a form of resistance to a six-day work
week beginning every day at 5:00 A.M. facing tubs of up to 1,800

pounds each of bread dough whose composition and rising time he faithfully had to monitor. Stories of what grew in the mustache, he said, were now legend in the bakery.

Obviously my friend's use doesn't prevent the circulation of shaving cream commercials reproducing and elaborating the details of a white, middle class system of relations between hygiene and social distinction, any more than the uses the two of us put "Be-Bop-a-Lula" to 25 years ago in junior high prevented the circulation of normative sexist attitudes. But "prevent" is at once a "natural" and an impossible term in these circumstances. For the reorganization of cultural production generally on the basis of an enormous, complex, expensive, and centralized apparatus of material means permits a mass circulation of social mythologies through a continual proliferation of detail, to some extent regardless of what uses anybody puts those details to. That is, the power to circulate the details isn't directly contingent on rationalizing their uses exhaustively, and as a result alternative uses—like my friend's, or for that matter extended ideological analysis of shaving cream commercials by English professors—can't immediately prevent circulation. But what this also means is that analysis is mistaken when it concludes from the fact that shaving cream commercials circulate very widely indeed, that thousands and thousands of people are "manipulated" into believing the commercials. Advertisers like Maloney know better than to assume that everybody out there "believes" the details of advertising, nor is the success of his work measured by "inducing" belief.

Popular cultures exist because there is no monopoly of cultural production; such production goes on all the time, in all kinds of locations, "even" bakery mixing rooms. It is not because a monopolized cultural production produces the details that constitute even the subjective sense of self and of identity to which consumers cling that circulation moves so smoothly, with so little visible resistance to what is circulated and the devices of realism that deliver its terms. What the new technologies of centralized cultural production permit, and what advertisers like Maloney rely on, is a monopoly, precisely, of *circulation*. Thus while it is surely significant that the cameras filming a TV shaving cream commercial frame "experience" in specific ways, produce its semiotic codes and directions, it's at least equally significant that what the cameras generate can be circulated to literally millions of locations simultaneously, in a way alternative forms of cultural production, like popular cultures, cannot possibly accomplish. Mass circulation exists as mass circulation, not necessarily because we've become a nation of "passive" consumers, living in an imagined world of imagined relationships naturalized from above, but because cultural production has concentrated and centralized a complex of material means to enforce a monopoly of mass circulation.

In any case the target of my friend's mustache, as evidenced most obviously in the stories of its inhabitants, was not the terms of framed "experience" in shaving cream commercials. The target was the local, specific conditions of work in the bakery, and both mustache and stories were the result of a calculated inventory of working conditions that prized out of the enormously detailed apparatus of management control over what seemed every conceivable point of decision about the work and the people who performed it a possibility of shifting to another territory within those conditions. Such a shift will seem a small achievement only if you work in a place like a university English department where no "management" exercises a similar control over the details of your work time. For a great many people, however, the place where they work is organized much more like a bakery mixing room than like a university English department. The material used, worked on, to make that shift was the detail of a TV commercial about shaving cream, but the end was a reclaiming of at least one of those decision points at the work location. Two male coworkers, my friend gleefully reported, both black army vets, were now in the process of claiming the same exception. They had, he discovered, used a similar tactic before to circumvent army regulations, playing off a "medical condition common to blacks," they told him, of ingrown facial hair that made shaving painful. The exchange of knowledges marks not only a process of countercirculation, but a step in a radical political education.

Had my friend sat down to reflect on the situation at length, it might have occurred to him to inquire into how the company rule specifying no facial hair in the mixing room instanced rather more than management control over the hygiene practices of workers who were in physical contact with the product. That in fact it could be connected to the very terms of the TV commercial itself, and beyond that to a whole ideology of the body in contemporary culture. It's not that my friend was unaware of these things, but they did not occasion, as they did for me, an extended reflection—even reading a few articles that helped focus my thinking, and rereading some passages in Foucault I had almost forgotten and that now loomed suddenly as more significant. For again, the conditions of my work (typing this now in an almost empty building, in my own private space in the building, on a weekend, still eight days before a new term) aren't determined in quite the same way by a thousand and one decision points always in someone else's hands. "One characteristic of workingclass writing," as Judy Grahn notes, "is that we often pile up many events within a small amount of space rather than detailing the many implications of one or two events."[7] My thinking wasn't more far-reaching than my friend's, probing much "deeper" into the situation. It moved in different ways because different working conditions yield different relations of work and use.

For me, given the expanse of extended cultural work time, the material of the TV commercial could be construed as undependable, an occasion to slow down its details, plot their lines of force, figure their field strength in a complex ensemble of relations, devise ways of using that analysis in the classroom. For my friend, in contrast, other kinds of events press, in a small amount of space indeed, and he construed the details of the TV commercial as eminently dependable. For unlike mine, *his* use, his cultural work, depended on those details being recognized by management in the terms in which they appeared in the commercial. Otherwise they wouldn't be any use at all. To distinguish the first sort of direction that I took as "genuine" work of cultural resistance and this latter use as at best an occasionally possible, even playful reshuffling of a stacked deck, is not only a consummate intellectual arrogance. It is also a way to doom the former to political ineffectiveness.

Bakery mustache stories may seem very far indeed from what goes on in university English classes in literature, but the question of course is why it seems that way. After all, the literature we teach— or at least could teach—is full of such things. And they don't always have to be subordinated everywhere to the study of the construction of a literary text as text. There is to be sure a lot more to be "got out" of *Ulysses* than watching Bloom turn over the permutations of a potential advertising jingle, and a lot to be understood by means of construing the text of *Ulysses* as undependable. But in a culture inundated with advertising jingles surely multiple ways exist to use Bloom's advertising stories besides folding them relentlessly into Joyce's irradiating decomposition of "realistic" textual codes. Likewise, when you read the first few lines of Stevens's poem "The Man on the Dump" out loud, they afford a perfect excuse—because "socially acceptable"—to be spitting all over the place. You might not get to the meaning of "The the" in the last line, and its relation to a Regime of Truth, in that way. But you've made more available a dependable gesture of disgust that can be used in lots of circumstances. Nobody learns to spit by reading Stevens; the point, as we've all been taught anyway, is that he can be used to broaden your horizons, as it were.

Further, the immediate material means of telling mustache stories in a bakery are not a lot different from the material means of classroom discussion in English. The material means of writing papers on Stevens or Joyce are not so very different either from the material means to write the letter my friend was asked to "put on record" in order to be excused from shaving his mustache. You need paper and a typewriter. (As Woolf reminds us in *A Room of One's Own*: "For ten and sixpence you can buy enough paper to write all of the plays of Shakespeare.")[8] The skills of work are obviously different, but real skills and imaginative energy can be involved in each case.

These connections, however, have proved easy enough to disguise, even obliterate. It is relatively rare by high school that students think of what they read and write about in English classes as having any relation at all to the poems and stories their teachers asked them to compose in third or fourth grade, to stories they invent for their friends, to notes passed in class, to "revised" song lyrics, elaborate jokes, dating "lines," impersonating parental or medical excuses for absences to teacher or principal—the whole complex of cultural work in which they are engaged. That there are differences between these things and a Stevens poem or a Joyce novel should need no particular emphasis. That there are also differences among these familiar activities that in specific circumstances might be equally significant, and that the whole range does have connections to the typical material worked on in literature classes does need emphasis.

For while there's nothing really new about noting them, in literature classrooms all too often the movement of connection, even when recognized, is a one-way street. That is, to the extent connection is emphasized at all, it's to the point of moving you further into the literary text, as if there and only there can the details assume their full force of meaning and significance. Hence making use of "The Man on the Dump" for a socially acceptable spit seems a kind of deliberately contrived shock tactic on my part, an extension —albeit a trivial one—of what Kenneth Burke used to call "perspectives by incongruity." But if you don't think of connections as necessarily always a one-way street, if the ultimate rationale isn't always understood as a matter of exploring still further the resonances of literary texts as comprehending the experiences they're connected to, then the example is neither particularly shocking nor particularly incongruous. It simply registers that what you do with a Stevens poem in the context of a literature classroom and what you might want to do with it in other contexts aren't necessarily at odds with each other, as two different ways to "read" Stevens. Poems, that is, are available to be "read," with specific values that can result from reading worth sustained struggle to circulate, as I argued in my last chapter. But that use doesn't exhaust the availability of poems to function in other ways in other contexts. Specific features can even themselves be a vehicle of circulation, a means of motion that often can and does escape from the rigorously controlled processes of circulation institutionalized in the social formation.

For English, again, occupies a marginal position in the larger, organizing apparatuses of cultural production and circulation within that dominant formation. And studying TV commercials or films or rock music or political speeches rather than a "traditional" literary canon does relatively little in and of itself to effect any social change. That sort of "territory shift" doesn't mean we're now playing for big stakes, in the very midst of the central propaganda offices of dominant culture. It just means we're playing for the same marginal stakes with new material to work on to produce a labor process, that the one-way street remains a dead end, unable to convey the work involved anywhere else. English is crucially positioned in the social circulation *of people*, in the distribution and certification of human capital resources, and whatever strategies of political praxis we can deploy occur precisely there. Which means among other things learning to be attentive to the availability of poems, or any other texts studied in English, for use in contexts where the systems of connection do not always have as a final end the "reading" of the text. The fact that *Ulysses* might be used to talk about advertising slogans or the notes high school students pass each other in class doesn't after all diminish the value of *Ulysses* as a text to be "read." For the point of such connections isn't just to suggest "new perspectives" on how to read *Ulysses* that might then turn out to be "inadequate" to the task. They suggest instead a lot of different tasks, to which at least some aspects of *Ulysses* might usefully contribute.

Thus the immediate reason for focusing on popular cultures as I have suggested is to emphasize and strengthen the connections to the forms of cultural work in which people can engage in the multiple locations of work, the multiple range of social positions they occupy. For one common denominator at least of people in those multiple work locations and social positions is passage through the discipline of English on the way. English is then a location where, if in necessarily diffuse and capillary forms, a monopoly of cultural *circulation* can be challenged. It can't be challenged by educating people to work like we do, by trying to circulate generally our practices of production, to teach others to produce "readings" of texts. But there are possibilities of forging alliances with the range of popular culture production. That is, what the authority of English in the social circulation of people affords is a location to educate a support structure for resistances elsewhere, a place of educative exchanges of knowledges and strategies, a position to exploit toward the end of complicating and breaking up a monopoly of the circulation of cultural constructions.

For after all, is there really any reason to expect a bakery mixing room attendant to join with others at his work place to help organize proletarian revolution when he is constantly made to feel that no one beyond the bakery can even see the point of telling mustache stories, let alone proletarian revolution? To expect secretaries to organize to smash patriarchal power when they are made to feel that no one can see why they might spend their "leisure time" making poems out of PBS nature shows? When they've been educated over and over from childhood that even such initial and local actions, so far from active resistance, are not "real" cultural work at all? Not really worth the bother? That they haven't a clue to what oppresses them and thus fall for every trick of embourgeoisement and complicity that comes rolling down the pike? No one in such positions needs English to invent "the new" that might enlighten and direct their practices, nor to explain to them the potential significance of cultural work, nor to legitimize the cultural work they do. To have any political consequences, work in English needs to forge connections to popular cultures as they exist in these locations, and to use the connections to educate a support structure for the next step, the next shift in territory in a prolonged war of position.

For "territory shift" as I've been coaxing the term along is a way of explaining how Gramsci's conception of a war of position is carried out when the struggles occur in the midst of the details of "lived experience." Thus the Russian Formalist notion of *ostranie*, for example, is a kind of territory shift, and some version or another of it has been incorporated into almost every critical theory since. Because it's one of the best ways to shift to *our* territory, to relocate the electronic rapidity of circulation and turnover time of the details of social mythologies within the conditions of an extended labor process where a slowing down of details will register their contradictions and gaps. My focus on popular cultures in contrast points to the exploitation of the "realistic" and familiar, on the premise that if you're working where you can't afford a slowdown in the same way, the material of the labor process in English isn't going to help you much unless you can do something else with it. The undependability that comes from making strange is only an advantage if you've got the time and control over work processes to dictate the subsequent direction of work. If you don't, then what you want from a Stevens poem say is not always a making strange, an invitation to work, an occasion for an extended labor process of reading, but rather, and like "Be-Bop-a-Lula" or a shaving cream commercial, a dependable set of details you can take and use in some other way where you are. That doesn't mean we should start publishing essays that revise a literary canon on the basis of spitting quotient, but that nobody else is likely to work at a place where you can press the advantage, as we can, of recognizing an anxious intertextuality in Stevens's poems.

The problem when you slow down the details of "lived experience," as that familiar pantheon of Masters of Suspicion reminds us, is that you find no single source but instead a branching mass of tributaries organizing a landscape of positions rather less amenable to anything like the simple notion of territory shift I've been describing. As Teresa de Lauretis explains early in *Alice Doesn't*, in the context of feminist theorizing, you can't just shift "out" of this larger territory any more than you can lure all the positions that diagram its frontiers into the same forest guerrilla trap of your own making.[9] The experience of constructing in narrative a monstrous mustache denizen might be exhilarating, and it might help reclaim at least one position in the manifold of work organization. But in itself it doesn't alter the fact that you're in the bakery at 5:00 A.M. staring fixedly at 1,800 pounds of bread dough that will make your boss rich and leave you just less than enough for the next payment on the machine that gets you to the bakery at 5:00 A.M. in the first place. Likewise, your demonstration that so far from "deep humanity," Fitzgerald's novels are tales of sexist stereotyping doesn't immediately alter the exploitation of women in home after factory after office throughout the country. The "irony"—if the word isn't too cheap for the context—is that the working conditions in English that can be used to produce this latter kind of long-range, slowdown, focusing vision occur because the work is relatively less constrained by what the vision reveals. That doesn't mean that it can see more. Nobody has to explain to secretaries the differences between themselves and their bosses, and nobody has to explain to my friend that his bakery work is exploitation. It means the price paid for what might be called, to invert Gramsci's familiar formula, an "optimism *of the intellect*"—a confidence in our work practices to trace all the intricacies of detail to the bottom of the matter, as it were—is a "pessimism of the will," slowdown become paralysis because it seems useless to try to move at all.

One result is that familiar sensation (one Gramsci occasionally records in his reviews, for example) in reading literary and critical texts that the "critique" they offer has been far more convincing than the "positive alternatives." In my own text, which I assume you've followed to this point and which has involved long, long elaborations of critique, I've of course taken advantage of the working conditions of English in order to slow down, precisely, the details of the organization of work in English. Thus the structurally appropriate slot to be filled by "positive alternatives" seems to occur as a few rambling memories of junior high street fights over "Be-Bop-a-Lula," an attenuated account of bakery mustache stories, and some Spit Around with Stevens. You can of course "deconstruct" this opposition of critique/positive alternatives, where for movement you

at least substitute a kind of prolonged and suspended fall in a forward direction. But the point I would emphasize is that you get into
the trap of critique/positive alternatives in the first place by an overvaluation of "the new" that functions to distribute the possibilities
of change into, first, a critique to prepare the ground, and then the
invention of "the new" to escape it.

For insofar as critique involves the slowdown of details to plot
their multiple positional sources, it is only the preparation for the
invention of the new, the "positive alternative," the territory just
beyond the shuttered world your critique has exposed. And to that
extent the new inevitably underdetermines what you can do with
those details in any given location, and undervalues the work of
popular cultures as political resistances that, unlike work in English,
find different uses for the details. That is, the values of the new
function internally to work practices in English as a structure of
repetition; they command you over and over again to begin again
somewhere else. Thus what I have argued from the beginning of the
book is indifferently *all* critique or *all* positive alternatives, for it
has nothing new to offer. It doesn't tell you to go anywhere else,
but to exploit the positional shifts of territory possible where you
are. For my assumption is that popular culture work helps make
visible where and how changes have begun, and that what we're in
a position to do is educate a support structure so they can continue.

Mustache stories and the like may be "backward and conventional" by the standards of the new, but they ought to be a source
of wonder that anybody has been able to coerce anything of the sort
out of the conditions of their working lives and with so little help
from anybody else in doing it. The function of Gramsci's dictum, a
"*pessimism* of the intellect," is less to chasten wishful thinking than
to realize among other things what such victories cost those who
obtain them in the circumstances, to realize why a support structure
to continue their directions of change is both a far more necessary
praxis and considerably more possible to accomplish in our positions in English than the dramatic vision of ourselves as in the very
revolutionary vanguard of change.

For given the specific conditions of work in university English
departments (especially the relative freedom of concrete labor in the
organization of work and the way in which its professional status
affiliates it with multiple other locations of professional work and

with other professionals), it *is* difficult to grasp just what "work" means for so many people so much of the time. It is difficult to recognize as a structurally imposed optical illusion what Blackmur some time ago identified as a perception of living in a whole world gone professional. Despite the hierarchies of privilege in English, the hazards of "careers," the often very obvious precariousness of certain work practices, work in English for a permanent labor force does not mark a comprehensive system of humiliation as work does for so many others. It can make dissatisfactions more acute; it can and often does refine the exclusions of gender and race within the discipline. But *work* in English is not a reminder of what began long before in the schools as a systematic destruction of expectations, and which continues through not only the workplace itself, but the thousand and one boundary signs of power and authority always somewhere else, of *always* being in a position to lose what you do to someone else. It is not the continual, palpable, tangible, intrusive presence of an enemy who seems to have been around every corner all your life. I can't think there is any reason to "identify" with work in these terms, to press the hazards of our jobs until they are made to yield an image of similar experience. They won't, and god knows why anyone would want them to. For one use at least of what socio-cultural values we can force into circulation is not to identify with the work of others, but to change the conditions of all our work. It is, by whatever means available in whatever specific locations, to destroy the organization of labor as it exists and construct one that values the lives and energies of people to each work for each other in a society.

Reference Matter

Notes

CHAPTER ONE

1. Karl Marx, *Capital*, trans. Ben Fowkes (New York, 1977), vol. 1, p. 1026. Marx's emphasis. Subsequently cited in the text as C.

2. Louis Althusser, "Ideology and Ideological State Apparatuses," in Althusser, *Lenin and Philosophy and Other Essays*, trans. Ben Brewster (London, 1971), pp. 127–86.

3. There is, of course, a considerable body of research documenting this role of education generally; for a now familiar example, see P. M. Blau and O. D. Duncan, *The American Occupational Structure* (New York, 1967).

4. Stephen Berg and Robert Mezey, eds., *Naked Poetry* (New York, 1969), pp. xii–xiii.

5. T. S. Eliot, "*Ulysses*, Order and Myth," in Robert H. Deming, ed., *James Joyce: The Critical Heritage* (London, 1970), vol. 1, p. 269. This volume is useful because it also contains Aldington's review to which Eliot was responding.

6. R. P. Blackmur, "The Artist as Hero: A Disconsolate Chimera," in Blackmur, *The Lion and the Honeycomb* (New York, 1955), p. 45. Subsequently cited in the text as AH.

7. Antonio Gramsci, *Selections from the Prison Notebooks*, ed. Quintin Hoare and Geoffrey Nowell Smith (New York, 1971), p. 7. Whenever possible I have used the *Selections*, subsequently cited in the text as SPN. Other references are my own translations of Gramsci, *Quaderni del carcere*, ed. Valentino Gerratana, 4 vols. (Turin, 1975), cited in the text as QC.

8. F. R. Leavis, *For Continuity* (Cambridge, 1933), pp. 184–85. Subsequent references are cited in the text as FC.

9. Yvor Winters, *In Defense of Reason* (Denver, 1947), p. 7.

10. In ibid.

11. Francis Mulhern, "Marxism in Literary Criticism," *New Left Review*, 108 (Mar.–Apr. 1978): 87.

CHAPTER TWO

1. Perry Anderson, "The Antinomies of Antonio Gramsci," *New Left Review,* 100 (Nov. 1976–Jan. 1977): 5. Subsequently cited as AAG.

2. References throughout will be to Gramsci's *Quaderni del carcere,* ed. Valentino Gerratana, 4 vols. (Turin, 1975), subsequently cited as *QC.* Whenever possible, I have used translations of Gramsci by Quintin Hoare and Geoffrey Nowell Smith from *Selections from the Prison Notebooks* (New York, 1971), cited in the text as *SPN.* All other translations are my own. I have included page numbers for *QC* along with the passages quoted from *SPN,* since occasionally it is important to my argument to note the location of the passage in *QC.*

3. Christine Buci-Glucksmann, *Gramsci and the State,* trans. David Fernbach (London, 1980), esp. pp. 10–48.

4. Karl Marx, *The Eighteenth Brumaire of Louis Bonaparte* (New York, 1963), p. 18.

5. Christine Buci-Glucksmann, "Sui problemi politici della transizione: classe operaia e rivoluzione passiva," in Franco Ferri, ed., *Politica e storia in Gramsci* (Rome, 1977), vol. 1, esp. pp. 102–6.

6. For the concept of "passive revolution" in Gramsci, see Buci-Glucksmann, "Sui problemi politici della transizione," and Franco De Felice, "Rivoluzione passiva, fascismo, americanismo in Gramsci," in Ferri, vol. 1, pp. 161–220. Anderson's account of the relation between "war of maneuver" and "war of position" does not deal at all with the problems posed by a "passive revolution."

7. For another account of "reciprocal education," see Alberto Granese, "I *Quaderni del carcere*: dalla 'convertibilità' come principio ermetico all 'egemonia' come educazione reciproca all'autogoverno," in Ferri, vol. 2, pp. 395–418.

8. In "The Antinomies of Antonio Gramsci," Anderson argues that the correct relation between "coercion" and "consent" in Western democracies can best be grasped through an analogy to the media of monetary exchange, gold and paper, where the former is the hidden support system of the latter (AAG, 43–44).

9. Gramsci's critical account of the *riforma Gentile* is especially important here, for in the next chapter I will discuss in at least some detail the various programs of reform that were involved in the development of a system of public education in the United States. The comparisons, of course, are not exact by any means. Nevertheless, Gramsci's particular focus on vocational education as a component of the *riforma Gentile* requires a parallel focus on the programs of vocational education as they emerged in the United States as well. So far from an adjunct, such programs were central to the formation of public education in the United States.

10. Frederick Engels, letter of Apr. 1888 to Margaret Harkness, in Marx-Engels, *Selected Correspondence* (Moscow, 1975), pp. 380–81.

11. Quoted in Giuliano Manacorda, ed., *Marxismo e letteratura* (Rome, 1975), p. 84.

12. Alberto Asor Rosa, *Scrittori e popolo*, 7th ed. (Rome, 1979), pp. 221–22.

13. Quoted in Manacorda, p. 334.

14. T. S. Eliot, "*Ulysses*, Order and Myth," in Robert H. Deming, ed., *James Joyce: The Critical Heritage* (London, 1970), vol. 1, p. 270.

15. James Joyce, *Ulysses* (New York, 1961), p. 378.

16. "Perspective" is of course the term Lukács also uses in *The Meaning of Contemporary Realism*, trans. John and Necke Mander (London, 1962). However, in that book at least the argument seems finally not to recognize any difference between a "perspective" as an aesthetic criterion and as a political criterion.

17. Elsewhere in the *Notebooks*, Gramsci argues, "Two writers can represent (express) the same historical-social moment, but one can be an artist and the other merely a fraudulent mouthpiece. To work out the question in detail, limiting oneself to describing that which the two represent and express socially, that is, summing up more or less well the characteristics of a determinate historical moment, means not yet even touching upon the artistic problem" (*QC*, 2187).

18. Judy Grahn, *The Work of a Common Woman* (Trumansburg, N.Y., 1978), p. 60.

19. See especially "Il carattere di totalità dell'espressione artistica," in Benedetto Croce, *Nuovi saggi di estetica*, 5th ed. (Bari, 1968), pp. 117–46.

20. Arcangelo Leone de Castris, *Croce, Lukács, della Volpe* (Bari, 1978), p. 7.

CHAPTER THREE

1. Karl Marx, *Capital*, trans. Ben Fowkes (New York, 1977), vol. 1, p. 163. Subsequently cited in the text as *C*.

2. James Boswell, *Boswell's Life of Johnson* (London, 1961; orig. pub. 1953), p. 230.

3. Richard Ohmann and Wallace Douglas, *English in America* (New York, 1976), p. 234. Subsequently cited in the text as *EA*.

4. Antonio Gramsci, *Selections from the Prison Notebooks*, ed. Quintin Hoare and Geoffrey Nowell Smith (New York, 1971), p. 42.

5. Similar hostility is of course evident in any number of interviews that appear in Richard Sennett and Jonathan Cobb's *Hidden Injuries of Class* (New York, 1972); Lillian B. Rubins's *Worlds of Pain* (New York, 1976); Andrew Levison's *The Working Class Majority* (New York, 1974); and Studs Terkel's *Working* (New York, 1972).

6. In *Criticism and Social Change* (Chicago, 1983), Frank Lentricchia begins by dividing educational thinking between those who believe education is a function of society and those who believe instead that society is a function of education—that is, between "conservatives" and "radicals." Liberals he dismisses as "nervous conservatives governed by an irresistible impulse to tinker, though when the chips are down, they usually find a way to resist their need to mess with the machine" (p. 1). It's possibly a good

division to identify ultimate ideological ends, but then such chips are rarely down all the way. Most of the ideas of education as "compensatory" involve a lot of liberal "tinkering." Whatever its ultimate colors, the tinkering *itself* has, I think, exercised the dominant influence in the actual history of education in the United States. English departments at least did not emerge from ultimate ideological ends, no matter how much we want to flatter ourselves about the ideological importance of English. Their position in education is much more like a result of the long machinery of tinkering. I like the notion that society *ought* to be a function of education; *making* it that way is another matter. I can't see how one can proceed very far by initially dismissing the conditions where the making must take place, to concentrate instead on a dramatically polar opposition.

7. Charles William Eliot, "Inaugural Address as President of Harvard College," in Eliot, *Educational Reform: Essays and Addresses* (New York, 1905), p. 1. Subsequently cited in the text as IA.

8. James Conant, *Education in a Divided World* (Cambridge, Mass., 1948), p. 168. Subsequently cited in the text as *EDW*.

9. In the next chapter, I discuss at length the relations of English as a "profession" to a clientele.

10. Burton Bledstein, *The Culture of Professionalism* (New York, 1976), p. 102. Subsequently cited in the text as *CP*.

11. William Riley Parker, "Where Do English Departments Come From?," *College English*, 28 (Feb. 1967): 339–51.

12. Alexander Inglis, *Principles of Secondary Education* (Cambridge, Mass., 1918), pp. 424–25.

13. James Conant, *The Revolutionary Transformation of the American High School* (Cambridge, Mass., 1959), p. 3. Subsequently cited in the text as *RT*.

14. In *Labor and Monopoly Capital* (New York, 1974), Harry Braverman has a long commentary on the development of systems of classification of work skills, pp. 428–43. Subsequently cited in the text as *LMC*.

15. Wallace Douglas, "Rhetoric for the Meritocracy," in Ohmann and Douglas, pp. 97–132.

16. In *The Culture of Professionalism*, Bledstein has a chapter discussing the connections between professionalism and "character."

17. James Conant, *The American High School Today* (New York, 1959), p. 37. Subsequently cited in the text as *AHS*.

18. Quoted in Braverman, p. 133n.

19. "Planning Post-War Education," *Proceedings of the Conference on Planning Post-War Education*, School of Education, University of California, Los Angeles, Jan. 10 and 11, 1944, p. 59.

20. Clarence J. Karier reproduces the card in "Testing for Order and Control in the Corporate Liberal State," in Roger Dale et al., eds., *Schooling and Capitalism* (London, 1976), p. 135.

21. Arthur R. Jensen, "How Much Can We Boost IQ and Scholastic Achievement?," *Harvard Educational Review*, 39 (Winter 1969): 14. Jensen is quoting with full approval from the report by O. D. Duncan, D. L. Featherman, and B. Duncan, *Socioeconomic Background and Occupational*

Achievement, written for the Department of Health, Education, and Welfare's Office of Education, May 1968. He goes on to argue that IQ, strictly, means intelligence as it can be measured, not the whole of any individual's mental abilities. The point, of course, is to facilitate a correlation between *measurable* intelligence and occupational achievement, a conclusion Samuel Bowles and Herbert Gintis strongly dispute. See the following note.

22. Samuel Bowles and Herbert Gintis, "I.Q. in the U.S. Class Structure," in Jerome Karabel and A. H. Halsey, eds., *Power and Ideology in Education* (New York, 1977), p. 218. Subsequently cited in the text as IQ.

23. Charles Babbage, *On the Economy of Machinery and Manufactures* (Philadelphia, 1832), p. 18. Subsequently cited in the text as *EMM*.

24. The National Commission on the Reform of Secondary Education, *The Reform of Secondary Education* (New York, 1973), p. 8. Subsequently cited in the text as *RSE*.

25. PMLA Commission on the Future of the Profession, "Report of the Commission on the Future of the Profession, Spring, 1982," *PMLA*, 97 (Nov. 1982): 942. Their emphasis.

26. L. P. Alford and John Bangs, eds., *Production Handbook* (New York, 1948), p. 576. "Therblig" is Gilbreth spelled almost backward, named by Frank Gilbreth and Lillian Gilbreth. The *Production Handbook* explains therbligs as follows: "Most manual labor can be performed with a relatively few elementary motions that are repeated over and over. The Gilbreths divided work into 17 classifications. Most of these are motions of the hands, some are the absence of motion, and others are mental reactions. To these they gave the name 'therblig' which is coined from the letters of their name, reversed. The word is represented by synonyms such as basic divisions of accomplishment, or fundamental motions, or Gilbreth elements. They serve as useful categories for the classification of similar types of motions for study and refinement" (p. 576). The Gilbreths' extension of Frederick Taylor's principles derived from the conviction that almost any form of concrete labor in production, no matter what the specific task, involved—as the *Production Handbook* puts it—"relatively few elementary motions that are repeated over and over." As a result, time-motion study could be generalized enormously, for data could be drawn from any one work process and applied elsewhere. Employers would not find it necessary to spend money and research time on documenting operations in their own particular plant, or on monitoring workers directly. Production standards could be set on the basis of already available data.

27. See Richard Rorty, *Consequences of Pragmatism* (Minneapolis, Minn., 1982).

28. See my "The Self-Evaluations of Critical Theory," *boundary* 2, 12–13 (Spring–Fall 1984): 359–78.

CHAPTER FOUR

1. Alexander Inglis, *Principles of Secondary Education* (Cambridge, Mass., 1918), pp. 440–41, 442. Subsequently cited in the text as *PSE*.

2. *The 1909 J. Walter Thompson Blue Book on Advertising*, in David A.

Aaker, ed., *Advertising Management* (Englewood Cliffs, N.J., 1975), p. 18. Subsequently cited in the text as *BB*.

3. Ibid.

4. Inglis, pp. 440–41.

5. Quoted in John S. Wright, *Advertising*, 4th ed. (New York, 1977), p. 72. Wright's *Advertising* is subsequently cited in the text as *A*.

6. Wright, p. 394.

7. Editorial, "What is Advertising? What Does It Do?," *Advertising Age*, November 21, 1973, p. 8. Subsequently cited in the text as WA.

8. Robert Scholes, *Textual Power: Literary Theory and the Teaching of English* (New Haven, Conn., 1985), pp. 15–16. Subsequently cited in the text as *TP*.

9. Thorstein Veblen, *Absentee Ownership and Business Enterprise in Recent Times* (New York, 1923), p. 306.

10. Rod Horton and Herbert Edwards, *Backgrounds of American Literary Thought* (New York, 1967), p. 324.

11. Harry Braverman, *Labor and Monopoly Capital* (New York, 1974), pp. 260–61, 265. Subsequently cited in the text as *LMC*.

12. Donald Kendall, "Statement Before the Federal Trade Commission," in Aaker, p. 395. Subsequently cited in the text as FTC.

13. John C. Maloney, "Is Advertising Believability Really Important?," *Journal of Marketing*, 27, 4 (October 1963): 1. Subsequently cited in the text as AB.

14. Douglas Tigert, "A Research Project in Creative Advertising Through Life Style Analysis," in Douglas Tigert and Charles W. King, eds., *Attitude Research Reaches New Heights* (Chicago, 1971), p. 227.

15. Theodore G. N. Chin, "New Product Successes and Failures—How to Detect Them in Advance," in Aaker, p. 108. Subsequently cited in the text as NP.

16. Cleanth Brooks, *The Well-Wrought Urn* (New York, 1947), p. 213. Subsequently cited in the text as *WWU*.

17. David Shumway and James Sosnoski, "Critical Protocols," in *The GRIP Report*, second draft, vol. 2, p. 12. Subsequently cited in the text as CP.

18. For a rather different understanding of the relation between "Theory of Modes" and "Theory of Symbols," see William A. Johnsen, "The Sparagmos of Myth Is the Naked Lunch of Mode: Modern Literature in the Age of Frye and Borges," *boundary 2*, 8 (Winter 1980): 297–311.

19. Raymond Williams, *Marxism and Literature* (Oxford, 1977), pp. 121–27. Subsequently cited in the text as *ML*.

20. Edward Said, *The World, the Text, and the Critic* (Cambridge, Mass., 1983), pp. 229–30.

21. Wayne Booth, "Arts and Scandals, 1982," *PMLA*, 98 (May 1983): 315.

22. R. P. Blackmur, "Toward a Modus Vivendi," in Blackmur, *The Lion and the Honeycomb* (New York, 1955), p. 8.

23. Northrop Frye, *Anatomy of Criticism* (Princeton, N.J., 1957), p. 27. Subsequently cited in the text as *AC*.

24. As in the previous chapter, my use of the term "cultural capital" differs somewhat from that of Pierre Bourdieu in *Distinction* (Cambridge, Mass., 1984), but it is not entirely incompatible with Bourdieu's understanding.

25. Heidi Hartmann, "The Unhappy Marriage of Marxism and Feminism: Towards a More Progressive Union," in Lydia Sargent, ed., *Women and Revolution* (Boston, 1981), p. 29.

26. Quintin Hoare and Geoffrey Nowell Smith, *Selections from the Prison Notebooks* (New York, 1971), p. 7. Subsequently cited in the text as *SPN*.

27. Michael Apple, "Work, Class, and Teaching," in Stephen Walker and Len Barton, eds., *Gender, Class, and Education* (Sussex, Eng., 1983), p. 54.

CHAPTER FIVE

1. Harry Braverman, *Labor and Monopoly Capital* (New York, 1974), pp. 25–26.

2. Karl Marx, *Capital*, trans. David Fernbach (New York, 1981), vol. 3, p. 135.

3. Terry Eagleton, *Literary Theory: An Introduction* (Minneapolis, Minn., 1983), p. 201.

4. Braverman, pp. 25–26.

5. The remark about professionals appears in R. P. Blackmur, "The Artist as Hero: A Disconsolate Chimera," in Blackmur, *The Lion and the Honeycomb* (New York, 1955), p. 45, and the use of "intellectual proletariat" appears throughout Blackmur's "Toward a Modus Vivendi," also in *The Lion and the Honeycomb*, pp. 3–31.

6. André Gorz, *Strategy for Labor* (Boston, 1974); Serge Mallet, *Essays on the New Working Class* (St. Louis, 1975); Nicos Poulantzas, *Classes in Contemporary Capitalism*, trans. David Fernbach (London, 1978); Erik Olin Wright, *Class, Crisis, and the State* (London, 1979); Barbara Ehrenreich and John Ehrenreich, "The Professional-Managerial Class," *Radical America*, 11, 2 (Mar.–Apr. 1977): 7–31, reprinted with a number of responses and a rejoinder by the authors in Pat Walker, ed., *Between Labor and Capital* (Montreal, 1978), pp. 5–45, rejoinder on pp. 313–34.

7. Judy Grahn, *The Work of a Common Woman* (Trumansburg, N.Y., 1978), p. 112.

8. Michèle Barrett makes good use of the Woolf passage toward a similar end in "Ideology and the Cultural Production of Gender," in Judith Newton and Deborah Rosenfelt, eds., *Feminist Criticism and Social Change* (New York, 1985), p. 77.

9. Teresa de Lauretis, *Alice Doesn't* (Bloomington, Ind., 1982), p. 7.

Index

In this index an "f" after a number indicates a separate reference on the next page, and an "ff" indicates separate references on the next two pages. A continuous discussion over two or more pages is indicated by a span of page numbers, e.g., "pp. 57–58." *Passim* is used for a cluster of references in close but not consecutive sequence.

Abstract labor: and concrete labor, 16–23, 92–94, 133–41 *passim*, 160–64, 223–28, 232–40 *passim*

Abstract labor form: as evaluations, 20–21, 24–26, 83–93 *passim*, 135–37, 157, 161–64, 213–47 *passim*, 251–52, 263

Advertising, 149, 249

Advertising Age, 149–50, 168–69, 174

Advertising agencies: as workplaces of circulation, 22, 140–41, 266–68; history of, 142–44, 146, 150–51, 166, 168–85; organization of work in, 144, 168–82; and teaching of literature, 144–49, 159–64 *passim*, 185–91, 211–13, 225–26, 237–39, 249–51; and clientele, 146, 156; and manipulation of consumers, 149–50, 159–68 *passim*, 176–82, 185; and psychological research, 170–74; and "failures," 179–82; and manipulation of production, 183–85

Aldington, Richard, 31

Alford, L. P., 134, 283

Althusser, Louis, 20, 26–27

Anderson, Perry, 45–59 *passim*

Arnold, Matthew, 30, 84, 192, 207f, 228

Asor Rosa, Alberto, 67

"Author industries," 198–200

Babbage, Charles, 122–27 *passim*

Balzac, Honoré de, 64ff, 72

Bangs, John, 134, 283

Berg, Stephen, 29

Blackmur, R. P., 31–33, 35, 39, 100, 198, 210–11, 256, 276

Blake, William, 214

Bledstein, Burton, 101, 103, 110

Blue Book on Advertising, The, 142–49, 157, 167ff, 176f, 182–89 *passim*, 201–2, 212, 225

Booth, Wayne, 209–10, 211, 229

Boswell, James, 84

Bourdieu, Pierre, 258, 285. *See also* Cultural capital

Bowles, Samuel, 119–25

Braverman, Harry, 110–11, 122, 127–32 *passim*, 166, 176, 248, 255–58

Brigham, C. C., 118

Brooks, Cleanth, 195, 198, 205–6

Buci-Glucksmann, Christine, 55, 71

Burke, Kenneth, 271

Burney, Charles, 84

Chin, Theodore, 174–76, 180, 266

Circulation: of people, 1, 6–7, 23–29, 91, 222, 238, 240–47, 249–55 *passim*, 264–65, 271; of grades, 6–7, 17–19, 90, 217–18; of texts, 7–8, 148, 151–54, 186–91, 218–21;

in and from English departments,
20–23; material means of, 41–43,
250–55 *passim*, 268. *See also* Marx,
Karl; Merit; "Sorting"
Class: as boundary, 26, 240–47; theory
of "new" working, 248, 255–58
Clerical work, 1f, 113–14, 125, 131–32,
134, 263, 272
Clientele: for literary study, 100, 105,
146–47, 152–60 *passim*, 193–96,
201, 203–4
Compensatory: education as, 91–101,
108–37 *passim*, 204
Composition, 101–8 *passim*, 117,
145–46, 253, 258–59
Conant, James, 97–110 *passim*, 114ff,
119, 124, 130, 139
Concrete labor: and abstract labor, 16–
23, 92–94, 133–41 *passim*, 160–64,
223–28, 232–40 *passim*
Consumer Reports, 178
Crane, Hart, 39, 216
Croce, Benedetto, 35, 54, 57, 62ff, 66,
73–76, 79f
Cultural capital, 223–37, 258. *See also*
Human capital
Cultural production, 7, 21, 77–80, 88–
89, 184–85, 189–90, 207, 212–13,
238–39, 248, 253, 260–72 *passim*;
material means of, 40–44, 249–55
passim
Cultural skills, 40–41, 102–4, 108, 111,
116–17, 120, 129
Cultures, popular, *see* Popular cultures
Curriculum: organization of, in literary
study, 109, 200–201

Deconstruction, 228–33
de Lauretis, Teresa, 273–74
Deleuze, Gilles, 229
Derrida, Jacques, 229
De Sanctis, Francesco, 62–66 *passim*,
72
Deutermann, Walter, 128
Doolittle, Hilda (H.D.), 216
Douglas, Wallace, 103–4

Eagleton, Terry, 251–52
Education: vocational, 60, 103, 106,
111–14, 125, 130–33, 154, 280; as
compensatory, 91–101, 108–37
passim, 204

Edwards, Alba, 102–3
Ehrenreich, Barbara, 256
Ehrenreich, John, 256
Eliot, Charles William, 95–98, 104
Eliot, T. S., 16, 31, 33, 36, 70, 99, 209,
216, 236–37
Engels, Frederick, 64–65, 71–72

Faulkner, William, 220–21
Ford, Henry, 111
Foucault, Michel, 269
Frye, Northrop, 201–6, 211–30 *passim*

Gatekeepers, English departments as,
5–7
Gender constructions: of women in
education, 26, 96–97, 98, 106, 113–
14, 242, 245–46, 263; of men in
education, 34–35, 95–96, 106, 246
Gentile, Giovanni, 60–61
Gintis, Herbert, 119–25
Gorz, André, 256
Grahn, Judy, 72, 269
Gramsci, Antonio: war of position, 16,
22–23, 27, 46–57, 59–62, 234–37,
273–74; traditional intellectuals,
34–37, 227, 243; popular culture,
43–44, 66–68, 69; "pessimism of
the intellect, optimism of the will,"
45, 62, 274–75; war of maneuver,
46–52, 53–54; coercion and consent,
47–49, 58–59, 231–32; "East" and
"West," 47–50; civil society and the
state, 47–52, 54–55; "dual power,"
49–52; intellectuals, 53–54, 79–80;
"passive revolution," 56; education,
57–62, 86; *riforma Gentile*, 60–61;
aesthetics and Marxism, 62–76;
realism, 68–73; organic intellectuals,
243–45; mentioned, 19, 85. *See also*
Croce, Benedetto
*Guide to Office Clerical Time Stan-
dards, A*, 132

Harkness, Margaret, 64
Hartmann, Heidi, 242
H.D., 216
Herrnstein, Richard, 119, 123
High schools, 5, 87, 98, 102–17 *passim*,
128–33, 144–56 *passim*, 260
Hoxie, Robert, 111, 113, 129
Human capital, 20, 23, 25, 242–43,

249, 257–60, 264, 271. *See also*
Cultural capital
Hunt, William, 102

Ideologies: of "the new," 15–22 *passim*,
27–31, 69–71, 94, 139, 219–21,
236–37, 275. *See also* Tradition
Inglis, Alexander, 5, 101–2, 103, 113–
14, 115, 142–56 *passim*, 162–65,
185–96 *passim*, 207, 225, 251
Institutionalization, 13–14, 18
Intelligence testing, 107, 117–25, 229–
35
Intrinsic value: in literary texts, 158,
160, 186–91, 196–204, 213, 215,
219–24 *passim*

Jensen, A. R., 118–20
Johnsen, William, 284
Johnson, Samuel, 83f, 222
Joyce, James, 31, 33, 70–71, 269–70,
272

Kendall, Donald, 168–69, 179ff, 188,
225
Kerner report, 132–33
Kettering Foundation report, 130–32
Krieger, Murray, 37

Labor, division of, 95–96, 106, 112–13,
122–25, 137–38
Laughlin, H. H., 118
Leavis, F. R., 35–39 *passim*, 84, 100
Leavis, Q. D., 35
Lenin, V. I., 49–50
Lentricchia, Frank, 281–82
Leone de Castris, Arcangelo, 74–75
Literary history, 100, 150–56 *passim*,
199
Lukács, Georg, 69, 71

Mallet, Serge, 256
Maloney, John, 171–77 *passim*, 185,
212, 266f
Mann, Horace, 91
Marx, Karl: circulation, 7f, 248–49;
transformation of labor, 13, 16–
17, 78ff, 92; abstract and concrete
labor, 16–20 *passim*; revolutionary
"content," 55, 68; commodity form,
78ff; productive and unproductive
labor, 87–88; reserve army of labor,

221–22; mentioned, 57, 110, 133,
143, 213, 223, 232, 239, 257
Merit, 95–96, 98, 108–10, 114–29
passim, 245–46. *See also* "Sorting"
Mezey, Robert, 29
Miami Vice, 40–41, 43, 254
Milton, John, 4, 8, 17ff
Modernism, 15–16, 31–33, 69–71, 101
Mötley Crüe, 4, 8
Mulhern, Francis, 36–37, 39–43

Nader, Ralph, 178
NEA Commission on the Reorganization of Secondary Education, 102f,
143
New Criticism, 8, 33–34, 35–39, 99–
101, 138, 194–201, 208, 209–10,
224
"New" working class theory, 248,
255–58

Occupational Outlook Handbook, 131
Ohmann, Richard, 85, 88, 92, 95, 101,
104, 109, 138, 159

Packard, Vance, 178
Parker, William Riley, 101, 104
PMLA Commission on the Future of the
Profession, 133
Poetry, contemporary, 15, 29–31, 39
Politz, Alfred, 172–73, 174
Popular cultures, 41–44, 140–41,
254–55, 260–75
Postmodernism, 15, 28
Poulantzas, Nicos, 256
Pound, Ezra, 31, 33, 254
Printer's Ink, 147f, 170, 177, 212
Professionalism, 85, 87f, 93–109 *pas-
sim*, 115–16, 128, 204–8
Psychographics, 173–74
"Public critic," 146, 151, 206–7

Racism: in education, 6, 26, 118–21
passim, 127–33 *passim*, 242, 257–58
Rambo, 261
Ransom, John Crowe, 35–36, 100
Readers: as consumers of literature,
144–47, 151–54, 187–90
Realism, 68–73, 265–67
Recruiting a labor force in English, 1,
8–9, 209–11

Reserve army of labor: in education, 127–33, 210–11
Richards, I. A., 99
Rorty, Richard, 137

Said, Edward, 208
Scholes, Robert, 159–60, 189–90, 218
Scrutiny, 36–37
Shaving cream, 266–69 *passim*, 273
Shumway, David, 199–200, 201
Snow, C. P., 38, 100
"Sorting," 91–92, 95–97; and training, 102, 104–9, 115–17, 120–25. *See also* Circulation, of people; Merit
Sosnoski, James, 199–200, 201
Stevens, Wallace, 3, 270–71, 274

Tate, Allen, 35–36, 39, 100
Terman, Lewis, 118
Theory: and organization of work practices, 205–13
"Therblig" classification system, 134, 283
Tigert, Douglas, 173–74
Time-motion studies, 2, 132, 134–35, 283

Tradition: and "the new," 30–31, 33, 37–44 *passim*, 160–61, 164. *See also* Ideologies
Tree frogs, 263
Twinkies, 19

Unemployment, 128ff

Veblen, Thorstein, 165–66
Vincent, Gene, 265, 267, 273f
Vocational education, *see under* Education

Warren, Robert Penn, 194
Williams, Raymond, 206, 208–9
Williams, William Carlos, 236
Wilson, Edmund, 36
Wimsatt, William, 201
Winters, Yvor, 36, 38f
Women writers: and the canon, 192–93
Woolf, Virginia, 270
Wordsworth, William, 197f
Work, clerical, *see* Clerical work
Wright, Erik Olin, 256
Writing for publication, 218–21

Library of Congress Cataloging-in-Publication Data
Watkins, Evan, 1946–
      Work time : English departments and the circulation of cultural
value / Evan Watkins.
      p.   cm.
Includes bibliographical references and index.
ISBN 0-8047-1691-9 (alk. paper)
      1. English philology—Study and teaching (Higher)—United States—
Evaluation.   2. Universities and colleges—United States—
Departments—Evaluation.   3. English teachers—United States—Job
descriptions.   4. College teaching—United States—Evaluation.
5. Work environment—United States.   I. Title.
PE1068.U5W37   1989   89-31002
820'.7'1173—dc 19   CIP